TIMELY MEDITATIONS

TIMELY MEDITATIONS

MARTIN HEIDEGGER AND
POSTMODERN POLITICS

Leslie Paul Thiele

PRINCETON UNIVERSITY PRESS   PRINCETON, NEW JERSEY

Library of Congress Cataloging-in-Publication Data

Thiele, Leslie Paul.
    Timely meditations : Martin Heidegger and postmodern politics /
Leslie Paul Thiele.
        p.   cm.
    Includes bibliographical references and index.
    ISBN: 0-691-08659-1 (alk. paper). — ISBN 0-691-04336-1 (pbk. :
alk. paper)
    1. Heidegger, Martin, 1889–1976—Political and social views.
    2. Political science—Philosophy.   I. Title.
    B3279.H494T45   1995
    320'.092—dc20   94-43133

For Susan ————————————————————————————

WHO ALWAYS KNOWS HOW SHE FEELS

Contents

Acknowledgments

I WOULD LIKE to thank William Connolly, Fred Dallmayr, Tracy Strong, and Paul Wapner for their insightful comments on various drafts of this work. I would also like to thank Al Damico, whose intellectual integrity and sense of justice have been inspirational. Finally, I would like to thank my wife, Susan, and son, Jacob. Sharing their lives has brought me into the world in ways that made the writing of this book possible.

An early version of chapter 1 appeared as "Twilight of Modernity: Nietzsche, Heidegger, and Politics," *Political Theory* 22 (1994): 468–90, © 1994 Sage Publications, Inc. Reprinted by permission of Sage Publications, Inc. An early version of chapter 3 appeared as "Heidegger on Freedom: Political, Not Metaphysical," *American Political Science Review* 88 (June 1994): 278–91. Generous support from the National Endowment for the Humanities and the Social Sciences and Humanities Research Council of Canada allowed the completion of this book in a timely fashion.

Abbreviations ──────────────

Index to Heidegger's Works

IN THE TEXT, abbreviated references are followed by page numbers, with the exception of the *Gesamtausgabe*, whose abbreviation is followed by volume number and page number.

BP   *Basic Problems of Phenomenology.* Trans. A. Hofstadter. Bloomington: Indiana University Press, 1982.

BT   *Being and Time.* Trans. J. Macquarrie and E. Robinson. New York: Harper and Row, 1962.

BW   *Basic Writings.* New York: Harper and Row, 1977.

DT   *Discourse on Thinking.* Trans. J. Anderson and E. Freund. New York: Harper and Row, 1966.

EB   *Existence and Being.* Washington, D.C.: Regnery Gateway, 1949.

EGT   *Early Greek Thinking.* Trans. D. Krell and F. Capuzzi. New York: Harper and Row, 1975.

EP   *The End of Philosophy.* Trans. J. Stambaugh. New York: Harper and Row, 1973.

ERS   *Nietzsche.* Vol. 2, *The Eternal Recurrence of the Same.* Trans. D. Krell. New York: Harper and Row, 1984.

G   *Gesamtausgabe.* 65 vols. Frankfurt am Main: Vittorio Klostermann, 1976–89.

HCT   *History of the Concept of Time: Prolegomena.* Trans. T. Kisiel. Bloomington: Indiana University Press, 1985.

HPS   *Hegel's Phenomenology of Spirit.* Trans. P. Emad and K. Maly. Bloomington: Indiana University Press, 1988.

ID   *Identity and Difference.* Trans. J. Stambaugh. New York: Harper and Row, 1969.

IM   *An Introduction to Metaphysics.* Trans. R. Manheim. New Haven: Yale University Press, 1987.

KPM   *Kant and the Problem of Metaphysics.* Trans. J. Churchill. Bloomington: Indiana University Press, 1962.

MFL   *The Metaphysical Foundations of Logic.* Trans. M. Heim. Bloomington: Indiana University Press, 1984.

MHC   *Martin Heidegger in Conversation.* Ed. R. Wisser, trans. B. Murthy. New Delhi: Arnold-Heinemann, 1970.

N   *Nietzsche*. Vol. 4, *Nihilism*. Trans. F. Capuzzi. New York: Harper and Row, 1982.

OGS   "'Only a God Can Save Us': The *Spiegel* Interview (1966)." Trans. William Richardson. In *Heidegger: The Man and the Thinker*, ed. T. Sheehan, 45–67. Chicago: Precedent, 1981.

PLT   *Poetry, Language, and Thought*. Trans. A. Hofstadter. New York: Harper and Row, 1971.

PT   *The Piety of Thinking*. Trans. J. Hart and J. Maraldo. Bloomington: Indiana University Press, 1976.

QB   *The Question of Being*. Trans. W. Kluback and J. Wilde. New York: Twayne, 1958.

QT   *The Question concerning Technology and Other Essays*. Trans. W. Lovitt. New York: Harper and Row, 1977.

SAG   "The Self-Assertion of the German University and the Rectorate, 1933–34: Facts and Thoughts." Trans. Karsten Harries. *Review of Metaphysics* 38 (March 1985): 467–502.

ST   *Schelling's Treatise on the Essence of Human Freedom*. Trans. J. Stambaugh. Athens: Ohio University Press, 1985.

TB   *On Time and Being*. Trans. J. Stambaugh. New York: Harper and Row, 1972.

WBG   "The Way Back into the Ground of Metaphysics." Trans. W. Kaufmann. In *Existentialism from Dostoevsky to Sartre*, ed. W. Kaufmann, 206–21. New York: Meridian, 1956.

WCT   *What Is Called Thinking?* Trans. J. Gray. New York: Harper and Row, 1968.

WL   *On the Way to Language*. Trans. P. Hertz. New York: Harper and Row, 1971.

WP   *What Is Philosophy?* Trans. W. Kluback and J. Wilde. London: Vision Press, 1958.

WPA   *Nietzsche*. Vol. 1, *The Will to Power as Art*. Trans. D. Krell. New York: Harper and Row, 1979.

WPK   *Nietzsche*. Vol. 3, *The Will to Power as Knowledge and Metaphysics*. Trans. J. Stambaugh, D. Krell, and F. Capuzzi. New York: Harper and Row, 1987.

TIMELY MEDITATIONS

Introduction

Many are the wonders of the world, but none
walks stranger than man.

. . . .

And the noblest of gods, the Earth—
ageless she is, and untiring—yet he wears her
away.

. . . .

He has taught himself language, and thought
as swift as the wind,
and the sentiments that form the city.

. . . .

Clever beyond all dreams is his inventive craft
which drives him this time and that to well or
ill.
    (Sophocles, *Antigone*)

STRANGE INDEED is the upright walker. With grasping hands and for-
ward-looking eyes, this most wondrous of creatures has developed the
sentiment, thought, speech, and craft needed to extend its reign across
the expanse of the earth and beyond. What are the limits to its power?
The ancients presumably had their answer. "Do not seek to be master
in every way," Creon had warned Oedipus. But Creon, we know,
would not follow his own advice. He met a fate no less dire than that of
the former king of Thebes. Any human pursuit that ignores limitations,
Sophocles suggests, inevitably brings doom. Well or ill may come of our
vast ingenuity. With tragic closure the chorus insists that "our happiness depends on wisdom all the way."

Contemporary liberalism easily marks the limits Creon transgressed
in his patriarchal and authoritarian pursuit of power. From the perspective of this hegemonic ideology of our era, the young Antigone appears
as the courageous voice of individual liberty. Creon rules as the despot
blinded to the inalienability of this liberty by the arrogance of power.
But justice prevails, and tyranny brings calamity to both king and kin.
The sentiments that allowed the city to form are vindicated. Surely this
interpretation is an anachronistic imposition. Nevertheless, liberalism

may rightly claim to have forged many of the needed restraints for despotic power in the modern world. And surely this is no small feat. Of late, however, in the midst of its most glorious, global vindications, liberalism has been challenged anew and from within. Its very success in valorizing individual liberty has potentially undermined both the sentiments needed to sustain political community and the wisdom needed to restrain the cumulative craft, consumption, and propagation of billions of individuals who are wearing away the earth. It is, I believe, an open question whether some form of liberalism can cultivate these sentiments and this wisdom. What is not in question is the need for such cultivation.

We call ourselves Homo sapiens, and by the latter term mean to indicate both the wisdom and the cleverness of our species. Wisdom and cleverness, as Sophocles observed, are far from the same thing. While the former denotes a capacity to discern limitations and live within them, the latter denotes an ingenuity and craft designed to shatter barriers. Today, the imbalance between wisdom and cleverness is more extreme and the shattering of barriers more dangerous than anything Sophocles imagined. Cultivating wisdom is, for us even more than for the ancients, an indispensable practice. Today, as E. F. Schumacher observes, "man is far too clever to be able to survive without wisdom."[1] Yet today, more than ever, we count on cleverness to compensate for a dearth of wisdom. We falsely believe, to paraphrase Schumacher, that a technological breakthrough a day will keep the political and ecological crises at bay. By comparison, the hubris of the ancient tyrant pales.

These practical concerns about political and ecological sustainability orient this work. Yet they stand enmeshed with a third concern, equally important but philosophic in nature. Wonder is the root of philosophic inquiry, and wonder at ourselves lies deep within all our wonder at the world. At the core of our concern about the caretaking of the earth and the caretaking of political community lies the philosophic enigma of that strangest of all creatures. Pondering this enigma is not idle musing. The political and ecological wisdom that would sustain the earth and its communities is, or at least may be, grounded in the contemplative wisdom that describes philosophy proper. I believe that these three concerns, political, ecological, and philosophic, confront us today with the mandate of addressing a single, increasingly pressing question: *How are we to understand and exercise our freedom?* It is our freedom—demonstrated in thought, speech and deed—that grounds our growing power over the earth, our capacity for political community, and our philo-

---

[1] E. F. Schumacher, *Small Is Beautiful: Economics as If People Mattered* (New York: Harper and Row, 1973), 32.

sophic disposition to question their meaning and limits. How we understand and exercise this freedom largely determines whether our ingenuity and craft will be balanced with the sentiments and wisdom needed to sustain a common earthly home.

In an attempt to grapple with the question of human freedom, I have chosen to expound and build on the thought of Martin Heidegger. Following Heidegger, who insists that "the question of the essence of human freedom is the fundamental question of philosophy, with even the question of Being entwined in it" (G 31:300), this book roots the question of freedom in the question of Being. In so doing, it departs from liberal theory, which is loath to ground politics in ontology. Yet it would be misleading, with this in mind, to characterize this book as an *anti*liberal tract. If a label is required for it, I would propose *post*liberal, signaling not so much an effort to undermine or subvert liberal claims to freedom as an effort to reach beyond them—redirecting their political and ecological implications by reordering their philosophic foundations. While the redirection of political and ecological implications is largely my own doing, the reordering of philosophic foundations is largely Heidegger's achievement.

Martin Heidegger was born at Messkirch in 1889, the same year Nietzsche was "received into the protection of the night of lunacy," to use Heidegger's description of Hölderlin's untimely exit (*EB* 282). Heidegger seldom left his German homeland, or his south German province of Baden Württemberg for that matter. He died there in 1976. His life was distinguished by a career spanning more than fifty years as a teacher and writer. In terms of his intellectual development, Heidegger, along with Wittgenstein and a few other philosophers, is known almost as much for the distinct phases of his work as for its substance. Through his late student years, Heidegger evidenced a Catholic and medievalist orientation with an early focus on logic. His key interests were Aristotelian and scholastic in nature. From about 1920 on, culminating with the publication of his magnum opus, *Being and Time*, in 1927, Heidegger demonstrated more Lutheran and Kierkegaardian existentialist concerns. His problem was with the meaning of Being. Influenced by, but also departing from, the phenomenological orientation of his mentor, Edmund Husserl, Heidegger attempted to develop a fundamental ontology. By the late 1920s, Heidegger had turned to Jünger and then to Nietzsche. For a time, his work took a distinct nationalistic and voluntaristic direction. Subsequently, Heidegger distanced himself both from the systematic search for a fundamental ontology and from its translation into a popular revolutionary force. He began to focus on the historical development of Western metaphysics. With the publication of the "Letter on Humanism" in 1947, and in many ways beginning in

1935 or 1936, Heidegger entered his final stage. From his reassessment of Nietzsche until his death, he engaged in the poetic-philosophic celebration of ontological disclosure while describing the threat posed to it by the hegemony of technological life.

We may, then, roughly divide Heidegger's work into three periods. The first culminates with *Being and Time* and the third begins with the "Letter on Humanism." They are separated by a transitional period marked by Heidegger's "turning," or *Kehre*. Heidegger himself first wrote publicly of his Kehre in the "Letter on Humanism," noting that a reorientation of his thought had already been "at work" in his thinking a decade earlier. He also maintained that his turning in no way constituted an abandonment of the concerns identified in *Being and Time*, but rather marked a progression of his thinking about them. One might describe Heidegger's shift in orientation as a recharacterization of human being, or *Dasein*, from the role of the heroic protagonist to that of a humble participant in the historical saga of Being's disclosure. In Heidegger's own words, the distinction made between the early period and the late one is "justified only on the condition that this is kept constantly in mind: only by way of what Heidegger I has thought does one gain access to what is to-be-thought by Heidegger II."[2] The distinct stages of Heidegger's work are, as Heidegger himself suggested, less striking than its continuity.

Apart from intellectual monuments, Heidegger's life was also marked, or rather marred, by his involvement with National Socialism, which he fervently supported while serving a year as rector of Freiburg University beginning in 1933. The controversy surrounding this period has been much heightened because of Heidegger's stubborn reluctance after the war to express remorse or come to terms with the meaning of his dangerous political escapade. The reader might then question, particularly in light of the proposed continuity of Heidegger's thought, what a largely unrepentant former Fascist might have to teach us about freedom. At this juncture, however, I shall say no more about the connection between Heidegger's biography and his philosophy. Indeed, an even briefer biographical introduction to his work might have been appropriate. A rendition of Heidegger's own preface to his lectures on Aristotle—that he "was born, worked, and died"—might have served best. The reason, as Heidegger himself writes with Nietzsche in mind, is that "the work as work closes itself off to us as long as we squint somehow after the 'life' of the man who created the work instead of asking about Being and the world, which first ground the work" (*WPK*

---

[2] Martin Heidegger, preface to *Heidegger: Through Phenomenology to Thought*, by William Richardson (The Hague: Martinus Nijhoff, 1963), xxii.

4). I do not think Heidegger was self-serving in making this remark; it is unnecessary and unfortunate to abridge or prejudice one's confrontation with a work of philosophy because of its author's regrettable choices in life or the character traits that made these choices possible or even likely.

Commentators have pointed out that Heidegger's own notion of authenticity precludes the separation of his politics from his philosophy.[3] Authenticity does indeed demand a holistic self-understanding and self-accounting. But the lesson to be drawn from Heidegger's discussion of authenticity is not that we should dismiss a person's philosophy on account of his or her politics. Holistic self-understanding and self-accounting demands the integration of one's philosophic and political insights and judgments. That this integration remains dogged by uncertainty is part of the burden of authenticity. There are no fast and easy formulas for translating a philosophy into a politics, and we are remiss if we peremptorily reject the former because of the shortcomings of the latter. For this reason I have postponed extensive biographical discussion until chapter 6. And there my purpose is neither to praise Heidegger in spite of his biography nor to bury him with it. Rather, I attempt to think through Heidegger's philosophy to arrive at sober political insights. Thus I invoke an interpreter's prerogative to derive from a philosophy sensibilities that its author has not earned, and might perhaps disown. In turn, I attempt to think through Heidegger's politics to arrive at sober philosophic insights. Thus I invoke an interpreter's prerogative to derive worthy theoretical lessons from unworthy practices.

This work grapples with the nature of human freedom, its philosophic foundations, and its political and ecological import. Why, the reader might ask, is such a task couched in an extended account of Heidegger's thought when other exigetical works already exist in abundance? One of Heidegger's more illustrious students, Hannah Arendt, once spoke of the need to think without bannisters. She believed that thought needed to escape from the dead weight of tradition and habit as well as from the fickleness of fashion, to move beyond conventions, whether those of one's times or those of one's teachers.[4] In many ways

---

[3] Karsten Harries, "Heidegger as a Political Thinker," in *Heidegger and Modern Philosophy*, ed. Michael Murray (New Haven: Yale University Press, 1978), 305.

[4] In a conference in Toronto on her thought, Arendt was criticized for "groundless thinking." She responded: "I have a metaphor which is not quite that cruel, and which I have never published but kept for myself. I call it thinking without a bannister. In German, *Denken ohne Geländer*. That is, as you go up and down the stairs you can always hold onto the bannister so that you don't fall down. But we have lost this bannister. That is the way I tell it to myself. And this is indeed what I try to do." Hannah Arendt, "On Hannah Arendt," in *Hannah Arendt: The Recovery of the Public World*, ed. Melvyn Hill (New York: St. Martin's Press, 1979), 336–37.

Arendt relied on bannisters herself; a long tradition of political and philosophic thought (including the thought of Martin Heidegger) stabilizes her work. Still, Arendt achieved an impressive intellectual autonomy. Frankly, I have not aspired to such heights. I have required the steady support of Heidegger's bannister in grappling with the quandaries of freedom and the meaning of our times. Hence this work remains significantly exigetical. Yet it does not shy away from identifying the dangers and shortcomings of Heidegger's assistance. My goal, in any case, is to gain enough support from a great philosopher's work to make departures both possible and productive.

In a postmodern age, this project might still seem strangely antiquated. Heidegger is often criticized for supplying an ontological metanarrative that, far from serving as a means of orientation, should be greeted with incredulity. As one commentator writes, the deconstructive strategy is to undermine "the assumption in philosophy . . . that a single foundation—'Being,' for example, in Heidegger—could be posited which saturates every aspect and moment of life and into which everything in the world ultimately resolves itself."[5] Reductivist strategies are indeed out of vogue. A central claim of this book, however, is that Heidegger's Being is anything but a stable foundation for our conceptual reductions and reconstructions. Being, as Heidegger understands it, remains fundamentally questionable. It is the ultimate deconstructive force. Indeed, to approach Being in any way but a questioning manner is both to miss the point of Heidegger's philosophic enterprise and to preclude the opportunity of its political redemption.

My purpose, then, is to take a man recently much accused of dogmatism and to develop three claims. First, philosophically speaking, Heidegger provides no answers, only better ways of posing questions. Second, philosophically speaking, better ways of posing questions are all that can be hoped for, and that is a great deal indeed. And third, Heidegger's philosophic achievements are, nonetheless, not without political implications. The political implications I draw from Heidegger's thought contrast sharply with the more infamous tendencies of his work and life. Even so, in negotiating this tension I have attempted to remain faithful to a basic tenet of Heidegger's work. In philosophic inquiry, there is no place for imitation. "When we hear of disciples, 'followers,' as in a school of philosophy," Heidegger maintains, "it means that the nature of questioning is misunderstood" (IM 19–20). If the interpretation of Heidegger that follows too often strays, it is because I have sought to avoid this fundamental misunderstanding.

[5] Michael Ryan, Marxism and Deconstruction: A Critical Articulation (Baltimore: Johns Hopkins University Press, 1982), 16.

My claim is that there is a politics to be discovered in Heidegger's philosophy, one quite at odds with the politics that Heidegger had occasion to champion. I say "discovered" with the understanding that, as Heidegger himself put it, in philosophy discovering necessarily means shaping (*ST* 38). Like all works of interpretive political philosophy, mine shapes a certain world out of things discovered in another's text. This shaping is best described as both a critical and a creative engagement. I approach the generally apolitical but occasionally quasi-fascistic orientation of Heidegger's writings by following Heidegger's own recommendation. He observes that "the most drastic way to reject a proposition is not to dismiss it rudely as disproven and merely brush it *aside*, but on the contrary to take it over and work it *into* a fundamental and grounded connection with one's own argument—that is, to take it over and work it in as the nonpresence [*Unwesen*] that necessarily belongs to the presence [*Wesen*]."[6] The democratic vision developed in the following pages is offered as that political nonpresence that belongs to, but remains largely unclaimed and occasionally betrayed by, the philosophic presence of Heidegger's work.

It would be fatuous at this point to defend the claim of a beckoning political content to Heidegger's thought. What follows might then best be introduced with the same caveat Heidegger impresses on *Being and Time*. The first task, he writes, is to find "a *way* of casting light" on a fundamental question. Then one must begin the journey of its development: "Whether this is the *only* way or even the right one at all, can be decided only *after one has gone along it*" (*BT* 487). I have chosen Heidegger's thought as a way of casting light on the question of human freedom in postmodern times. The justification for this choice can only be found within the work as a whole.

[6] Martin Heidegger, "On the Being and Conception of Φύσις in Aristotle's Physics B, 1," trans. Thomas Sheehan, *Man and World* 9 (August 1976): 263–64. Translation emended.

Part One ————————————————————————

THE TWILIGHT OF MODERNITY

One

Nietzsche's Legacy

He who sees me, knows me,
he who knows me, names me
The homeless man.
. . . .

No one may dare
Question me where
My home is.
I am simply not confined
To space and fleeting time.
   (Friedrich Nietzsche, "Without a Home")

NIETZSCHE once said that he fought so fiercely with Socrates because the Greek philosopher always stood so close to him. I have come to form a similar relationship with Nietzsche. Consequently, this book was conceived with Nietzsche antagonistically in mind. During its gestation, Nietzsche prodded and poked and pried, like the mischief maker who tripped up the tightrope walker and cautioned Zarathustra. Heidegger also established this sort of relationship with Nietzsche. He was both excited and worried by Nietzsche's mischief. For this reason, Heidegger's characterizations and criticisms of Nietzsche are at times unfair. His accolades, at other times, seem exaggerated. In any case, Nietzsche serves as the subject of the greatest single share of Heidegger's published work. He is a crucial figure who receives the epithets, among others, of the "last German philosopher," the "only essential thinker after Schelling," and the "West's last thinker" (*SAG* 474; *ST* 3; *WCT* 46). Nietzsche, Heidegger states, was the first to recognize and the only philosopher to think through to its awesome conclusions the role of nihilism in the history of humankind (*WCT* 57). Heidegger also claimed that his lecture courses on Nietzsche, beginning in the mid-1930s, marked "for all who could hear at all" his initial "confrontation" with National Socialism (*OGS* 53). More generally, Nietzsche is held responsible (or coresponsible with Hölderlin) for the Kehre in Heidegger's thought. In short, Heidegger's struggle with Nietzsche largely defines the development of his thought. One must pass through Nietzsche,

Heidegger insists, if one is to come to terms philosophically with modernity and its aftermath.

Many believe that coming to terms with the politics of postmodernity also requires a passage through Nietzsche. Yet if one sets out with a democratic destination in mind, the passage becomes an uneasy affair. Those who take on this challenge generally celebrate aspects of Nietzsche's iconoclasm while redirecting its ruthlessly aristocratic force to other purposes. Anyone so engaged, however, must worry about joining the ranks of those Nietzsche considered his *"worst readers . . . who proceed like plundering soldiers: they pick up a few things they can use, soil and confuse the rest, and blaspheme the whole."*[1] Indeed, those who once approached Nietzsche with a political purpose diametrically opposed to that which I have in mind—the Nazi sympathizers of the 1930s and 1940s—did plunder him unscrupulously. Today the political theorist's choice of Nietzsche as a mentor or companion is more honorably based on the importance of his philosophic deeds. Nietzsche is acknowledged as constituting a radical break in the history of thought, thereby opening new vistas in the realm of political life.

The results obtained so far in this area of philosophy have been strikingly limited. The reason has to do with a commonly held premise regarding the nature of Nietzsche's philosophic achievement. Nietzsche is generally understood as the destroyer of metaphysics and the saboteur of any ethics resting on metaphysical foundations. As a means of introducing Heidegger's thought, I shall argue that this position obscures as much as it reveals about Nietzsche and saddles one with what might be called the postmodern political dilemma.

Nietzsche's Rupture

Writing to his friend Paul Deussen on September 14, 1888, Nietzsche made the claim that his recent works had "split the history of mankind in two halves."[2] A month later, shortly before his mental collapse, Nietzsche frenetically began to write his literary autobiography, *Ecce Homo*. Here the phrase describing his historically unique and cataclysmic role would again appear, among Nietzsche's many claims for him-

---

[1] Friedrich Nietzsche, *Human, All Too Human: A Book for Free Spirits,* trans. R. J. Hollingdale (Cambridge: Cambridge University Press, 1986), 245; translation from *On the Genealogy of Morals: A Polemic,* trans. Walter Kaufmann and R. J. Hollingdale (New York: Vintage, 1967), 175.

[2] Friedrich Nietzsche, *Nietzsche Briefwechsel, Kritische Gesamtausgabe,* ed. Giorgio Colli and Mazzino Montinari (Berlin: Walter de Gruyter, 1975–84), div. 3, 5:426.

self, in the section "Why I Am a Destiny." An "event without parallel" that set its discoverer "apart from the whole rest of humanity" is announced. Specifically, Nietzsche claims that his "uncovering" of Christian morality has broken human history in two. Christian morality, Nietzsche accuses, evidences the enfeeblement of basic instincts to the point where worldly life becomes depreciated. It is a form of *ressentiment*. In an effort to take revenge for the pain and unpredictability of life, the Christian moralist indignantly strikes out against it, attempting to control life's fractious power and harness its mysteries by means of an ethical code. Appeal to this code both justifies and promises compensation for the moralist's worldly impotence and suffering.

The early Greeks, Nietzsche argues, had a much healthier, more worldly, and consequently less decadent culture. Yet we must surpass even the Greeks' tragic heroism, he believes, to survive the looming menace of modern nihilism. Nietzsche's promotion of the life-affirming god Dionysus, in lieu of "the Crucified," is meant to constitute the world-historic onset of a new age. It is to initiate the transformation of thought, such that great thought might grasp and overcome nihilism, as well as the transfiguration of culture, such that great culture might foster a breed of human beings capable of harboring such thought. The revived tragic and heroic affirmation of life, not its resentment-induced calumny and morality-ridden bureaucratization, would constitute the future of humanity—if humanity were to have a future.

Though Nietzsche's world-historic aspirations proved overly ambitious, his crucial position within the history of thought remains intact. Yet for the most part, and increasingly so, the rupture Nietzsche is celebrated for occasioning is not that between Christian morality and its aftermath. This breach has been surpassed in significance by Nietzsche's detonation of metaphysics. Nietzsche originally viewed his attacks on the metaphysical foundations of modernity as skirmishes that prepared the ground and readied the warrior for the approaching war with Christian morality. Yet in the midst of contemporary cultural diversity and religious entropy, the significance of Nietzsche's holy war is lost on many of his readers. The more amorphous fissure between the modern and the postmodern has become his most celebrated handiwork.

The break between modernism and postmodernism, somewhat contrived in form but not without substance, is that which loosely marks off most of the twentieth century from its Cartesian (that is, rationalist and modernist) origins. The modern/postmodern dichotomy distinguishes the Western cultural regime of knowledge and power that lays claim to rationally accessible foundations, generally mediated through a metaphysically grounded ethics, from an emergent, disparate (anti)regime that admits no such pretensions. If postmodernity, in Jean-François Lyotard's popular definition, is chiefly constituted by an "incredulity toward metanarratives,"[3] then Nietzsche is held largely responsible for fostering this suspicion. Nietzsche is perhaps most famous for his announcement of the death of God. But Nietzsche recognized the chasing away of God's lingering shadows—the remnants of metaphysics—to be his more important feat. In this way he undermined any possible foundation for grandly constructed stories harboring the truth of humankind and dictating its ethics. Nietzsche's postmodern credentials are certified by his burning the bridge (while still standing on it) between the previous era of metaphysical belief and the present era of skeptical reserve. This is the major rupture for which Nietzsche, who announced himself not a man but dynamite, is held responsible. And it is from the dangerous crevices of this rupture that much of the cautious thinking about postmodern politics has emerged.

Nietzsche's substitute for rationally accessible metaphysical foundations is a Heraclitean world, stripped of stability, purpose, and predictability. Herein life becomes a terrifying and tragic experience amid the constant flux of becoming. But such a world also regains its lost innocence and resuscitates freedom. Indeed, though fearsome, it bestows the greatest liberty possible. In Nietzsche's world, humanity becomes free to create itself anew; it is constrained neither to a transcendent nature nor to a teleological program. Nietzsche espouses "the absolute necessity of a total liberation from ends: otherwise we should not be permitted to try to sacrifice ourselves and let ourselves go. Only the innocence of becoming gives us the *greatest courage* and the *greatest freedom*."[4] Life, Nietzsche insists, is an awe-inspiring adventure. It is decidedly not a clearinghouse within which one may drive one's hardest ethical bargain, fulfilling present obligations and accumulating promissory notes to be redeemed in ideal, future worlds. The upshot of Nietzsche's attack on modern metaphysics is his subversion of modern ethics. In Nietzsche's Heraclitean world, human society becomes an exercise in creative freedom, "an experiment . . . *not* a 'contract.' "[5]

The irony is that Nietzsche, the severest critic of Western culture, would champion the West's most cherished value: freedom. Nietzsche's brilliance is most evident in his analysis of the constraint, sacrifice, and slavery elicited and maintained in the name of reason, morality, and their metaphysical truths. The task taken on by many of Nietzsche's

[3] Jean-François Lyotard, *The Postmodern Condition: A Report on Knowledge* (Minneapolis: University of Minnesota Press, 1984), xxiv.

[4] Friedrich Nietzsche, *The Will to Power*, trans. Walter Kaufmann and R. J. Hollingdale (New York: Vintage, 1968), 416.

[5] Friedrich Nietzsche, *Thus Spoke Zarathustra: A Book for Everyone and No One*, trans. R. J. Hollingdale (New York: Penguin, 1969), 229.

postmodern readers is to demonstrate the liberating effects of his de-struction of metaphysics. Applauding Nietzsche for this feat, however, leaves one rather disadvantaged in the effort to establish or renew social and political sensibilities. Nietzsche's brand of freedom is simply too powerful an elixir to be left unregulated within the polity. It serves, alternately, as an anesthetic or an intoxicant.

The difficulty, then, is twofold. First, Nietzschean freedom may prove a debilitating anesthetic. It comes at the expense of teleological justifica-tions and moral applause. Precisely for this reason, it remains a heroic achievement.[6] Those without the heroic capacities and tragic disposi-tions needed to celebrate an ultimately meaningless life will discover that Nietzschean freedom reduces them to a state of jaded skepticism, cultural despair, and political apathy. Indeed, defenders of Nietzsche who find postmodernism to inspire just such disintegration and pas-sivity have for this reason sought to deny his paternity of it.[7] Effectively they are critical of postmodernists who adopt a Nietzschean skepticism without also adopting his heroic demeanor. Too suspicious of involve-ment and action, these postmodernists escape to literary diversions. They end up fiddling with tropes while Rome burns.

When the "ceremony of innocence is drowned," W. B. Yeats foresaw in "The Second Coming," "things fall apart." Then "The best lack all conviction, while the worst / Are full of passionate intensity." Hence the second problem with the political inauguration of Nietzschean freedom: while some succumb to apathy and inaction, others engage in action without boundaries. While the best lack all conviction, the worst, drunk with freedom, lack all restraint. While the former fail to rise to heroic heights because of their skeptical reserve, the latter exercise their heroic natures unchecked by principle. When freedom becomes an intoxicant, liberty becomes license. Everything is permitted. Nihilism looms.

If politics is defined by the exercise of freedom and responsibility in tandem, then a freedom gained at the expense of responsibility is a free-dom ill suited to political life. Yet this is the raw, unrestricted, and often debilitating freedom that Nietzsche delivers to us at the grave of meta-physics. Consequently, commentators on Nietzsche have been stymied

---

[6] Albert Camus explains that for Nietzsche "total acceptance of total necessity is his paradoxical definition of freedom. The question 'free of what?' is thus replaced by 'free for what?' Liberty coincides with heroism." Albert Camus, *The Rebel* (New York: Vin-tage, 1956), 72.

[7] Robert Solomon understands postmodernism to be "an excuse not to believe in any-thing, to avoid both personal and political involvement and take refuge in apathy, despair, or mere ambition." Robert Solomon, "Nietzsche, Postmodernism, and Resentment: A Genealogical Hypothesis," in *Nietzsche as Postmodernist: Essays Pro and Contra,* ed. C. Koelb (Albany: State University of New York Press, 1990), 292.

by the challenge of describing how his writings might be viewed as the epitaph of metaphysics but not of responsible judgment and accountable action. But in Nietzsche's world of constant flux and absolute liberty, where are we to find the criteria and standards that would allow critical evaluation and social obligation? Certain postmodern Nietzscheans, following Michel Foucault, propose aesthetic criteria to regulate our freedom. Art is to substitute for the fallen idols of ethics and metaphysics. For modernists this is an unsatisfying gesture, impractical at best and dangerous at worst. The kind of judgment elicited by art, like judgments of taste, is held to be without the normative force required to stabilize political life.[8]

The task of refitting Nietzsche with a political (and all-too-human) face, modern critics argue, has met with little success. Most efforts may be accused of wanting to eat their metaphysical and moral cakes and destroy them too. A satisfactory nonethical substitute for ethics, as the motivating and controlling element of politics, and a nonmetaphysical substitute for metaphysics, as the foundation for such an ethics, remains missing from postmodern recipes.[9] To the extent that postmodern theorists are successful in defending Nietzsche's destruction of metaphysics, they disable themselves from producing a viable politics. Alternatively, if they are intent on promoting a democratic political vision, they are forced to call a halt to Nietzsche's assault on metaphysics and ethics. Either the promotion of Nietzschean freedom leaves one at a loss as to

[8] Charles Taylor writes of the "unrestrained, utterly self-related freedom that this ideal [Foucault's notion of the self as a work of art] entails. . . . To the extent that this kind of freedom is held up as the essence of 'post-modernity,' as it is by Jean-François Lyotard, it shows this to be a prolongation of the least impressive side of modernism." Charles Taylor, *Sources of the Self: The Making of the Modern Identity* (Cambridge, Mass.: Harvard University Press, 1989), 489. Though his assessment is apposite, Taylor does not adequately spell out the nature of the "prolongation." I attempt this in chapter 3.

[9] William Connolly denies that a recipe is sought in the first place. The aim, Connolly maintains, is not to develop "from scratch" a philosophically grounded ethics and politics. Instead of seeking a basis for a binding morality, Connolly proceeds from the assumption of "a world already permeated by ethical proclivities" to argue for an ethic of "cultivation" rather than one of "command." William E. Connolly, *Identity\Difference: Democratic Negotiations of Political Paradox* (Ithaca: Cornell University Press, 1991), 10, 15. The appropriate politics for this ethics, Connolly proposes, is a Foucaultian "agonism" that balances itself between the requirements of responsibility and the threats of normalization and exclusion. Predictably, Connolly cannot give a satisfying reply to those (modernists) who ask what this political "balance" would look like in practice or precisely what procedures are required for an ethic of cultivation. But Connolly's choice of Foucault as a model is well taken; Foucault has supplied us with the richest description of a democratic politics inspired by Nietzsche's thought to date. I have offered an analysis of the Nietzschean background to Foucault's development of an aesthetic and agonistic politics in "The Agony of Politics: The Nietzschean Roots of Foucault's Thought," *American Political Science Review* 84 (September 1990): 907–25.

how a responsible politics might be fostered, or the extent of the adulteration of Nietzsche's thought found necessary for his domestication leaves us unconvinced that his philosophy constitutes a useful starting point for a political inquiry.

It is my conviction that such efforts will continue to be unsatisfactory, their increasing sophistication notwithstanding. The problem is not with the imaginative political uses to which Nietzsche is put, but with the traditional premises on which these efforts rest. In short, Nietzsche's role as a watershed in the history of thought is misunderstood. Nietzsche is not the destroyer of metaphysics. He is at once its fiercest rival and its unwitting spokesperson. My claim is that only when we see how and to what extent Nietzsche remains entangled in metaphysics may his efforts serve a promising political purpose. Nietzsche's lingering metaphysics has not been completely ignored by postmodernists. In attributing to Nietzsche an *unconsummated* victory over metaphysics, however, they tend to confront us with a spurious dilemma. We are forced to choose between saving metaphysics from Nietzsche and saving Nietzsche from metaphysics. The former is the modern mission, which postmodernists (and I) reject as vain. The postmodern alternative thus appears to win by default. But the project of blotting out Nietzsche's metaphysical residues is self-defeating. Any effort to give metaphysics the coup de grâce that uses a Nietzschean strategy for the attack will only iterate Nietzsche's own reinvestment in metaphysics. The appropriate task, I propose, is to understand Nietzsche as a prodigal son of the Western metaphysical tradition. His political significance is better illuminated if one outlines his affiliation with this tradition than if one celebrates his disjunction from it. To explore the potential of a postmodern politics we must first unlearn the lesson of Nietzsche's destruction of metaphysics, and subsequently reach beyond the *homelessness* of his position.[10]

Nietzsche found humanity "sitting between two chairs." Here, as always, his investigation was characterized by an effort to push what was beginning to fall. Then the *"diagnosis of the modern soul"* would begin by way of a "vivisection of the *most instructive* case."[11] Nietzsche was in this instance referring to his former friend, the composer Richard Wagner. But we might equally view Nietzsche in such a vulnerable position, and it will be instructive to turn our knives in his direction. Such

[10] As may be gathered from certain aspects of my previous work, I have had some unlearning to do myself regarding the nature of Nietzsche's relation to the metaphysical tradition (see especially 34 n. 2 of *Friedrich Nietzsche and the Politics of the Soul: A Study of Heroic Individualism* (Princeton: Princeton University Press, 1990).

[11] Friedrich Nietzsche, *The Case of Wagner*, trans. Walter Kaufmann (New York: Vintage, 1967), 192.

delicate surgery, if it is to aid us in our political theorizing, demands focused vision. Heidegger provides the needed lens.

Heidegger's lens magnifies certain facets of Nietzsche's thought and obscures others. I propose its use, therefore, with a caveat. Nietzsche does not take easily to pigeonholes. He is a protean thinker, harboring profound ambiguities and ambivalences. When approaching Nietzsche we should recall his observation that intellectual sophistication and integrity are confirmed by the ability to forgo exclusive opposites and dichotomous categories. Heidegger indulged in categorical statements and oppositions. We should be wary of them. But the specific and elusive goal set by Heidegger remains: we must strive to "*see beyond everything that is fatally contemporary in Nietzsche*" (WPA 127). Nietzsche's tragic genius is evident in his capacity to demonstrate the maladies of the modern world by exhibiting his own contamination by it. The present effort largely ignores Nietzsche's inspiring struggle with this infection in order to concentrate on how and why he proved unable to overcome it.

Nietzsche maintains that one cannot evaluate life as a whole because an objective perspective is wanting: "Judgements, value judgements concerning life, for or against, can in the last resort never be true: they possess value only as symptoms. . . . One must reach out and try to grasp this astonishing *finesse, that the value of life cannot be estimated.* Not by a living man, because he is party to the dispute, indeed its object, and not the judge of it; not by a dead one, for another reason."[12] This observation does not lead Nietzsche to adopt a Stoic indifference to life. He desperately seeks to affirm life as a whole, despite its suffering. Indeed, what separates his philosophy from the Stoics' is his determination not merely to accept the inevitable pain of life with equanimity but to prize it as a means to life's fuller affirmation. The challenge is not simply to bear suffering with resignation, but heroically to seek it out because it offers an opportunity to test, display, and improve one's mettle.[13] What allows Nietzsche to celebrate life despite any objective grounds for its evaluation is this heroic disposition. To be heroic, tragically heroic, is constantly to taste the terrible mystery of life and willingly to risk all in the adventure. There is no moral redemption in a Heraclitean world, but the tragic hero nevertheless achieves greatness through his deeds. And his greatest deeds are those that transform suffering into life affirmation. *"What makes one heroic,"* Nietzsche in-

[12] Friedrich Nietzsche, *Twilight of the Idols; or, How to Philosophize with a Hammer,* trans. R. J. Hollingdale (New York: Penguin, 1968), 30.
[13] Friedrich Nietzsche, *Gesammelte Werke,* 23 vols. (Munich: Musarion, 1920–29), 1:244.

sists, is "going out to meet at the same time one's highest suffering and one's highest hope."[14]

The highest suffering is spiritual. We suffer most from our inability to endow our mundane afflictions with cosmological meaning. Hence the invention of morality, which gives meaning to our pain by providing an alleviating sense of guilt. Punishment is easier to bear than senseless suffering. With the modern disintegration of morality, Nietzsche foresaw that the terrible abyss of a Heraclitean world, a world of suffering without meaning, might become unbearable: "Nihilism appears at that point, not that the displeasure at existence has become greater than before but because one has come to mistrust any 'meaning' in suffering, indeed in existence. One interpretation has collapsed; but because it was considered *the* interpretation it now seems as if there were no meaning at all in existence, as if everything were in vain."[15] A single remedy for this debilitating mistrust exists. One must lift oneself up by one's bootstraps and greet a meaningless and painful life not merely with equanimity but with joy. There is no *reason* that justifies this comportment. Indeed, it is the absence of any rational justification that makes for the heroic, and ultimately tragic, nature of Nietzsche's solution.

Nietzsche's philosophy of tragic heroism is both inspiring and intimidating. For the purposes of this discussion, I will restrict myself to two of its most significant consequences. First, it produces a radically individualistic worldview. Nietzsche's heroic ideal befits only a wanderer and a solitary. In creating of himself, philosophically and biographically, a heroic and hermitic figure, Nietzsche attempts to leap beyond the realm of good and evil, beyond political community, social mores, customs, religion, even beyond personal habits and friendships. He shuns his affiliation with humanity, abandons all idols, and spurns any divinities that might accompany him on his odyssey. His is an itinerancy of such isolation that it forbids itself a companion and a resting place both on earth and in the heavens.

Nietzsche's individualism amounts to an extreme homelessness. I will spend little time at this point discussing the nomadic character of Nietzsche's philosophy and existence; in his writing and his life Nietzsche frequently described, often applauded, and in the end tragically celebrated this fate. In any case, its nature will become evident as I explore the second ramification of Nietzsche's heroic perspective. Despite his

[14] Friedrich Nietzsche, *The Gay Science*, trans. Walter Kaufmann (New York: Vintage, 1974), 219.
[15] Nietzsche, *Will to Power*, 35.

effort to leap beyond the realm of good and evil—indeed, in large part because of it—Nietzsche proves incapable of escaping metaphysics. The radical individualism embraced to ensure the success of his journey forever envelops Nietzsche in the subjectivism that grounds the Western metaphysical tradition. To be sure, Nietzsche distinguishes himself from all previous metaphysicians by the extremism of his nomadic pursuit. His worldly and self-referential perspective, an effective reversal of the Platonic ideal as Nietzsche sees it, is offered as the evidence of his having left metaphysics behind. Even those few "metaphysical comforts" in which he himself once indulged, Nietzsche insists in his 1886 "Attempt at a Self-Criticism," have been dispatched "to the devil."[16] But Nietzsche's extreme position, most evident in his celebration of the Overman, is just that: the furthest point on a line of metaphysical musings that forever court and in the end consummate a relationship to subjectivism. Though he believes himself only a visitor who might later shake the dust from his feet, Nietzsche ends up a rather permanent guest in the house of metaphysics. Incapable of escaping, yet unwilling to accept metaphysics as his abode, Nietzsche precariously straddles his modern origins and his postmodern legacy. In tribute to Nietzsche, I shall adopt here his own tactic of pushing what is beginning to fall. Heidegger's understanding of Nietzsche's role in the history of metaphysics provides the lever.

Subjectivism and Metaphysics

Unlike all other beings, Heidegger observes, human being is interrogatively occupied with its own existence. Existence, as an ontic or factual category, is something humans share with all beings. Only human being, however, is ontologically disposed to its life, oriented questioningly to itself. In questioning its very being, human being cannot help questioning that which serves as the ground for all being, for beings as a whole. Heidegger writes in *Being and Time:* "Dasein is an entity which does not just occur among other entities. Rather it is ontically distinguished by the fact that, in its very Being, that Being is an *issue* for it. . . . *Understanding of Being is itself a definite characteristic of Dasein's Being.* Dasein is ontically distinctive in that it *is* ontological" (*BT* 32). The distinctiveness of human being, then, is not simply that it is aware of itself, but that its awareness is fundamentally interrogative. Human being is not simply self-conscious, but is conscious of

---

[16] Friedrich Nietzsche, *The Birth of Tragedy,* trans. Walter Kaufmann (New York: Vintage, 1967), 26.

a self that questions its own ground and the ground of beings as a whole.

The ontological thought of human being, in its most profound and most basic form, may be reduced to a single question: What is the Being of being? (*Was ist das Sein des Seienden?*)[17] This query pursues the "isness" of everything that is but tolerates no final answer. Oriented to the Beingness of being (*die Seiendheit des Seienden*), the questioner glimpses that the universe, all that *is,* material and otherwise in its manifold states, is fundamentally unified in its partaking of "isness," of Being. In the history of Western thought, Heidegger believes, this search for the Being of being first truly begins with Parmenides. Heraclitus, though distinct in his approach, shares with Parmenides this fundamental project. To the extent that other words might be ascribed to the Being of being, these thinkers indicate it to be an upsurgence, a revealing or presencing, an unconcealment. The original names given to the Being of being were *physis* and *alētheia.* Physis, often translated as "nature," signifies not simply geological or biological processes, but the upsurgence of all beings as they come to presence. Alētheia, often translated as "truth," likewise refers to an unconcealment. For these ancient thinkers, Being is that which fosters the disclosure of beings. Being, therefore, is truth itself. What gives unity and wholeness to the universe of beings is that they come to presence. Being, most fundamentally, is an emerging into unconcealment.

The original thought of Parmenides and Heraclitus would soon undergo a change. This change marked the beginning of Western metaphysics, and, as the terms are often synonymous for Heidegger, the beginning of Western philosophy. With the rise of Sophism, and particularly with the rise of Socratic and Platonic thought, the focus on Being as unconcealment was lost (*WP* 53).[18] A distinct effort was made to grasp hold of the fundamental nature of a universe of entities, of beings. The focus, in other words, shifted from a questioning relationship to truth as an ongoing disclosiveness to the conception of truth as the underlying reality of beings as a whole. Concern was transferred from presencing as such to that which became manifest through presencing, to being thought of as the stable feature of a universal set of extant

[17] In the interest of consistency I have throughout this book emended certain English translations of Heidegger's works (namely Heim's, Hofstadter's, Kisiel's, and Manheim's) to correspond to Macquarrie and Robinson's translation of *Being and Time. Sein,* alone and in its hyphenated phrases, is translated as "Being." *Seiende* is translated as "being" or "beings," depending on the context.

[18] Given Heidegger's evaluation of Parmenides' role in the history of thought, the trenchancy of the following remark is apparent: "To present Parmenides as a pre-Socratic is even more foolish than to call Kant a pre-Hegelian" (*WCT* 184).

things. With Plato, Heidegger writes, "Being means *ousia*, the presence of what endures in the unconcealed. . . . *Because Being is presence of what endures in the unconcealed, Plato can therefore interpret Being, ousia (beingness), as* idea" (*N* 161, 162). Plato's original thought was that Ideas, conceived as that which endures amid change and flux, constitute the ultimate reality. The essence of Being here became a "what." The first great step on the long metaphysical road to modernity had been taken. Being received its first "master-name." It would receive many others in the development of Western metaphysics, culminating in Nietzsche's notion of the will to power. In each case the attempt was to give an answer to the question, "What is being?" And in each case the question was answered with an eye to an enduring, unchanging thing. The original Parmenidean and Heraclitean orientation to Being as unconcealment, to presencing as such, was abandoned.

Opposed to the metaphysical understanding of the Being of beings as an enduring presence that may be represented by an idea, Heidegger proposes Being as nonrepresentable, as "the pure 'Other' than what-is" (*EB* 360). We never actually perceive this pure Other (as a thing or a representation). Rather, "Being is there [*gibt sich*] primordially and in itself, when it gives access to its beings. Nor with regard to these beings can one investigate their Being in itself. We always know only beings, but never Being as a being" (*MFL* 153). Being, to the extent that it is made available to human being, is always revealed as *hidden*. Whenever we confront beings, there remains for us the *question* of their Being. Being becomes manifest to human being neither as an external ground that lies beyond us (*TB* 6), nor as a representation or idea that lies within us. Rather, Being reveals itself as the mystery of its own hiddenness within beings. Heidegger dubs human being the "persona" or "mask" of Being (*WCT* 62). Even if we could rip away the mask of Being, however, no discernible features would be revealed beneath. Being is nothing extant. Yet it is precisely the disclosure of Being's hiddenness in beings that human being assumes as its essential task. What "makes its claim on man, calling him to its essential being," Heidegger writes, is "Being itself—that is to say: the presence of present beings, the two-fold of the two in virtue of their simple oneness" (*WL* 30).

Throughout the history of Western metaphysics, Heidegger claims, we witness a persistent rejection of this truth. By way of its preoccupation with enduring being(s), metaphysics refuses to "think Being" (*WPK* 207). Rather than follow the long trail of philosophers and philosophic epochs that constitute this history, I shall leap from the ancient Greeks to the onset of modernity and then to Nietzsche, for Nietzsche's thought is spawned from, and instinctively returns to, the metaphysical tradition that began in Greece and reached its apogee in modern times.

Descartes's philosophy most clearly marks the beginning of modernity. His conception of truth as the certitude of a subject is premised on the metaphysical understanding that all truth is representational. Truth, for Descartes, is derivative of the clear and distinct mental representations of the self-conscious human subject. Modernity, Heidegger maintains, is thus founded on "two mutually essential determinations" present within Cartesian philosophy: "first, that man installs and secures himself as *subiectum*, as the nodal point for beings as a whole; and secondly, that the beingness of beings as a whole is grasped as the representedness of whatever can be produced and explained" (*WPK* 178). Modernity's ascription of subjectivity to human being and its ascription of truth to the subject's representational perceptions ironically find their culmination in Nietzsche's attempt to undercut the latter premise by pushing the former to its extreme. In so doing, Nietzsche most clearly demonstrates the continuity of metaphysics amid its many historical permutations. As Heidegger explains, "the new orientation toward consciousness in modern philosophy since Descartes is not a radically new beginning over against antiquity, but only its extension and transference to the subject" (*HPS* 136).

Truth, for Plato, was the correspondence of reality to the transcendent Idea. In turn and after numerous reformulations, truth, in the seventeenth century, became the correctness of human perception, its correspondence to an objective reality. But, as Heidegger notes, the understanding of truth as objectivity necessitates a reliance on the notion of subjectivity. The modern subject becomes the arbiter of what is to appear as true. This is a far cry from Plato's attempt to place truth beyond the perverting effects of our worldly senses and appetites in a transcendent realm of Forms. But the point is that the uneven and tortuous road leading from Plato to Descartes and Nietzsche requires no leaps, only time, to traverse. Heidegger offers this survey:

> Being, then, for Plato, has its real essence in its What. . . . And so the unhidden is conceived primarily and solely as what is perceived in the act of perceiving the ιδέα. . . . But in so far as this approach is necessarily carried out through a "seeing," unhiddenness is hitched to the "relation" to seeing, and is "relative" to this. . . . Truth becomes ὀρθότης, correctness of the ability to perceive and to declare something. . . . As unhiddenness truth is still a basic feature of beings themselves. But as correctness of "looking" truth becomes the label of the human attitude towards beings. . . . From now on the mold of the essence of truth becomes, as the correctness of representing through an assertion, the standard for all of Western thinking. . . . A statement of St. Thomas Aquinas holds true for Medieval Scholasticism: . . . "truth is really met with in the human or in the divine understanding." . . . At

the beginning of modern times Descartes sharpens the above quotation by saying: . . . "Truth or falsehood in the real sense cannot be anywhere else except in the understanding alone." Truth no longer is, as unhiddenness, the basic feature of Being itself, but it is, in consequence of having become correctness by being yoked under the Idea, from this time forth the label of the recognizing of beings. . . . Plato's thinking follows the change of the essence of truth, which change becomes the story of metaphysics and which has begun its unconditional fulfillment in Nietzsche's thinking.[19]

There is a seldom-noticed symmetry to the continuities and discontinuities marking Heidegger's history of metaphysics. Just as Descartes's subjective humanism would have been abhorred by Plato, so Nietzsche's radical perspectivism would have been abhorred by Descartes. Yet each of these thinkers did not so much transcend his predecessor's thought as expose and extrude its core.

Heidegger finds Nietzsche to be as much a victim of Western metaphysical conceptions as his forerunners were. While acknowledging Nietzsche's "vibrant rapport with the personalities of the Preplatonic philosophers" (EGT 14) and his understanding of "the great age of Greek beginnings with a depth that was surpassed only by Hölderlin" (IM 126), Heidegger nevertheless criticizes Nietzsche for failing to grasp the essence of Parmenidean and Heraclitean thought. The claim is that Nietzsche was charmed by metaphysics because of his misunderstanding of the origins of Western thinking. In short, Nietzsche became "a victim of the current (and false) opposition between Parmenides and Heraclitus" (IM 26). Nietzsche rejects Parmenides' assertion that everything partakes of Being in favor of what he holds to be Heraclitus's view: with everything in flux there can be no such thing as Being, stable and unchanging. Being and becoming, as opposites, must exclude each other.

If Being (and truth) are the enduring realities claimed by metaphysicians, then simple logic forever divides Being from becoming. If, on the other hand, Being (and truth) are a coming to presence, less a *what* than a *how*, then becoming is not only compatible with Being but constitutes its very essence. Heidegger maintains the need to escape the metaphysical dichotomy that still trapped Nietzsche: "Becoming is a manner of preserving Being, serviceable to Being, not the simple opposite of Being as it might easily appear if Being and becoming are only distinguished in formal respects and Being is understood as objective presence. . . . Nietzsche . . . never got out of the network of formal dialectic at this

---

[19] Martin Heidegger, "Plato's Doctrine of Truth," in *Philosophy in the Twentieth Century*, ed. William Barrett and Henry Aiken (New York: Random House, 1962), 262, 265–67, 269.

point" (*ST* 123). Nietzsche approaches Heraclitus through Plato. His strong identification with the former is largely a by-product of his passionate rejection of the latter. Becoming is embraced in opposition to Being because Being, with Plato, got firmly attached to idealism and its counterpart, moralism. Plato reduces Being to the rigid realm of Forms. A further ossification is signaled by the reduction of the Platonic good (*agathon*) to an idea with strictly moral import. With such a bloodless alternative before him, Nietzsche gladly embraces Heraclitus's heroic world of change and strife. In so doing, he rejects any attachment to stagnant ideals and transcendent realms in order to establish a transient, worldly, and sensuous life as its own reference.

Here we observe Nietzsche's "reversal of Platonism" wherein the sensuous becomes the true world and the suprasensuous becomes the untrue world. Physics replaces metaphysics. Becoming replaces Being. But by turning Plato on his head, Nietzsche, though ousting the notion of transcendent truth, actually exaggerates the subjectivism implicit in the metaphysical tradition. He remains, as Heidegger observes, "thoroughly caught in metaphysics" (*EP* 92). Nietzsche, in his most doctrinaire moments, proposes his own (meta)narrative with the will to power playing the part of the enduring (meta)physical truth of being. Ethical ideals and epistemological principles are discarded so that a world of ungrounded beings may exercise their drive for growth. For most earthly inhabitants the will to power is a primordial dictate executed unconsciously as the rule of life. For humankind, however, and for "higher types" in particular, it becomes a terrible truth. Their tortured consciousness of human limitation might cause these rare individuals to perish were it not for their heroic capacity to thrive on nothing but the play of their will in the world. Such individuals, Overman-like in their demeanor, are isolated and self-sufficient subjects capable of establishing a private world of truth, and perhaps remaking the world of others in its image.

Radical Individualism and Homelessness

Heidegger's assessment of Nietzsche appears straightforward and unyielding. He declares that *"we must grasp Nietzsche's philosophy as the metaphysics of subjectivity"* (*N* 147). Yet Nietzsche is a thinker of multiple tendencies and few, if any, enduring positions. Like Emerson, he believes a foolish consistency to be the hobgoblin of little minds. Nietzsche originally proposes the will to power as an experiment in thought, not a dogmatic statement of transcendent truth. More to the point, he frequently criticizes facile formulations of subjectivism, disparaging the

tendency to presume a "doer" simply because one observes a "deed."[20]
In turn, he proposes that the vocabulary of subjectivity itself is merely a
fabrication erected as a bulwark against the unknown.[21] One could argue that dogmatism increasingly overtook thought during the last years
of Nietzsche's productive life. But my point here is not that we must
accept the metaphysically consolidated Nietzsche as the only Nietzsche,
even though Heidegger, at times, does. The point is that Nietzsche was
unable to resist the lure of metaphysics, though his never-ending battles
with it evidence greater and lesser degrees of attachment. Nietzsche illuminates the nature of subjectivism not because he naively endorses it,
but because in constantly wrestling with it he proves incapable of doing
without its support.

To grasp the significance of this view, we must first ask how Nietzsche's philosophy may at one and the same time espouse the metaphysics of subjectivity and spurn the other side of the modern coin: a
belief in an ultimate reality begetting an objective truth. After all, the
effort to secure a passkey to an objective realm was the reason for devising subjectivist criteria for establishing truth, such as Cartesian certitude, in the first place. Nietzsche had bit deeply into Cartesian doubt.
But unlike Descartes, he felt himself too honest to posit an evil demon
as an epistemological vandal and a moral God as the prevailing police-
man. "Why does man not see things?" Nietzsche asks, not unlike Descartes. But Nietzsche's answer differs markedly: "[Man] himself is in
the way: he conceals things."[22] We remain prisoners within ourselves,
and serve as our own wardens. Our truths are nothing but our conventions. According to Nietzsche, "The habits of our senses have woven us
into lies and deception of sensation: these again are the basis of all our
judgments and 'knowledge'—there is absolutely no escape, no backway
or bypath into the *real world!* We sit within our net, we spiders, and
whatever we may catch in it, we can catch nothing at all except that
which allows itself to be caught in precisely *our* net."[23] The individual
remains ensconced within its own cave. Projects carried out therein necessarily bear the marks of their shadowy origins. Metaphysical exercises
aimed at leaving the cave to gaze at objective truth evidence only a
decadent yearning for the unattainable. "In the final analysis," Zarathustra reminds us, "one experiences only oneself."[24] For this reason
Nietzsche avers that his own work is written with blood. Nor, we learn,

[20] Nietzsche, *On the Genealogy of Morals,* 45.
[21] Nietzsche, *Will to Power,* 267–72. See also chapter 3, n. 31, below.
[22] Friedrich Nietzsche, *Daybreak: Thoughts on the Prejudices of Morality,* trans. R. J.
Hollingdale (Cambridge: Cambridge University Press, 1982), 187.
[23] Ibid., 73.
[24] Nietzsche, *Thus Spoke Zarathustra,* 173.

could it be otherwise: "No matter how far a man may extend himself with his knowledge, no matter how objectively he may come to view himself, in the end it can yield him nothing but his own biography."[25]

Nietzsche grasped the legacy of modern thought. Subjectivism is a curse for modern humans, who have lost the innocence needed to deny its nihilistic claims. The heroic response, however, is not to bewail this plight but to transform it. Nietzsche attempts to make a virtue out of the subjectivist isolation in which he finds himself and modern humanity to be languishing. He proclaims, "No longer the humble expression, 'everything is *merely* subjective,' but 'it is also *our* work!—Let us be proud of it!'"[26] Faced with the prison of subjectivity, one has the opportunity to make it a paradise. But the task is awesome. There are no foundations on which to build. There are no paradigms to emulate. Each, Zarathustra insists, must become a law unto himself. Each must take responsibility for the creation of a self and its world of meaning. Indeed, the world has collapsed into the self. Only the strongest can survive this freedom.

It follows for Nietzsche that the degree of one's strength and the mettle of one's character are determined by the intensity of one's solitude. "He shall be the greatest who can be the most solitary," Nietzsche flatly declares.[27] The first question concerning the order of rank pertains to the extent of one's isolation. More precisely, the question of the order of rank pertains to the depth of one's affirmation of the inescapable individuality of human being. Community with fellow humans or with gods, Nietzsche insists, is an illusion in any case. "Fundamentally," Nietzsche writes, "all our actions are altogether incomparably personal, unique, and infinitely individual; there is no doubt of that. But as soon as we translate them into consciousness *they no longer seem to be.*"[28] The intellectual and spiritual integrity that dictates rejection of the illusion of community, coupled with sufficient will to power to create and maintain a world of beauty and meaning for oneself, is the mark of the highest type. At the same time, Nietzsche's heroic individual must remain connected enough to his culture to rise above it. The "pathos of distance" separating the individual from "the herd" is a creative force. It brings forth the "ripest fruit," which is, for Nietzsche, the "*sovereign individual.*"[29] Thus the "production of genius," the nurturing of "great redemptive men," becomes the sole purpose of culture. A people be-

[25] Nietzsche, *Human, All Too Human,* 182.
[26] Nietzsche, *Will to Power,* 545.
[27] Friedrich Nietzsche, *Beyond Good and Evil: Prelude to a Philosophy of the Future,* trans. R. J. Hollingdale (New York: Penguin, 1972), 125.
[28] Nietzsche, *Gay Science,* 299–300.
[29] Nietzsche, *On the Genealogy of Morals,* 59.

comes merely "a detour of nature to get to six or seven great men."[30] The solitude of these great men is as severe as their freedom is unconstrained.

Nietzsche informs us that *Thus Spoke Zarathustra* was written as a "dithyramb on solitude."[31] The same might be said of his philosophy as a whole. Nietzsche's writings are panegyrics dedicated to the solitude incarnated in himself and envisioned in the Overman. In the urge to "perfect self-sufficiency" of the Nietzschean Overman, subjectivism finds its apotheosis. Herein Nietzsche reinvests himself in Cartesian thought with a vengeance. But now there is no deus ex machina to ground the subject's certitude and vouch for the accuracy of its mental representations. The Overman experiences a solitude so severe that he refuses—as Nietzsche said of himself—to allow even a god into his company.[32] The subjectivism that Nietzsche inherits from his modern origins is distilled into a near-solipsistic individualism. Heidegger describes the ironic result: "No matter how sharply Nietzsche pits himself time and again against Descartes, whose philosophy grounds modern metaphysics, he turns against Descartes only because the latter *still* does *not* posit man as *subiectum* in a way that is complete and decisive enough. . . . Modern metaphysics first comes to the full and final determination of its essence in the doctrine of the Overman, the doctrine of man's absolute preeminence among beings. In that doctrine, Descartes celebrates his supreme triumph" (*N* 28). Far from denying the subject as the locus of truth, then, Nietzsche celebrates this relation. But now truth, no longer a representation of objective reality, becomes the individual's fabrication of a subjective reality. The need for a shared foundation for truth, be it metaphysical or religious, is spurned as the symptom of an atrophied will to power.

Nietzsche believed that the intellectual integrity involved in his rejection of transcendent realms and divinities would indisputably separate him from his metaphysically and religiously disposed predecessors. But in denying that truth is a reflection of an objective reality in the mirror of the human mind, Nietzsche was toppling only one of the twin pillars supporting the metaphysical edifice. Nietzsche's tug-of-war with metaphysical thought is largely carried out along this single axis, with Nietzsche confident that in crossing the line to ungrounded subjectivity he would have defeated the metaphysicians pulling him toward objective

[30] Friedrich Nietzsche, *Untimely Meditations*, trans. R. J. Hollingdale (Cambridge: Cambridge University Press, 1983), 161–63; *Beyond Good and Evil*, 81.

[31] Friedrich Nietzsche, *Ecce Homo*, trans. Walter Kaufmann (New York: Vintage, 1967), 234.

[32] Nietzsche, *Nietzsche Briefwechsel*, div. 3, 3:63.

standards. What Nietzsche failed to realize was the extent to which a metaphysics of subjectivism underlay the entire field of his struggle.

Nietzsche's battle with Descartes, in this regard, is not unlike his battle with Plato. He rejects Plato's idealism only to find himself inextricably entangled with materialism. He rejects Descartes's notion of objectivity and certitude only to find himself enmeshed in a vastly exaggerated form of subjectivism. In this sense, both Plato and Descartes deserve a place of honor at the wake Nietzsche prepares to celebrate God's demise. Heidegger indicates the philosophic legacy to which Nietzsche proved a reluctant heir: "in the brief statement: 'God is dead' it remains to ask whether Nietzsche does not rather pronounce here the word that always, within the metaphysically determined history of the West, is already being spoken by implication" (*QT* 57; cf. *N* 72). In his least-reserved articulation of the same point, Heidegger writes: "*Metaphysics as metaphysics is nihilism proper.* The essence of nihilism *is* historically as metaphysics, and the metaphysics of Plato is no less nihilistic than that of Nietzsche. In the former, the essence of nihilism is merely concealed; in the latter, it comes completely to appearance" (*N* 205).

Nietzsche, like Heidegger, perceives the nihilism lurking within the metaphysical tradition. But Nietzsche responds with a direct attack. In place of otherworldly hopes or Platonic ideals that underscore worldly deficiencies, Nietzsche celebrates the sensuous and self-sufficient individual. He attempts to distinguish himself from his forerunners by denouncing their betrayal of the earth in the name of higher realms, truths, and deities. Those who cannot affirm a worldly life in and for itself, he accuses, project heavenly ideals in compensation. Not he, but these metaphysicians, theologians, Platonists, and romantics are the true nihilists, Nietzsche inveighs, "because they all have glorified the concept contrary to life, *nothing(ness),* as end, as highest good, as 'God.'"[33] The charge of nihilism is leveled against all those who deprecate life because of their inability to partake of its tragic celebration in the absence of foundations. Experiencing existential vertigo, they grasp for idols. Their desperate efforts constitute a new form of impiety.

Zarathustra entreats his followers to "*remain true to the earth.*" They should forgo the temptation of "superterrestrial hopes." Such hopes profane life: "Once blasphemy against God was the greatest blasphemy, but God died, and thereupon these blasphemers died too. To blaspheme the earth is now the most dreadful offence."[34] Nietzsche announces the

---

[33] Nietzsche, *Gesammelte Werke* 14:328.
[34] Nietzsche, *Thus Spoke Zarathustra,* 42.

death of God as a plea for humanity to establish a mundane home. He believes that this home will never come to be while eyes are still lifted toward heaven. "The concept of 'God,'" Nietzsche charges, was "invented as a counterconcept of life. . . . The concept of the 'beyond,' the 'true world' invented in order to devaluate the only world there is—in order to retain no goal, no reason, no task for our earthly reality!"[35] The irony is that Nietzsche's radical individualism also has the effect of leaving us without a sense of place and without criteria to determine what remaining "true to the earth" might mean. Consequently, it too strips mundane tasks and goals from our hands.

With this in mind, a more revealing description of Nietzsche's subjectivist solitude emerges: it is a form of homelessness. The self-isolation of the "higher types" makes them "wanderers" accompanied only by their shadows. These itinerants have no home in the world because they share no world with others. At best, they can hope for a home in a future world where they might live in memory among friends, posthumously. Nietzsche considered himself and his meditations "untimely." Indeed, being without place in the present is considered by Nietzsche to be not simply a fate, but a duty. "What does a philosopher demand of himself first and last?" Nietzsche asks. "To overcome his time in himself, to become 'timeless.'"[36] Nietzsche's philosophy, as the subtitle of *Beyond Good and Evil* indicates, is intended as a "philosophy of the future." His voyage beyond good and evil, and beyond all that could establish for him an abode among his contemporaries, is Nietzsche's celebration of a temporal homelessness.[37] Only self-isolation allows the intellectual and spiritual distance necessary to allow one to recognize and assess the delusions of those who have taken refuge in the present day and its conventions: "If one would like to see our European morality for once as it looks from a distance, and if one would like to measure it against other moralities, past and future, then one has to proceed like a wanderer who wants to know how high the towers in a

---

[35] Nietzsche, *Ecce Homo*, 334.

[36] Nietzshe, *Case of Wagner*, 155.

[37] In an excellent analysis of Nietzsche's individualism, Werner Hamacher writes: "Only in setting new goals for itself, only in tracing the design of a future into which it projects itself, proving itself free of conventions, customs, and morals, free for its own future self, does the individual become the monstrously significant single being in which the whole process of its becoming places itself under the sign of its own futurity." Werner Hamacher, "'Disgregation of the Will': Nietzsche on the Individual and Individuality," in *Friedrich Nietzsche*, ed. Harold Bloom (New York: Chelsea House, 1987), 172. Hamacher goes on to quote Nietzsche's description (from *Will to Power*, 403) of the type of individual capable of living its future: "The individual both *is* and *produces* what is wholly *new*; he is absolute, all acts wholly *his own*. The isolated one draws the values that guide his acts ultimately only out of himself."

town are: he *leaves* the town."[38] Leaving town, for Nietzsche, became a lifelong endeavor.

Leaving town prohibits one from keeping companions, from establishing foundations on which to build, and from dwelling in one's time. It is a dangerous refusal. Under the heading "*We who are homeless,*" Nietzsche describes the task: "Among Europeans today there is no lack of those who are entitled to call themselves homeless in a distinctive and honorable sense. . . . We are children of the future, how *could* we be at home in this today? We feel disfavor for all ideals that might lead one to feel at home even in this fragile, broken time of transition; as for its 'realities,' we do not believe that they will *last*. The ice that supports people today has become very thin; the wind that brings the thaw is blowing; we ourselves who are homeless constitute a force that breaks open ice and other all too thin 'realities.' "[39] What is most remarkable in Nietzsche's wanderings, however, is not that he rejects the comfortable refuge of certain social norms, moral prescripts, or epistemological tenets; surely philosophy's task is to question all-too-thin realities. What is remarkable is that Nietzsche's rejections are so complete: nothing remains but a nomadic self, cut off from meaningful rapport with others, proscribed from finding any residence in the world and in the present time, held together from disintegration by the sheer force of its will.

Many have chosen homelessness in one realm in order to find their proper abode in another. Diogenes of Sinope, the founder of Cynicism, reputedly lived in a tub and was homeless in his native land so that he might declare himself a *cosmopolites*. Not unlike Diogenes, Nietzsche held familiar and customary things in disdain. For Nietzsche, however, the rejection was total and unrelenting. Through the power of will he sought to overcome and do without not only morality and metaphysics, but also social and political community. Unlike Diogenes, Nietzsche denied himself refuge in universal citizenship and the realm of natural law. He allowed himself no home whatsoever. Nietzsche speaks of the will to power as the "strangest of all guests." Heidegger's assessment reveals the core of this thought: "It is called the 'strangest' because as the unconditional will to will, it wants homelessness as such" (*QB* 37).

Heidegger insists that the homelessness evidenced generally in contemporary life and specifically in Nietzsche's philosophy is a "symptom of the oblivion of Being *[Seinsvergessenheit]*" (*BW* 218). More precisely, homelessness is a product of the subjectivism that isolates humans from each other and from their world. Heidegger traces its devel-

---

[38] Nietzshe, *Gay Science*, 342.
[39] Ibid., 338.

opment to the disengagement of Being from becoming, the subsequent preoccupation with the enduring reality of beings over the presencing nature of Being, and the transformation of these orientations into an understanding of truth as representational and ultimately subjective. That is to say, homelessness finds its roots in the sustained reign of metaphysical thought. The remedy for homelessness entails transcending the subjectivist tradition. However, Heidegger insists that transcendence of metaphysics is not to be achieved in direct battle with it. The only possible result of such a tactic, as Nietzsche demonstrates, is more metaphysics, albeit with its nature obscured by the struggle. A "regard for metaphysics still prevails even in the intention to overcome metaphysics," Heidegger writes. "Therefore, our task is to cease all overcoming, and leave metaphysics to itself" (TB 24).

The preeminent spiritual nomad, Friedrich Nietzsche, could not leave metaphysics alone. He hoped to escape its inherent nihilism through a heroic struggle with it. He identified the essence of this struggle as a celebration of life out of the depth of his suffering. His disdain for his time derived from his belief that modern humanity retained neither the capacity for deep suffering nor the heroic passion for worldly life. Nihilism tortured Nietzsche in large part because he foresaw that it would soon become accepted with complacency. The Last Man would announce his happiness, his comfort, and blink. As Heidegger describes life after Nietzsche: "What was once the scream 'The wasteland grows. . . ,' now threatens to turn into chatter" (WCT 49). Nietzsche's rejection of a worldly home intensified as his world turned into a wasteland before him. Indeed, he was forced to incorporate homelessness so radically and celebrate homelessness so tragically in his own life and philosophy because, in the end, he could in no other way tolerate its menace.

Complacency in homelessness threatens to become the postmodern condition. The alternative to such homelessness entails acknowledging the world as the place of human dwelling. Such an acknowledgment would maintain humanity as the discloser of the world, rather than its master and possessor; the earth as an abode in need of caretaking, rather than a resource awaiting exploitation; and human relations as the partnerships—undeniably agonistic at times—allowing for the discovery of our tasks and potentials, rather than raw material for administration. The learning of such guardianship in the realm of worldy things is inseparable from the learning of guardianship in the realm of thought. And this entails leaving metaphysics alone.

Leaving metaphysics alone, however, is not a passive affair. On the contrary, it entails the active exploration and exercise of human freedom in thought, speech, and action. The transcendence of metaphysics is, for this reason, a wordly event, both philosophical and political in nature.[40]

The Use and Abuse of Nietzsche for Life

At this point the reader might resist the attempt to translate Heidegger's controversial philosophic interpretations into a political sensibility. Undeniably Heidegger's understanding of homelessness as a state reflective of our forgetfulness of Being may sound rather metaphysical itself. The account of the rise and fall of metaphysics that culminates in our nomadic condition may appear as Heidegger's own historical metanarrative. No doubt the comprehensiveness of Heidegger's account lends itself to this interpretation. But it is important to remember that Heidegger's history of metaphysics is an account of contingent events, not the working out of a transcendental dialectic (*WP* 63). Indeed, Heidegger disparages as "onto-theological" any historical narrative that harbors such necessity (*ID* 42–76). Furthermore, representational truth, truth conceived as an enduring reality accessible to the constructs of the human mind, is the foundation on which metanarrative rests. Clearly Heidegger does not subscribe to this.

Nevertheless, I believe Heidegger is often misunderstood in this regard and he occasionally encourages such misunderstandings. He maintains, for example, that in "the poet's and thinker's struggle for a word for beings as a whole" the result is not "a private view of the person" but a fulfillment of the "destiny" of Being: "This means that the Being of this thinker and of every essential Western thinker consists in an almost *inhuman* fidelity to the most covert history of the West" (*WPK* 18–19). Despite Heidegger's denial, the cunning of reason seems to be at work here. History appears as the mystical play of Being rather than the product of human endeavor. But we must remember that Heidegger's description of the relation of Being (*Sein*) to human being (*Dasein*) is not primarily one of historical achievements and events, but of phenomenal essence. Heidegger maintains that "man belongs to the history of Being only in the scope of his essence which is determined by the claim of Being, and not with regard to his existence, actions, and accomplishments within beings" (*EP* 82). Heidegger distances himself

---

[40] Hans Jonas's *Imperative of Responsibility: In Search of an Ethics for the Technological Age* (Chicago: University of Chicago Press, 1984) meets this challenge in many respects. However, Jonas, Heidegger's former student, does not acknowledge his pedagogic debt, and his account suffers for it.

from the notion that human history is foreordained and metaphysically grounded. His position is not that our political and historical possibilities are predetermined by an otherworldly thing called Being. But they are nourished or stinted by the worldly relationship we come to form with Being.

Even if Heidegger's project does not constitute a metanarrative in the traditional sense, one might still argue that some peculiar form of Heideggerian metaphysics looms so large that we see Nietzsche, and more generally postmodern life, too darkly through it.[41] Heidegger is not averse to admitting that his own philosophy is metaphysical in some sense of the word. But this admission is made with the proviso that Heideggerian metaphysics is understood to be something quite distinct from the mode of thinking that structures the tradition of Western philosophy. That Heidegger's Nietzsche is noticeably his own, however, is a charge Heidegger himself did not even want to parry. Great thinking, he states, entails taking what is greatest in the work of another and transforming it in an original manner (*WPA* 35). The hermeneutic task is not to "understand a thinker in his own terms," which Heidegger insists is "impossible." Rather, the aim is "to take up a thinker's quest and to pursue it to the core of his thought's problematic" (*WCT* 185). This pursuit, Heidegger maintains (with Nietzsche), unavoidably results in "violence." But interpretive violence should not be arbitrary. Rather, it must be "animated and guided by the power of an illuminative idea" that "is confirmed by its own power of illumination" (*KPM* 207). Heidegger writes:

> We are accused of reading into it [in this case, a Parmenidean fragment] things that an "exact interpretation" can never determine. This is true. In the usual present-day view what has been said here is a mere product of the farfetched and one-sided Heideggerian method of exegesis, which has already become proverbial. But here we may, indeed, we must ask: Which interpretation is the true one, the one which simply takes over a perspective into which it has fallen, because this perspective, this line of sight, presents itself as familiar and self-evident; or the interpretation which questions the customary

[41] There has been no dearth of commentators who have decided this to be the case. Walter Kaufmann tersely describes Heidegger's writing on Nietzsche as "important for those who want to understand Heidegger." Walter Kaufmann, *Nietzsche: Philosopher, Psychologist, Antichrist,* 4th ed. (Princeton: Princeton University Press, 1974), 500. Echoing Kaufmann, Bernd Magnus notes that "Heidegger's Nietzsche studies are often inseparable from the author's own position," and that "it should be rather clear, if we reverse our standpoint for a moment and judge Heidegger by Nietzsche's standards, that Heidegger's Being-question is an eminently metaphysical one." Bernd Magnus, *Heidegger's Metahistory of Philosophy: Amor Fati, Being, and Truth* (The Hague: Martinus Nijhoff, 1970), 130–32.

perspective from top to bottom, because conceivably—and indeed actually—
this line of sight does not lead to what is in need of being seen. (*IM* 176)

Heidegger's is a forceful interpretation. The sweep of his survey, despite
its meticulous detail and discriminating insight, is notoriously broad
and assuming.[42] Certainly the unnecessarily monolithic identities he as-
cribes to historical personages often illuminate his concerns as much as
their own. Nietzsche, in this respect, is occasionally reduced to a foil for
Heidegger's attack on modernity.[43] In his effort to fit Nietzsche and
other Western thinkers onto a single trajectory that culminates in his
own work, Heidegger occasionally takes on the role of Procrustes.
"Whoever really knew the reason for [Nietzsche's] breakdown and
could conquer it intelligently," Heidegger wrote in 1936, "would have
to become the founder of the new beginning of Western philosophy"
(*ST* 3). Heidegger at times thought himself the most likely candidate for
this task. The categorical nature of his writing may well betray his need
to convince himself as much as his readers.

With this in mind, Heidegger's story of originary Greek thinking and
its subsequent metaphysical developments is perhaps best understood as
quasi-mythical. Indeed, Heidegger eventually came to admit as much.
Not known for self-criticism or retractions, Heidegger nonetheless acknowledged that there was never a pristine and transparent relation to
Being at the Greek beginnings of Western thought. He would admit by
1954 that "that which really gives us food for thought did not turn
away from man at some time or other which can be fixed in history—
no, what really must be thought keeps itself turned away from man
since the beginning" (*WCT* 7). In his lecture "Time and Being," given in
1962, Heidegger was more specific: neither Homer, nor other Greek
poets, nor everyday Greek speakers employed alētheia in the sense of
unconcealment. They, too, largely understood it as correctness of representation, as *òrthótes*. Heidegger admits that his earlier assertion about
the "essential transformation" of the historical understanding of truth
from unconcealment to correctness is "untenable" (*TB* 70).

Interpretive violence always begs defense. Heidegger's is no exception
to this rule. The quasi-mythical nature of Heidegger's historicizing (and
the deplorable political uses to which it had once been put)[44] do not,

[42] As Stanley Cavell aptly put it, "Heidegger writes philosophy according to the myth of
having read everything essential." Stanley Cavell, *This New Yet Unapproachable America*
(Albuquerque: Living Batch Press, 1989), 19.

[43] It might also be argued that Nietzsche serves as the fall guy for Heidegger's own
misadventures in politics, with Nietzsche announcing the will to power that Nazism
would perversely incarnate.

[44] As John Caputo writes: "It cannot be forgotten that it was in the context of the
National Socialist seizure of power that Heidegger narrowed down the beginnings of the

however, justify our turning our backs to Heidegger's originality and importance. The significance of his distinction between thinking Being as unconcealment and the metaphysical and ultimately subjectivist pursuit of being as an enduring reality remains intact, philosophically if not historically. We need not, in other words, impeach the originality and importance of Heidegger's thought on account of his unfortunate tendency to paint his forerunners and their philosophic epochs with such monochromatic strokes.

But why should we worry about the effects of metaphysics if metaphysics, whenever or wherever it began, terminates with Nietzsche? To speak of Nietzsche's thought as "the end of metaphysics," in turns out, is somewhat misleading. In no sense has metaphysics been destroyed or left behind. The essence and limits of metaphysics have simply been revealed. Nietzsche marks the culmination of metaphysics more than its termination. As Heidegger acknowledges: "our talk of the end of metaphysics does not mean to suggest that in the future men will no longer 'live' who think metaphysically and undertake 'systems of metaphysics.' Even less do we intend to say that in the future mankind will no longer 'live' on the basis of metaphysics. . . . It means the historical moment in which the essential possibilities of metaphysics are exhausted. The last of these possibilities must be that form of metaphysics in which its essence is reversed" (N 148). This reversal was performed by Nietzsche when he substituted the celebration of an isolated and self-sufficient subject for the Platonic identification of reality with the transcendent Idea. Despite this reversal, metaphysical thought continues to structure Western culture, and through the West's effective imperialism, global culture. Heidegger put the point severely in an interview toward the end of his life. "Today's society," he proposed, "is only an absolute image of modern subjectivity" (MHC 39). Heidegger would identify technology as the most powerful force operating within modern society, a force testifying to the continuing reign of metaphysics and modern subjectivism. As important as any such force is, however, in the realm of thought it remains "epigonal" (TB 57). That is, it remains a variation on a theme whose essential meaning already has been established. For the most part, its meaning was established prophetically by Nietzsche.

W. H. Auden once remarked that the books you read are not necessarily the important ones. The important books are the ones that read you. Nietzsche's works, Heidegger suggests, read us well. Referring to

West to a single 'Origin'—*Anfang* and *Ursprung*—purely Greek, without Jewish or Christian contamination, and tied the future of the West to the German future, to the German capacity for thinking and questioning Being." John D. Caputo, *Demythologizing Heidegger* (Bloomington: Indiana University Press, 1993), 4. I explore this feature of Heidegger's thought further in chapters 5 and 6.

the status and meaning of the will to power, Heidegger writes that "the present age has not taken over Nietzsche's doctrine, but the other way around" (*ST* 179). Nietzsche's importance, in other words, is not to be grasped as twentieth-century culture reaching back to find its roots in nineteenth-century philosophy. Rather, Nietzsche forecast and captured the emerging dynamics of contemporary life. The same might be said regarding the status and meaning of postmodern homelessness. Nietzsche's solitude and itinerancy, experienced by an individual, is the precursor to the homelessness experienced at a cultural level today. Eventually the will to power would prove insufficient to hold together Nietzsche's soul. He would escape its burden in the sanctuary of madness. Nietzsche's subsequent decade of silence finds its cultural analogue in the jaded complacency of postmodern times. The cultural analogue of Nietzsche's furious attempt at self-creation, in turn, is to be found in the understanding of freedom that drives contemporary technology.

Conclusion

To assert that Nietzsche remains caught within metaphysical subjectivism is to suggest neither that we have nothing to learn from him nor that he was a proponent of the technological forces that shape and misshape our world today. Nietzsche's thought is not to be equated with the thoughtless quest for technological mastery. His doctrine of the will to power, albeit the apogee of subjectivist thought, remains fundamentally within the governance of a spiritual regime. Despite an effort to describe Nietzsche's philosophy as that which prepares man to assume total mastery of the earth, Heidegger firmly maintains that the will to power extolled as a form of active nihilism by Nietzsche is distinct in form and thrust from that which exhibits itself in the contemporary technological will to knowledge and the "total organization" this knowledge craves (*QB* 47). Yet we must resist Nietzsche nevertheless. His radical individualism invites a homelessness with grave political and ecological implications. Surmounting this homelessness begins with the discovery that the Being-in-the-world fundamental to human being constitutes an equally fundamental Being-with-others.

Nietzsche insists that we criticize a man most sharply when we sketch out his ideal. Remaining true to Nietzsche, in this context, entails following his own genealogical procedures to excavate the man behind the masks in an effort to limn his inspiring and terrible visions. These visions, I have argued, are of the severest subjective solitude. Rejecting the subjectivist foundations on which Nietzsche built his philosophic edifice, however, does not preclude our marveling at the heights he was able to reach and the breadth of vision gained from these heights. Nietzsche was a self-styled tragic hero who struggled to escape the constraints of human life, a "buffoon" who encouraged us to dance and frolic as participants in his gay science, and a solitary who, in the end, saw the world he attempted to create collapse on him. He is, in short, a man whose contradictions ultimately prove more instructive than his truths.

Nietzsche's contradictions prove so instructive because he pushed them beyond his own capacity to escape their havoc.[45] In his philosophy these contradictions become terribly alive for us. Nietzsche was at once the most homeless of men, yet one who saw most keenly, felt most painfully, and combated most heroically the nihilistic abyss of modern homelessness. Nietzsche desperately sought to establish his place among us. But like Persephone, who was forbidden to return permanently to the earth after eating the pomegranate seeds of Hades, Nietzsche paid dearly for indulging in the fruits of the underworld. He became a victim of the metaphysics he had tasted but sought to leave behind, and was tragically fated never to establish his abode in the world. Solitude and wandering became for Nietzsche a vocation. Being with others remained an illusion. The world of politics was spurned, or rather internalized, in Nietzsche's constant battle to overcome himself.

The task of confronting Nietzsche is daunting. Heidegger sets the stakes: "If in Nietzsche's thinking the prior tradition of Western thought is gathered and completed in a decisive respect, then the confrontation with Nietzsche becomes one with all Western thought hitherto" (*WPA* 4). Without attributing an unwarranted uniformity to Nietzsche's thought or to the philosophic tradition he resisted, we may nevertheless acknowledge the decisive respect in which Nietzsche proves himself our most instructive case. Nietzsche is indeed a watershed in the history of thought. But Nietzsche is a watershed because he straddles two worlds, not because he fully embodies one or completely transcends the other. Nietzsche plants a foot firmly, if reluctantly, in the tradition of Western metaphysics whose "epigonal" features we still bear. His other foot is left unsupported by anything but his own strength, stretched over the abyss of nihilism, groping for a foothold in the future. Nietzsche's balance is precarious. He is able to maintain it only because of the support he finds in the world he pushes away. To tout

---

[45] Heidegger would admit his wonder at this aspect of Nietzsche's terrible genius, writing: "We are not yet mature enough for the rigor of a thought of the kind found in the following note that Nietzsche wrote down at about the time when he was doing the thinking for his projected masterpiece, *The Will to Power*: 'Around the hero everything turns into tragedy; around the demi-god, into a satyr-play; and around God—what?— perhaps into "world"?' (*Beyond Good and Evil*, Aph. 150, 1886)" (*QT* 94).

Nietzsche as the destroyer of metaphysics is to miss half the story—and perhaps the more important half. Alternatively, the attempt to succeed where Nietzsche fails in the destruction of metaphysics courts the most debilitating effects of postmodernism. In sum, to misunderstand the nature of Nietzsche's balance and its implications for our world is to misdirect our efforts to foster new social and political sensibilities grounded in philosophic insight.

The task at hand, then, is neither to seek a primordial (Greek) understanding of Being with the hope of regaining a lost homeland, as is the nostalgic remedy; nor to depreciate Nietzsche's insights into our current predicament, as is the modern response; nor yet to attempt the consummation of Nietzsche's effort to destroy metaphysics, as is a postmodern endeavor. Nor were any of these Heidegger's choices. Despite his romantic mythologizing, Heidegger explicitly rejects any attempt to leap back to the early days of Western thought as "vain and absurd" (*WBG* 210). His efforts to expound Nietzsche should be indication enough that he understood the importance of passing through Nietzsche's labyrinth. And Heidegger insists that metaphysics cannot willfully be destroyed. Its epitaph, written by Nietzsche, does not mark its disappearance but rather the end of its capacity for creative regeneration. We are not actually living in postmodernity. Modernity is still in its twilight. Peering into its dusk we may only speculate on the gifts and dangers of the dawn.

Two

Heidegger's Vision

BEING-IN-THE-WORLD

In the beginning is the relation.
  (Martin Buber, *I and Thou*)

WHILE FIERCELY BATTLING with the Western metaphysical tradition, Nietzsche became infected with its subjectivism. He subsequently distilled what he had absorbed into a radical individualism, extending its reach from the realm of epistemology to ethics. Higher man determines his own truths, Nietzsche insists, and these truths are uniquely his. But higher man also distinguishes himself ethically from "the herd" by his rejection of social standards and moral precepts. The sovereign individual, Nietzsche writes, is "like only to himself, liberated again from morality of custom, autonomous and supramoral (for 'autonomous' and 'moral' are mutually exclusive)."[1] Epistemologically, the heroic individual becomes its own point of reference. Ethically, the heroic individual becomes a law unto itself. Thus the individual finds freedom in solitude or, as Nietzsche indicates in his more telling moments, in domination. To keep regret, and hence resentment, of life's suffering from taking hold, pity, Nietzsche famously states, must be banished from the soul. Freed from pity, the hero's soul has all the more room for the affirmation of life. But one wonders how, in this hardened soul, love might ever take root. One suspects that fellow feeling will not find safe haven in Nietzsche's universe.

The Problem of Empathy

True community is an illusion, Nietzsche insists. It is the invention of those too weak to face the terrible truths of existence on their own. But the illusion of community, Nietzsche explains, has powerful effects. For the most part, and for quite practical reasons, humans live together. They attempt to translate this togetherness into community by subscrib-

---

[1] Nietzsche, *On the Genealogy of Morals*, 59.

ing to common laws, beliefs, conventions, and habits. In other words, society makes community possible by normalizing its members. Nietzsche observes that the fundamentally individualistic nature of humankind, on those rare occasions when it is not repressed by the herd mentality, becomes dangerous. Indeed, the radical independence and freedom of the individual constitutes the greatest threat to society. Morality is continuously deployed in counterattack. As Nietzsche put it, through morality individuals are forever being forced into social straitjackets. Weaker souls, which is to say the vast majority of human beings, quickly capitulate to the temptation of securing comfort and safety within the confines of the collective conscience. To the extent the "higher man" remains true to himself, however, he will continually rend himself from the weave of the social fabric. He remains, and struggles to remain, a solitary figure.

In making his ethics every bit as individualistic as his epistemology, Nietzsche proves more consistent than his metaphysical forerunners. The Western tradition, though implicitly embracing an epistemological subjectivism, resisted defining morality in like terms. Given its own epistemological foundations, however, Western metaphysics has always courted the danger of ethical subjectivism and moral relativism. Hitherto, most political philosophers have resorted to myth to evade its menace—from Plato's creation of a hierarchical, organic society by means of the noble lie to John Rawls's creation of a pluralist, liberal society by means of the veil of ignorance.[2] Throughout its long life, metaphysical thought has been burdened with the translation of a subjectivist epistemology into a social or transcendental morality. Indeed, metaphysics and metaphysically based political theories have been largely defined by this Sisyphean task. How to proceed from an epistemologically isolated subject to a morally permeable one? How can one recast the subject/object dichotomy for moral purposes, effectively bridging the chasm that separates the individual from a populated world? How, given a subject that regulates its own criteria for truth and well-being, may one instill sufficient concern for the well-being of others to make social and political life feasible and justifiable? How, to put morality in a nutshell, is one to learn to care deeply about human beings even though only one of them happens to be you? To simplify, we

---

[2] John Rawls, in his well-known article "Justice as Fairness: Political not Metaphysical," *Philosophy and Public Affairs* (Summer 1985): 223–51, has denied that his *Theory of Justice* sought a metaphysical foundation for its republic. Without entering into the protracted debate surrounding this claim, suffice it to say that Rawls's success in escaping metaphysics has left him quite busy defending the arbitrary and ethically relativist nature of his "political" alternative.

may call this ethical and political quandary haunting metaphysical thought the problem of empathy.

The problem of empathy has been made somewhat tractable by the belief in representational truth. If all subjects may share in the same image of an objective reality, there is hope that human interaction may be organized by common standards, procedures, and practices. Representational truth, metaphysicians implicitly assume, provides the bridge that allows isolated subjects to meet on neutral ground and strike ethical bargains. Indeed, it would be fair to say that many if not most of the great achievements of metaphysical thought over the ages have been variations on this theme. With Nietzsche's undermining of the notion of representational truth, however, morality threatens to follow epistemology down the road to radical subjectivism. Having taken the first step with the metaphysicians, one finds the next move dictated by the Overman. At this point, retreat to anything like a social morality is made impossible. At the bottom of this slipperiest of slopes, one confronts nihilism: a world in which everything is permitted, ethically no less than epistemologically.

What happens if we refuse to take the first epistemological step with metaphysics and consequently are not induced to fall in line with Nietzsche on the question of ethics? What happens if we deny that we exist as subjects isolated against the backdrop of an objective reality? What if we posit worldly reality as an intrinsic aspect of human being? This is the solution made available by Heidegger. Human being, Heidegger maintains, is a Being-in-the-world (*In-der-Welt-sein*). To be human means to exist in relation to a world, to "dwell alongside." Traditional metaphysics abstractly defines the whole by way of dichotomized parts: subjects and objects, observers and observed, spirit and matter. Heidegger insists that the whole, human-being-in-the-world, concretely defines the parts, as relations of interdependence and mutual signification.

Worldly Being and the Context of Knowledge

Being, for Heidegger, is a disclosiveness or unconcealedness. Human being, or Dasein, literally "there-being," is the *place* of Being's disclosure. Human being is the worldly opening (*Offene*) in which Being's truth is revealed (*WBG* 213). Only in human being does the world of beings achieve such disclosure. Without human being, Heidegger avers, there would be no world: "A stone is worldless. Plant and animal likewise have no world; but they belong to the covert throng of a surrounding into which they are linked. The peasant woman, on the other hand, has a world because she dwells in the overtness of beings, of the things that are. . . . By the opening up of a world, all things gain their lingering and hastening, their remoteness and nearness, their scope and limits" (*PLT* 45). But this sounds, if not subjectivist, rather solipsistic at the species level. Heidegger is not suggesting, however, that human beings must exist for there to be a universe of extant things. But human being is the only place where the Beingness of beings comes to presence, revealing a contextual world of meaning. As for beings themselves, their concrete existence remains unaltered by the unique role of human being in their ontological discovery.

Human being and Being always coexist, in the sense that the latter depends on the former for its revealing and the former on the latter for its meaning. Only through human being does Being come to presence. In turn, without the opportunity to disclose Being, human being would cease to be what it most fundamentally is. "And the fundamental idea of my thinking," Heidegger summarizes, "is exactly that Being, relative to the manifestation of Being, *needs* man and, conversely, man is only man in so far as he stands within the manifestation of Being" (*MHC* 40). To say that Being *needs* human being is not to say that human being is in itself necessary, that human being always already was, or is fated forever to persist. Indeed, to be human means to live with the expectation of death, of one's ceasing to be in the world. Human being is mortal by nature, and there are no physical or metaphysical laws that preclude an extinction of the entire species. However, if and whenever human being exists, it does so embedded in and revealing of a world. As Heidegger explains, "it is not intrinsic to the essence of Dasein as such that it factually exist; it is, however, precisely its essence that in each case this being can also not be extant. The cosmos can be without humans inhabiting the earth, and the cosmos was long before humans ever existed. . . . 'Dasein is, in its basic constitution, Being-in-the-world,' is not an affirmation of its factual existence. . . . Rather, I am saying: If Dasein in fact exists, then its existence has the structure of Being-in-the-world. . . . Dasein is therefore not a Being-in-the-world because it in fact exists, but conversely" (*MFL* 169). The universe existed in various forms long before the human race evolved. Once there is human being, however, and as long as human being persists, then Being has the opportunity to come to presence. This coming to presence of Being takes place through the uncovering of worldly beings by an always already-in-the-world being. Human being, in other words, does not exist in any "neutral" sense apart from its concrete, embedded reality (*MFL* 37). Dasein is not a substance but a relation, a disclosive weddedness to the world.

With the exchange of subjectivity for worldliness the problem of empathy is en route to being solved. But doubts persist. How does one really know that the disclosed world actually exists, that anything is what it seems to be and is not merely the product of one's imagination? In other words, how does one overcome recurring Cartesian doubts about the reality of the world? Heidegger's answer is that one does not try. An unassailable demonstration of the world's existence is impossible. "A sceptic can no more be refuted," Heidegger straightforwardly admits, "than the Being of truth can be 'proved'" (*BT* 271). But refutation is unnecessary and unwarranted. Indeed, it is illegitimate, for implicit in any attempt to prove the existence of the world is the unfounded premise of an isolated subject engaged in the effort of proving. The skeptic's problem of worldly reality is effectively dissolved by Heidegger's refusal to entertain this premise. Heidegger refuses to posit the primacy of an isolated "I" or "ego" that subsequently comes to doubt the reality of its world, for any such doubting exposes its precondition, namely, an already-in-the-world doubter. Heidegger writes: "To wish to prove that the world exists is a misunderstanding of the very questioning. For such a questioning makes sense only on the basis of a being whose constitution is Being-in-the-world. . . . World in its most proper sense is just that which is already on hand for any questioning" (*HCT* 215). Faced with the impossibility and illegitimacy of proof of an external reality, we are not to assume that the only available alternative is a leap of faith. Any leap of faith would necessarily be grounded in the supposed preexistence of a leaper. Again, the (potentially faithful) subject is already illegitimately posited in distinction to its world. "With such presuppositions," Heidegger explains, "Dasein always comes 'too late'; for in so far as it does this presupposing as an entity (and otherwise this would be impossible), it is, *as an entity,* already in a world. 'Earlier' than any presupposition which Dasein makes, or any of its ways of behaving, is the *'a priori'* character of its state of Being" (*BT* 249). The metaphysical tradition, as Heidegger summarizes the problem, must always first "bury the 'external world' in nullity 'epistemologically' before going on to prove it" (*BT* 250). Heidegger wants to be done with this metaphysical sleight of hand.

The metaphysical trick works only because it has been carefully prepared. First, Being is reduced to beings. Subsequently, beings are reduced to things defined only by their extantness, their "presence-at-hand" *(Vorhandenheit)*. With Being fully encompassed by presence-at-hand, and this presence verifiable only by the perceiving subject, reality appears to the individual as a subjective experience, as being "merely 'inner'" (*BT* 250). Having first created the conditions for this subjectivist doubt, metaphysics then presents us with the impossible task of welding together subjective experience with objective reality. Rather than take on this task, Heidegger begins with a relation of Being-in-the-world. He rejects the metaphysical supposition, first articulated by Plato, that "man is, in the first instance, a spiritual Thing which subsequently gets misplaced 'into' a space" (*BT* 83). It is a grave mistake to separate epistemologically the perceiving and knowing subject from its concrete worldliness and it is a vain effort to try to bridge this chasm once it is formed. Hence Heidegger insists that we do not *have* bodies. Rather, "we 'are' bodily" (*WPA* 99). Likewise, we do not *have* a world. Rather, we "are" worldly.

Our concrete, spatial existence is not separate from our perceiving, mental existence. A structural unity exists (*BP* 164). Knowledge, therefore, is not something gleaned by mind from a separate, external reality, but something absorbed in the midst of worldly existence. In Heidegger's words, "the Dasein is not also extant among things with the difference merely that it apprehends them. Instead, the Dasein exists in the manner of *Being-in-the-world,* and this *basic determination of its existence* is the *presupposition for being able to apprehend anything at all*" (*BP* 164). The upshot is that "every act of knowing always already takes place on the basis of the mode of being of Dasein which we call Being-in, that is, Being-always-already-involved-with-a-world" (*HCT* 161). To know or to question is already to have evidence of one's situated, worldly being and to undercut any prerogative to a more radical doubt. Heidegger's understanding of Being-in-the-world allows him to reject both radical (Nietzschean) individualism and Cartesian dualism.

Rethinking the nature of knowledge and perception is called for. Metaphysics posits knowledge in terms of a subject's representational apprehension of an external state of affairs. Heidegger insists in contrast that "what is knowable and what knows are each determined in their essence in a unified way from the same essential ground. We may not separate either one, nor wish to encounter them separately. Knowing is not like a bridge that somehow subsequently connects two existent banks of a stream, but is itself a stream that in its flow first creates the banks and turns them *toward* each other in a more original way than a bridge ever could" (*WPK* 83). The image Heidegger presents here is remarkable. But it remains somewhat misleading of his intent. One is still asked to conceive of a subject distinct from its object, represented as opposing banks of a stream, separated yet joined by something called knowledge. Perhaps a better way to understand the unified structure of Being-in-the-world, equally inspired by Heidegger's own imagery, is to visualize human being as a diffused radius of disclosure (*N* 93). The world of beings is disclosed as it comes to presence in the diffusely illuminated "there" of human being. What comes to presence always stands within this populated clearing (*Lichtung*). Not everything is disclosed at once, of course. There are horizons to an individual's

world. And certain features within the lighted area will be partially obscured by shadows, which give depth to what is illuminated. In turn,
perspective plays its part. What is revealed is revealed in the context of
its particular surroundings, a context ambiguous but always in evidence. Finally, what appears does so not as a singular object but as part
of an environment that surrounds, structures, and sustains it. Importantly, the clearing symbolizes not simply the visual perceptions of human being, nor even simply its complete sensory field, but also its demeanor, comportment, and mood. Its lighting never outlines an object
standing completely apart from it, as a spotlight would. The primary
relation is not that of observer to observed. Rather, human being illuminates its world by way of its holistic embeddedness. Like light travers-
ing empty space, human being would be dark indeed without its world.

Human being illuminates its world in various ways. Things come to
presence according to their various natures and relationships. Dasein
may reveal things as part of an instrumental assemblage or system, as
things *ready-to-hand (zuhanden)*. Much of what we encounter in our
daily lives consists of such "equipment." The ready-to-hand is disclosed
as we operate with and among artifacts without reflecting on their nature. Being ready-to-hand means being part of a network of things that
relate to each other with functional interdependence. As a hammer relates to nails, lumber, houses, and barns; as a word processor relates to
paper, printers, desks, and books; as a theory relates to hypotheses,
conceptual analysis, and logic; as trees relate to paths, shade, and orien-
tational aids; so the ready-to-hand is defined as part of a world being
managed, dealt with, navigated, or simply lived in a day-to-day manner.
The ready-to-hand, then, like human being or Dasein, is less a what
(object) than a how (form of coming to presence). The question here is
less *what is* this thing encountered, than *how is* this thing revealed in its
employment or circumspection. The ready-to-hand is revealed as an integrated, functional part of a navigated world.

Though the daily environment of human being is largely composed of
the ready-to-hand, the intentional detachment of something extant for
intensive scrutiny remains possible. Herein things come to be revealed
not as parts of a functional whole made available for use, but as isolated objects that permit focused observation or contemplation. Heidegger calls this the "present-at-hand" (*Vorhanden*). Despite its tendency
to stand apart from the lived world, the present-at-hand comes into
focus for abstract consideration only with its context already established and, generally, taken for granted. Scientific investigation of genes,
for instance, only occurs within the context of the ready-to-hand of
microscopes, formulas, and theories, and also within an environment of
other present-at-hand objects of study such as organisms, cells, chromo-

somes, and molecules. The narrower, concentrated light illuminating the present-at-hand (genes) simply causes the surroundings (microscopes, organisms, etc.) to fall into shadow and be temporarily obscured. Indeed, this is the very meaning of something revealed as present-at-hand. It arises out of a context. The obscurity of the surroundings serves further to define the object of attention, just as shadows more clearly demarcate that which is lit.

We call the act of focusing attention on and giving meaning to particular objects interpretation. Interpretation, then, is a bringing into focus of something that exists contextually. Heidegger insists that interpretation is not a matter of imposing meaning on a passive world lying before us: "In interpreting, we do not, so to speak, throw a 'signification' over some naked thing which is present-at-hand, we do not stick a value on it; but when something within-the-world is encountered as such, the thing in question already has an involvement which is disclosed in our understanding of the world, and this involvement is one which gets laid bare by the interpretation" (BT 190–91). The hammer is revealed as ready-to-hand when it is employed for hammering nails. It may also be revealed as present-at-hand if it is scientifically investigated as to its durability, weight, or chemical composition. Or it may be philosophically interpreted in the manner of the present discussion. In each case, the question is less what the thing is than how it comes to be revealed. In the latter two cases, consciously directed interpretation is facilitated by a background of interpretive activity (the act of hammering) of a less formal sort.

Heidegger's word for this primitive interpretation and the understanding it begets is "preontological." Human beings do not first stand opposite their world, as the subjects of present-at-hand objects, and then become further involved in it through their use of intrusive interpretive techniques. Rather, human beings always already exist in a ready-to-hand world. Only subsequently do they engage in the interpretive distillations that carry them beyond preontological understandings. A crucial feature of (formal) interpretation, then, is that any confrontation with the present-at-hand necessarily takes place from the position of one who, prior to any decision to interpret the world, is already involved with it. Only this primordial, one might say unpremeditated, interpretive activity that takes one outside the self and into the world may serve as the foundation from which formal interpretation, whether scientific or philosophical, may arise.

To exist as a being that is ineluctably integrated—functionally and interpretively—in a world is to exist as "thrown" into a world. Human being is defined by its "thrownness" (Geworfenheit) or "facticity" (Faktizität). Being-in-the-world means being always already situated, always already integrated into a there. Human being, most fundamentally, is a there-being, a being that exists in a world, as part of a world, and, importantly, by way of its worldliness.

Communication, Care, and the With-World

In disclosing its world, Heidegger maintains, human being also discloses itself. It reveals the world by revealing its place in the world, its "there-being." Human being is always engaged in a self-revealing, and may be defined, for this reason, as "a self-interpreting, self-articulating being" (*HCT* 302). Apart from the ready-to-hand and the present-at-hand, there is then a third way in which things are in the world. Human being may reveal itself or another human being as Dasein, as a self-interpreting being. A human being may also be revealed as something present-at-hand, as a thing isolated for investigation, say, as the object of a scientific study of mammalian bipeds. A human being may also be revealed as something ready-to-hand, as a functional element of a system, say, as a slave working in a mine, or a pedestrian treated as an obstacle to be avoided on a busy street. To reveal a human being as Dasein, however, is to reveal a being sharing one's world in a self-interpreting manner.

To understand Dasein as self-interpreting is not to suggest that human being is defined by a solely inward-looking comportment. Self-interpretation is as much a reaching outward as a turning inward. Human being exists as human being only by participating in a shared world. The horizon of the individual Dasein is always in fusion with the horizons of others. Communication among self-interpreting beings, therefore, is not the transference of information or knowledge from one formerly isolated subject to another. Rather, it is the codiscovery of meaning. To disclose the Being of beings is to discover meaning. But meaning is always discovered in the context of a world. Indeed, meaning is the bringing to light of a worldly context.

For Heidegger "the basic structure of worldhood, the Being of the entity which we call world, lies in meaningfulness. . . . *Meaningfulness is first of all a mode of presence* in virtue of which every entity of the world is discovered. . . . what is primary is Being in the world, that is, concerned understanding and Being in the context of meanings" (*HCT* 203, 210). What is crucial to communication is the shared meanings that emerge from a common world. Heidegger explains that "communications are not a store of heaped up propositions but should be seen as possibilities by which one Dasein enters with the other into the same fundamental comportment toward the entity asserted about, which is unveiled in the same way. . . . For 'thou' means 'you who are with me in a world'" (*BP* 210, 298). Communication, interpretation, and discovery of meaning originate from and continually evidence the embeddedness of human being in a shared world. This remains true regardless of the particular arrangements of speakers and listeners. Whether we are talking to friends, to ourselves, or to a wall, the social nature of language and meaning remains. A soliloquy no less exposes this nature than does an open debate. Whether the audience is imagined or actual, whether the words are spoken or silent, language discloses a shared world.

To discover meaning is to uncover an aspect of one's Being-in-the-world and implicitly, if not explicitly, to communicate this to others. Heidegger writes: "Discourse as a mode of being of Dasein qua Being-with is essentially *communication*. . . . The understanding of communication is the *participation in what is manifest*. . . . It is not a matter of transporting information and experiences from the interior of one subject to the interior of the other one. It is rather a matter of Being-with-one-another becoming manifest in the world, specifically by way of the discovered world, which itself becomes manifest in speaking with one another" (*HCT* 263). As an interpretive being, human being is always involved with language and communication. Human being, it follows, is inherently a social being. Whatever its concrete situation, human being remains embedded in a common world of meanings.

The social nature of human being may be summarily derived from Heidegger's ontology. In its interpretive occupation with its own capacity to be, Heidegger states, human being is necessarily occupied with its world. But this world is populated. In its occupation with worldliness, therefore, human being is necessarily occupied with others. "Dasein is with equal originality," Heidegger concludes, "Being-with others *and* Being-among intraworldly beings" (*BP* 297). Put most succinctly, "The world of Dasein is a *with-world* [*Mitwelt*]. Being-in is *Being-with-Others*" (*BT* 155). Our world is a world corevealed with other human beings, and this is true not only when individuals actually congregate. Rather, human being itself exists structurally as a Being-with-others, even in the midst of physical solitude. Heidegger is firm on this point: "Being-with is an existential characteristic of Dasein even when no Other is present-at-hand or perceived. Even Dasein's Being-alone is Being-with in the world" (*BT* 156–57). Solitude constitutes a removing of oneself from the physical presence of others. Indeed, solitude may often also constitute a removing of oneself from the emotional, moral, or cognitive presence of others. These retreats, however, are always carried out in the context of an initial and continuing relation to the with-world. Just as soliloquy, no less than debate, is rooted in shared meaning, so solitude, no less than association, is rooted in Being-with. What is achieved in solitude is not the nullification of the ontologically social nature of human being, but the counteracting of some of its "factical" features. For the solitary, a certain aspect of human being, its Being-with, is intentionally brought to the fore so that certain of its ramifications, say the tendency to converse, play, or empathize, might be counteracted or placed in abeyance. But the world of the solitary remains populated and shared to the extent that the solitary continues to exist in a world of meaning. If anything, solitude sharpens our sense of the with-world so we may better distance ourselves from its effects or resist certain of its temptations.

Opposed to the principles of methodological individualism, Heidegger denies that Dasein first exists as a solitary individual that subsequently bridges the chasm between itself and others through social involvement. Being-with is primordial. Heidegger responds to the metaphysical quandary of the isolated subject seeking communicative and moral access to other human beings in the same way that he responds to the metaphysical quandary of the isolated subject seeking epistemological access to an external world. He simply denies the atomistic presuppositions: "It is assumed that a subject is encapsulated within itself and now has the task of empathizing with another subject. This way of formulating the question is absurd, since there never is such a subject in the sense it is assumed here. If the constitution of what is Dasein is instead regarded without presuppositions as Being-in and Being-with in the presuppositionless immediacy of everydayness, it then becomes clear that the problem of *empathy* is just as absurd as the question of the reality of the external world" (*HCT* 243).[3]

This is not to say that empathy is synonymous with Being-with. Empathy is an emotional and ethical disposition. Heidegger calls it ontic, signifying that which does not directly address the ontological fundamentals of human being but rather pertains to its concrete possibilities. Being-with, on the other hand, is an ontological category. Nevertheless, empathy, as an ontic capacity, is made possible only on the basis of the ontological structure of Being-with. Just as solitude is a mode of Being-with that is asocial, so empathy is a mode of Being-with

---

[3] Hubert Dreyfus expresses the point well in his commentary on *Being and Time:* "There is no such thing as *my* world, if this is taken as some private sphere of experience and meaning, which is self-sufficient and intelligible in itself, and so more fundamental than the shared public world and its local modes. Both Husserl and Sartre follow Descartes in beginning with *my* world and then trying to account for how an isolated subject can give meaning to other minds and to *the* shared intersubjective world. Heidegger, on the contrary, thinks that it belongs to the very idea of a world that it be shared, so *the* world is always prior to *my* world." Hubert Dreyfus, *Being-in-the-World: A Commentary on Heidegger's* Being and Time, *Division I* (Cambridge, Mass.: MIT Press, 1991), 90.

that is, as it were, hypersocial. To be empathetic is to extend a self already embedded in a social world in such a way that emotional and ethical connections to others come to the fore and achieve prominence. Empathy reflects the emotional and ethical extension of a self *beyond* the ontological sharing of worldly life that defines human being. The stimulus for empathy may often be the desire to offset the egoistic or immoral dispositions frequently encountered in social life. As Heidegger notes, "Dasein, as Being-in-the-world, already is with Others. 'Empathy' does not first constitute Being-with; only on the basis of Being-with does 'empathy' become possible: it gets its motivation from the unsociability of the dominant modes of Being-with" (*BT* 162). Empathy and egoism, in other words, are two possible ways that human being may experience its Being-with-others. The prominence of one or the other, historically or phenomenologically, constitutes neither a confirmation nor a refutation of the more fundamental nature of Being-with.

Heidegger defines human being's shared Being-in-the-world as *care* (*Sorge*). Human being cares to the extent that it concerns itself with its worldly nature. This entails a concern for its Being-with-others as well as a concern for the meaning of this ontological structure.[4] By care Heidegger means the always-already-interpretive comportment of human being. Human beings care because they are involved with the world and its meanings, including the meaning of their own worldly existence. Heidegger offers this concise definition: "*Care is the term for the Being of Dasein pure and simple. It has the formal structure, a being for which, intimately involved in its Being-in-the-world, this very Being is at issue*" (*HCT* 294). To have one's Being as an issue is constantly to be involved with the meaning of one's Being. As such, human being can be said to live "*for the sake of its own self . . . so far as it is, it is* occupied with its own capacity to be" (*BP* 170). But being occupied with one's own capacity to be, like being self-interpreting, is not the same as being self-absorbed. Rather, to care is to be concerned with the meaning of oneself *in* the world. The focus of human being's self-interpretation and self-articulation is not a detached self, but a situated one. To be for the sake of the self is to care about worldly existence as a whole.

Heidegger states that care is the "primary *totality* of the constitution of Dasein, which as this totality always adopts this or that particular way of its can-be" (*HCT* 306). The particular "can-be" of an individual Dasein refers to its ontic possibilities, which, though always founded on

---

[4] Concern, for Heidegger, is care as it displays itself in the world: "*Concern itself is but a mode of being of care.* . . . To put it better, care *qua* structure of Dasein is Being-in as concern. Caring as it is in the world is *eo ipso* concern" (*HCT* 294).

the ontological structure of care, remain distinct from it. Thus Heidegger attempts to distinguish between ontological descriptions and ethical dictates. "Being towards oneself constitutes the Being of Dasein and is not something like an additional capacity to observe oneself over and above just existing. Existing is precisely this being towards oneself," Heidegger writes. "Only because Dasein, constituted by the for-the-sake-of, exists in selfhood, only for this reason is anything like human community possible. These are primary existential-ontological statements of essence, and not ethical claims about the relative hierarchy of egoism and altruism" (*MFL* 190). Being for the sake of the self, then, is the only possible foundation out of which anything like ethical obligation within human community might grow. Human being always already exists as an embodied, social, worldly relation, and this ontological description is neither more nor less valid simply because particular human beings deny or obscure their social and worldly nature or repudiate its practical extension to an explicitly moral realm. To be altruistic is to choose to channel one's thoughts, feelings, and actions into one's capacities for empathy. To be egoistic means to redirect this energy elsewhere. Neither activity changes the fundamental structure of human being as care, a Being-in-the-world-with-others fundamentally concerned with the meaning of its Being.

Heidegger does not suggest that we abandon our moral predispositions in order to engage in ontological questioning. But neither should we attempt to escape ontological investigation behind the supposed security and stability of ethical concepts and formulas. "Should we not safeguard and secure the existing [ethical] bonds, even if they hold human beings together ever so tenuously and merely for the present?" Heidegger asks. "Certainly," he responds, and then adds: "But does this need ever release thought from the task of thinking what still remains principally to be thought, as Being prior to all beings, is their guarantor and their truth?" (*BW* 232). We should not abandon morality. But neither should we subordinate ontology to it—for practical as much as for philosophic reasons. Before we determine the principles and rules by which we ought to live with others, we need to understand who we are, as questioners of Being, and what our Being-in-the-world-with-others means. Heidegger believed that "ethics as a mere doctrine and imperative is helpless unless man first comes to have a different fundamental relation to Being" (*WCT* 89). Establishing this fundamental relation is a type of ethics itself. Expanding the etymology of "ethics" (*ethos*) to include not solely a customary way of being with others but a characteristic way of being in the world, Heidegger considers his work an "original ethics" (*BW* 234–35). Human being finds its abode in the world as a sharer of meaning, which is to say, as a discloser of Being.

Heidegger's ontology might then be construed as a form of ethics—if ethics pertains not simply to the customs of the human collective but to the character of the human condition.

Authenticity and Community

Despite Heidegger's extensive discussion of Being-with, certain readers remain convinced that he promotes a radical individualism reminiscent of Nietzsche's antisocial orientation. His philosophy, like Nietzsche's, is identified with the advocacy of "*self-sponsored* heroism."[5] Heidegger explicitly denies that his is a "heroic" philosophy (*EB* 355). Nevertheless, this mischaracterization of Heidegger as a radical individualist is typically defended with reference to Heidegger's discussion of the "authentic" (*eigentlich*) individual, most prominent in *Being and Time*.

To be authentic is to resist the perspective of the "they" (*das Man*), which is the predominant mode of human being in its "everydayness" (*Alltäglichkeit*). The everyday refers to the normal—that is, the most frequent and customary—mode of human being. It is the realm of coping with day-to-day existence, including all of its necessities, banalities, passions, and perversions. Inauthenticity is characterized by Heidegger as a "falling" (*Verfallen*), a way of routinely "Being-alongside" entities without bringing their or one's own Being into question. Inauthenticity is a losing of the self into a way of being that is primarily *public*, in the sense of conventional. It is a falling back into the habits and conformities—perceptual and behavioral—of routine social existence. Authenticity, on the other hand, is a "resolute" maintenance of the self out of this stream of unselfconscious habituation that brings forth ontological questioning.

With these understandings as a background, Heidegger becomes misinterpreted to say that authentic being, in escaping the conformism of the "they," comes to disparage the social nature of human being. The authentic individual is falsely assumed to dislocate itself from Being-with. In fact, Heidegger's notion of authenticity in no way signals a retreat from his fundamental understanding of human being as a Being-with-others. Social life is indeed anchored in convention, and Heidegger readily acknowledges its ubiquity and indispensable utility. But social convention is simply an unavoidable game soliciting participation, not a jealous god demanding unthinking fidelity. To be authentic is neither to deprecate nor to escape social life, but simply to experience it in a par-

---

[5] George Kateb, review of *Martin Heidegger* by George Steiner in *New Republic*, May 12, 1979, 35.

ticular manner. Indeed, the authentic individual is chiefly characterized by the recognition and acceptance of its inevitable *thrownness* in the with-world. Being authentic means thinking and acting with awareness that human being, as a thrown Being-in-the-world, is both a contingent being without stable foundations and a Being-with-others whose meanings are always codiscoveries. Authenticity, in other words, necessitates an acceptance of the ontologically social basis of life, including its ineradicable tendency to inauthenticity. Far from requiring that one close oneself off from the shared world, authenticity solicits one to inhabit this world self-consciously, to acknowledge the social constitution of human being while at the same time refusing to become lost in the dominant modes of coping that inhibit its ontological reflection.

Heidegger, therefore, firmly rejects the position that authenticity entails denying or ignoring the collective, public constitution of our being. Indeed, it is precisely *inauthenticity* that begets the delusion of individual sovereignty and autonomy when all the while one remains swept along by the zeitgeist and actuated by social and cultural conventions. Thus Heidegger observes that the heroic denial of or attempted escape from social life, far from being an authentic act, is generally indicative of a deprivation. Actual participation in one's social environment, an ontic involvement, is correctly understood as compliant with rather than antagonistic to the ontologically social structure of human being. A straightforward example given by Heidegger illustrates this point. The ontic capacity for listening is a fundamental component of communication that, in turn, is phenomenologically illustrative of the nature of human being as a Being-with. "This listening to one another, in which Being-with cultivates itself," Heidegger writes, "is more accurately a compliance in Being-with-one-another, a co-enactment in concern. The negative forms of enactment, non-compliance, not listening, opposition, and the like are really only privative modes of belonging itself" (*HCT* 266).[6] Heidegger's notion of authenticity, therefore, strongly militates against any understanding of the human condition as a state of radical individualism, existential isolation, or heroic self-sufficiency.

To become authentic, not only must we reject radical solitude but we must come to feel at home in a shared world. "Being-with-one-another is not a tenacious intrusion of the I upon the thou," Heidegger insists; "instead, existence as together and with one another is founded on the

[6] Richard Wolin, among many others whose relation to Heidegger is fundamentally polemical, completely inverts the status of Being-with-others. Wolin writes: "The more closely one examines the role played by 'Being-with-others' in Heidegger's existential ontology, the more unequivocally it appears as a *deficient* mode of Selfhood or Being-a-Self." Richard Wolin, *The Politics of Being: The Political Thought of Martin Heidegger* (New York: Columbia University Press, 1990), 50.

genuine individuation of the individual. . . . Individuation does not mean clinging obstinately to one's own private wishes but being free for the factical possibilities of current existence" (*BP* 288). Authenticity entails an acknowledgment of the with-world, not as a constraint on individuality but as the chief medium of its expression. Heidegger explicitly states that "only in its Dasein with others can Dasein surrender its individuality in order to win itself as an authentic self."[7] In other words, only through Being-with-others do we come to know ourselves as individuals. "Knowing oneself [*Sichkennen*]," Heidegger insists, "is grounded in Being-with" (*BT* 161). Because our social being is the ground for self-knowledge, it is also the ground for self-reflective activity. Whether this activity is cooperative, competitive, or individualistic, it is carried out in authenticity (and I might add here in freedom, though this will be explained and justified later) when it is self-consciously embedded in human plurality.

Resistance to the full ramifications of our thrownness in the with-world is inherent in everyday life. Such resistance is the normal means we have of coping with daily affairs. Ontological concerns force us disruptively to interrogate rather than pragmatically to engage our agency, to underline its contingency rather than establish its viability. They must be placed in abeyance while we cope. However, any self-conscious denial or rejection of our Being-with constitutes a delusive, or even pathological, inauthenticity. It marks the destructive attempt to gain one's autonomy at the expense of one's worldly contextuality. When Nietzsche engaged in exposing the illusion of community, he occasionally lapsed into this pathology. As Albert Camus observes, Nietzsche "confused freedom and solitude, as do all proud spirits."[8] In one of his most-important and least-recognized confrontations with Nietzsche, Heidegger offers ontological therapy for this pathological confusion.

The human mind and body evolved together in a world of codiscovered meaning. To exist humanly is to exist socially and culturally, in both a phenomenological and a historical sense. Thought, speech, and action, even when riddled with doubt and uncertainty, remain embedded in a shared world. In defending these statements, Heidegger exposes the illusion of solitude and deconstructs its sovereign freedom. The politics that I claim lies submerged in Heidegger's philosophy emerges from this deconstruction.

[7] Martin Heidegger, *The Essence of Reasons*, trans. T. Malick (Evanston: Northwestern University Press, 1969), 131.
[8] Camus, *Rebel*, 75.

Part Two

POSSESSIVE MASTERY AND DISCLOSIVE FREEDOM

Three _____

Heidegger on Freedom

POLITICAL, NOT METAPHYSICAL

> When individuals and nations have once got
> in their heads the abstract concept of full-
> blown Liberty, there is nothing like it in its
> uncontrollable strength.
>   (G. W. F. Hegel, *Philosophy of Mind*)

IN 1958, Isaiah Berlin delivered his now famous essay "Two Concepts of Liberty." From the hundreds of senses of the words *liberty* and *freedom* that historians of ideas have recorded, Berlin selected two for analysis and evaluation: "positive" and "negative" liberty.[1] Such timely conceptual distinctions, Berlin insisted, have significant political ramifications. Attending to ideas in order critically to assess their meaning may prevent their acquiring an "unchecked momentum and an irresistible power over multitudes of men that may grow too violent to be affected by rational criticism."[2] Berlin was reflecting on Heine's observation of the relationship between Rousseau's thought and Robespierre's deeds, and on Heine's prediction that the romanticism of Fichte and Schelling would one day turn the Germans against the liberal culture of the West. More to the point, Berlin had the then closing Iron Curtain on his mind, and he critically evaluated positive liberty as its ideological foundation.

With a similar concern for the social and political effects of our thinking, I shall reexamine the concept of liberty. My worry, however, is less with past fascist threats or looming totalitarian menaces to Western liberal culture. I am more concerned with liberalism's success. To be specific, I am concerned with the danger posed to our social and political life, our world and our earth, by the prevalent notions of freedom that underlie Western political culture. My intent here is not to add to

---

[1] T. H. Green first popularized these terms. However, Immanuel Kant had already spoken of "positive" and "negative" concepts of freedom in the *Metaphysic of Morals*. Berlin makes numerous references to Kant, but fails to note this fact.

[2] Isaiah Berlin, "Two Concepts of Liberty," in *Four Essays on Liberty* (Oxford: Oxford University Press, 1969), 119.

the prodigious debate surrounding Berlin's seminal essay but to employ his schema for other purposes. The analysis will not pit positive liberty against negative liberty, but will contrast positive liberty, negative liberty, and their postmodern counterpart with an understanding of freedom for which Martin Heidegger serves as the spokesperson.

Heidegger is seldom acknowledged as a philosopher of freedom. There are chiefly two reasons. The first is Heidegger's own political biography. For many, Heidegger's prerogative to investigate freedom should be irreversibly revoked because of his fervent support of National Socialism while serving as rector of Freiburg University and his subsequent reluctance to atone for or even come to terms with the significance of this involvement. Heidegger's political biography and its relation to his philosophy has provided material for volumes of discussion and diatribe. For the moment, I shall skirt these issues, arguing later, in chapter 6, that our outrage at his political transgressions is, in any case, best grounded in and most productively developed by way of Heidegger's own reflections on freedom. In thinking about human freedom, Heidegger, after some missteps, demonstrates the need for a fundamental rearticulation of what in the West we find most essential to our historical and political being. How to voice this rearticulation of freedom within one's own political life is, of course, neither for Heidegger nor for his biographers to decide.

The second reason for the frequent dismissal of Heidegger's contribution to our understanding of freedom is that Heidegger articulates freedom in a way that takes us beyond traditional formulations—formulations of which he remains consistently critical. As such, either his discussions are considered overly idiosyncratic and hence irrelevant to standard debates, or his perspective (particularly given his understanding of technology) is held to leave little room for liberty of any ilk. As one commentator curtly observed in dismissing Heidegger's relation to the Western world's preeminent political value, "you can't be a very effective spokesman for freedom when your philosophy tells you that it doesn't exist."[3] While such perceptions are not uncommon, they remain unfounded.

Heidegger offers extended discussions of freedom in his philosophic writings. When he does not speak directly to the issue, the question of freedom still supplies impetus and structure to his thought. Heidegger explicitly testifies to the general philosophic importance of freedom as well as the central importance of freedom to his philosophy. He maintains that "philosophical . . . knowledge is grasped in its genuine con-

[3] Frederick Crews, "The New Americanists," *New York Review of Books,* September 24, 1992, 33.

tent only when in such knowledge the whole of existence is seized by the root after which philosophy searches—in and by *freedom*" (*MFL* 18). Elsewhere he insists that "philosophy is only to be brought about through freedom and that carrying it out is an act of highest freedom" (*ST* 10–11). The relationship between philosophy and freedom is secured for Heidegger because "the problem of Being" is itself *"a problem of freedom"* (*G* 31:300). This equation is grounded in Heidegger's understanding of human being, for the disclosive relationship of human being to Being is only gained in and by freedom. As Heidegger explains, *"freedom is the condition of possibility of the disclosure of the Being of beings, of the understanding of Being"* (*G* 31:303; cf. *BW* 128). Thus Heidegger admonishes his readers to investigate freedom as the ground of the possibility of human being, "as what is even before Being and time" (*G* 31:134). What follows is an effort to explore the philosophic meaning and demonstrate the practical relevance of these claims.

Freedom: Negative, Positive, and Postmodern

Negative liberty, simply put, is freedom from constraint. It signifies the (political) space accorded the individual to pursue desires unhindered by the impositions of others. Its particularly modern formulation, stemming from the Renaissance and the Reformation, encompasses the notion of privacy, a sacrosanct area of personal freedom over which the individual has complete jurisdiction and which demands protection from all external interference, whether by the church, the state, or society. Negative liberty denotes the individual's unchallenged control over his or her (immediate) environment. It forbids trespassing. Berlin identifies negative liberty as the core of liberalism.

Positive liberty, in contrast, is not a freedom *from,* but a freedom *to.* It signifies a freedom to do. But positive liberty entails doing not only what one desires, unhindered by external constraints, but what one *should* desire, unhindered by internal constraints such as irrational drives or delusions, weaknesses of character, false consciousness, or even shortsighted judgment. Free will is only truly free, in other words, when it actualizes the individual's "objective" interests. Positive liberty necessitates both the discovery of one's real needs (and desires) and the capacity to see them fulfilled. If, with Rousseau, we discover that our true interests coincide with the general will, then we may find ourselves in the curious position of being forced to be positively free. If, with Marx, we discover that our true interests are determined by our nature as species beings *(Gattungswesen),* then we may attain positive liberty only by overcoming bourgeois egoism and achieving a radical equality and fraternity such that each gives according to his or her abilities and receives according to his or her needs. Finally, if, with the Nazi ideologues, we discover that our true interests lie with the expansion and rise to power of the people or *Volk*, then we shall discover our positive liberty only in the life-and-death struggle for lebensraum. Positive liberty is freedom to be the most one can be. Attaining this goal—often a group effort—entails both the discovery of one's higher self and the actualizing of its mastery over one's lower (deluded) self.[4] Berlin thus identifies positive liberty with "the wish on the part of the individual to be his own master."[5] As an isolated ideal, self-mastery would appear difficult to disparage. The problem is that the indiviudal selves being mastered within the social whole are frequently understood to be identical in desires, needs, and reason. Historically, Berlin notes, the quest for positive liberty has therefore led to a "prescribed form of life" that too often serves as "a specious disguise for brutal tyranny."[6]

It comes as no surprise that Berlin opts for negative liberty. He advocates the pluralism it assumes and fosters. Positive liberty, he acknowledges, has its place, but it is a place of subordination to its negative counterpart. The positive liberty to participate in government, for example, is identified not as an end in itself—that of citizens realizing their full political nature—but rather as the only tried-and-true means of protecting negative liberties.[7] Yet Berlin is not a radical libertarian. He means to argue against the conflation of meanings and values and he deprecates the radical libertarian tendency to thrust negative liberty

[4] Berlin observes that in theory negative liberty might have similar requirements, demanding knowledge of *which* self is not to be interfered with or constrained. Historically, however, this has seldom proved the case. Those interested in negative liberty have simply identified the empirically demonstrative self as the true self. Hobbes offers the most straightforward and radical formulation of negative liberty, maintaining there to be no internal requirements for freedom at all. According to Hobbes, liberty signifies no more than the absence of "external impediments of motion," and therefore applies to "rational" and "irrational" creatures alike. Thomas Hobbes, *Leviathan*, ed. C. B. Macpherson (New York: Penguin, 1968), 261.

[5] Berlin, *Four Essays on Liberty*, 131.

[6] Ibid. Berlin is mostly interested in the seamy side of positive liberty and focuses on the political heritage of Marx's thought. As such he ignores advocates of positive liberty who reject the prescribed life, such as Marx's onetime rival, Mikhail Bakunin. Bakunin strongly contests the (Marxist) social control Berlin finds dangerous. Yet Bakunin consistently subscribes to a positive sense of liberty, maintaining that "the only liberty worthy of that name [is] liberty consisting in the full development of all the material, intellectual and moral powers latent in every man." Mikhail Bakunin, *The Political Philosophy of Mikhail Bakunin: Scientific Anarchism*, ed. G. P. Maximoff (Glencoe, Ill.: Free Press, 1953), 270.

[7] Boswell reports that Samuel Johnson espoused the strongest formulation of this view, wherein "political liberty is good only so far as it produces private liberty." James Boswell, *The Life of Samuel Johnson* (New York: Penguin, 1979), 140.

onto an unassailable pedestal. Freedom is freedom, and it is good. But it is not the only value we have or should have. Justice is also good, and its instantiation might at times require a diminution of negative liberty. To underline the point, Berlin observes that we force children to go to school. In so doing we must admit to restricting their freedom for the purpose of elevating another value, namely the diminution of ignorance. To maintain that in forcing children to attend school we are in fact not curtailing freedom (because freedom is effectively increased by the growth of knowledge) serves only to conflate the meanings of positive and negative liberty in a dangerous way.[8] Like most good things, freedom is to be enjoyed in proper measure. In this regard Berlin agrees with Edmund Burke. "Liberty," Burke writes in his "Letter to the Sheriffs of Bristol," "must be limited in order to be possessed."[9]

The concepts of negative and positive liberty, Berlin writes, gave rise to "the great clash of ideologies" that dominated his time. In 1958, Berlin could suggest that the view of those who reject negative liberty and favor its positive counterpart "rules over half our world."[10] Concerns are significantly different today. History has rerouted the Marxist yearnings for positive liberty and swept away their institutional perversions. As if these momentous political events of our times were not enough, events within the postmodern intellectual community have further undermined the viability of positive liberty. Whereas Berlin feared that the rational self was endangered by collective prescriptions for its mastery, postmodernists have declared this self an outright fiction. The notion of a fixed rationality that typically grounded the search for a mastered self has become thoroughly suspect. Rationalities may exist, but not a rationality that transcends culture, gender, history, and power. In the postmodern world, we learn, there simply is no self left to be mastered. It has been deconstructed. The pursuit of positive liberty is set adrift without anchor.

If the postmodern world has set positive liberty adrift, however, it has left negative liberty in equally dire straits. As Michel Foucault best demonstrates, contemporary power does not limit itself to prohibiting the fulfillment of desire: it engages in the stimulation and production of desire itself. Power, Foucault insists, should no longer be viewed solely as a juridical and repressive force, symbolized by a king who restricts

---

[8] Berlin's views on this matter have been hotly disputed. Many, taking issue with Berlin, have straightforwardly concluded that "to give up, for the sake of justice, some freedom to act is not to diminish liberty." Gary Frank Reed, "Berlin and the Division of Liberty," *Political Theory* 8 (1980): 376.

[9] Edmund Burke, *Selected Writings of Edmund Burke*, ed. W. J. Bate (Westport, Conn.: Greenwood Press, 1960), 211.

[10] Berlin, *Four Essays on Liberty*, 131, 141.

the movements or rights of his subjects. Increasingly, "bio-power" manifests itself as an insidiously creative force, evidenced in the social and
political apparatuses and technological networks that shape contemporary lives.[11] The postmodern worry is that both the individual and the
social body have become the vehicles and chief effects of power—objects of its stimulation, manipulation, and production. Power today is in
the business of creating subjects, not simply constraining them.

Berlin affirms that negative liberty consists of an actual political or
public space within which unconstrained thought, speech, and action
may occur. Freedom is not simply the ability to do as one wishes, a
formulation Berlin correctly attributes to John Stuart Mill.[12] Berlin reasons that if freedom is a function only of desire and not of (external)
empirical possibilities, then any contraction of desire necessarily becomes an increase in freedom. His worry is that tyrants could suppress
us so efficiently such that certain desires would atrophy. Under the de-
sire-dependent definition of negative liberty, we would then be considered free(r) because we would feel ourselves to be free(r), expressing
little or no inclination for (the abolished) political space, opportunities,
and rights. Freedom, Berlin might have paraphrased Rosa Luxemburg,
is truly freedom only if one can *actually* think, speak, or act differently.
The point is well taken. Any political freedom worth its name must
allow for the thinking and saying, and to a lesser extent the doing, of
what contests the popular and the prescribed.

But the postmodern world presents a more complex picture, which,
while not obviating the perennial concern of linking liberty to opportunity, casts any straightforward relationship in doubt. Not only the
repression of desire but its manipulation and hyperproduction are increasingly in evidence today. The image Berlin supplies to illustrate his
point is that of the ascetic philosopher-slave Epictetus who, by Berlin's
reckoning, mistakenly imagines himself free because he has learned severely to restrict his wants. If we are to hark back to first-century Rome
for illustrations of contemporary threats to liberty, however, then the
debauched Nero perhaps better serves our purpose. A surfeit of desire
that robs one of meaningful community and politics might better limn
postmodern (Western) patterns of unrestrained production and media-
driven consumption. Our subjectification in a technological world—the
administration of our identities as desirers, producers, and consumers—
is insufficiently addressed by the vocabulary of negative liberty.

How, then, are we to formulate the question of liberty today, sup-

[11] See Leslie Paul Thiele, "Foucault's Triple Murder and the Modern Development of
Power," *Canadian Journal of Political Science* 19 (June 1986): 243–60.
[12] See chapter 5 of John Stuart Mill, *On Liberty* (Indianapolis: Bobbs-Merrill, 1956).

planting or supplementing the negative liberty that allows personal control over a private domain? Foucault suggests that we understand freedom less as a thing to be secured, like the individual rights and opportunities of Berlin's negative liberty, than as an activity in which to be
engaged. "Liberty," Foucault insists, "is a *practice*"; it is "what must be
exercised."[13] With this in mind, Foucault preferred not to speak of an
"essential freedom" to be safeguarded so much as an "agonism" inherent in all social and political relations.[14] Freedom today, he maintains, is
to be experienced in the ongoing struggle against the techniques of subjectification. It is to be discovered in "resistance" to the productive
forces of power that manipulate and produce our identities.

Foucault's resistance should not be misunderstood as a completely
negative concept. It is the counterpart to power, and may be equally
productive of identities. For Rousseau (and in various ways for Cicero,
Montesquieu, Locke, and Kant), freedom entailed subordination to a
law of one's own making. Foucault adopts the Nietzschean premise that
the self, not merely the law, must be of one's own making. With the self
no longer given (as the gift of God, nature, or history), freedom is manifest only through the "invention" of the self. Invoking Nietzsche as his
mentor, Foucault thus admonishes us "to create ourselves as a work of
art."[15] However, Foucault effectively politicizes Nietzsche's philosophic
struggle. Freedom is a product of creative resistance to power. Freedom
arises primarily in the social and political arenas wherein identities become the spoils of battle. Foucault's genealogical efforts to destabilize
and contest modern modes of subjectification are consequently aimed at
giving "new impetus, as far and wide as possible, to the undefined work
of freedom."[16]

Foucault's understanding of freedom bears features of both negative
and positive liberty. He adopts the "exercise-concept" of positive liberty
wherein freedom is found not in the absence of external hindrances (the
"opportunity-concept" of negative liberty) but in an activity itself.[17]
However, this activity does not entail the actualization of a true or

[13] Michel Foucault, *The Foucault Reader*, ed. Paul Rabinow (New York: Pantheon,
1984), 245.
[14] Michel Foucault, "On the Genealogy of Ethics: An Overview of Work in Progress,"
in *Michel Foucault: Beyond Structuralism and Hermeneutics*, ed. Hubert Dreyfus and
Paul Rabinow, 2d ed. (Chicago: University of Chicago Press, 1983), 222.
[15] Ibid., 237; see also Michel Foucault, *The History of Sexuality*, vol. 2, *The Use of
Pleasure* (New York: Vintage, 1984), 10–11. For an account of Foucault's reliance on
Nietzsche, see Thiele, "Agony of Politics."
[16] Foucault, *Foucault Reader*, 46.
[17] I take these characterizations of Berlin's two concepts from Charles Taylor's "What's
Wrong with Negative Liberty," in *The Idea of Freedom: Essays in Honour of Isaiah
Berlin*, ed. Alan Ryan (Oxford: Oxford University Press, 1979), 175–93.

higher self. Like the negative libertarians, Foucault resists defining the nature of freedom or its practice as a function of the individual's completed (rational, moral, or political) development. Indeed, Foucaultian freedom entails the struggle to remain free from definitions of the self that prescribe its telos. Rather, freedom is found in the construction of a protean self as it evolves by way of the dynamic clash of productive power and resistance. I will call this Foucaultian (and Nietzschean) understanding of freedom the postmodern concept of liberty. In contrast to the freedom *from* (constraints) of negative liberty and the freedom *to* (master a rationally or collectively defined self) of positive liberty, postmodern liberty might be thought of as a freedom *in*. Primarily, freedom is actualized *in* the struggle of self-creation. Foucault, a student of Nietzsche's tragic school of thought, celebrates this freedom in the seemingly futile and endless attempt to create a self that necessarily remains forever enmeshed in the webs of power. Accordingly, Foucault advocates a "hyper- and pessimistic activism."[18] Postmodern liberty is found in the heroic attempt to create a self as a work of art, or it is not found at all.

Commenting on Berlin's thesis, Alan Ryan observes that "the simplest characterization of positive libertarians is that they identify freedom with control."[19] Ryan's remark is apt, for positive liberty refers to one's control of one's desires and needs, and perhaps of the world required to fulfill them. What Ryan, like most other participants in this debate, fails to observe is that negative libertarians also identify freedom with control. Negative liberty signals the individual's control of his or her immediate environment, of his or her "private" space and time. For John Stuart Mill, liberty is evident whenever "over himself, over his own body and mind, the individual is sovereign."[20] For Bertrand de Jouvenal, the essence of liberty "lies in our will not being subject to other human wills: in our will ruling alone over our actions. . . . Liberty is . . . the direct, immediate, and concrete sovereignty of man over himself, the thing which . . . gives him mastery over and responsibility for his destiny."[21] Negative liberty, in other words, pertains to sovereign control of a personal realm. This is the realm of private property, which includes, following John Locke's formulation, the property of one's self. The key difference between negative and positive libertarians, then, has to do with the kind of self that is assumed to pursue control. Positive libertarians advocate a transcendent, socially defined self that achieves

---

[18] Foucault, "On the Genealogy of Ethics," 232.

[19] Ryan, *Idea of Freedom*, 5.

[20] Mill, *On Liberty*, 13.

[21] Bertrand de Jouvenal, *On Power: The Natural History of Its Growth* (Indianapolis: Liberty Fund, 1993), 352.

mastery over itself and its world by way of self-given law. Negative libertarians advocate an empirical, atomic self that achieves mastery over a private domain through the expression of will.

According to Foucault, and for postmodern thinkers in general, the transcendent self is too mythical and the empirical self too malleable for positive and negative concepts of liberty to cut much ice; thus the need for creative resistance to the productive power that envelops us. But herein postmodern liberty displays its greatest affinity to positive and negative liberty by way of its own, albeit more subtle, pursuit of control. The postmodern liberation from teleological ends is achieved only by way of the subject's reinvestment in an ideal of artistic mastery. The sovereign control of the ungrounded but creative self over its own invention and constitution now becomes the Sisyphean task.

Agonistically engaging those "techniques and practices" that constituted the self in the West, Foucault asks us to join him in charting "the conditions and the indefinite possibilities of transforming the subject, of transforming ourselves."[22] This move is perhaps best understood as the postmodern extension and radicalization of the self-mastery originally sought by the Stoic philosophers, whom Berlin correctly identifies as epitomizing positive liberty and on whom Foucault chooses to focus in his last works. Stoic self-mastery entails the disciplined sculpting of the self into an impervious image of natural law. Postmodern libertarians dismiss natural law (along with the gods and transcendent norms). But the nucleus of the Stoic task remains intact. The postmodern attempt to mold the self into a work of art orients the individual to itself as a malleable object of production. One must invent a self and constitute an identity, as Foucault's students have suggested, by means of the "*stylized repetition of acts*," a project modeled on Nietzsche's effort to stylize his character according to "the constraint of a single taste."[23] Fire, it seems, must be fought with fire. In order to combat the techniques of power, we must become technicians of our own being, dandies of a sort, sculpting ourselves into admirable aesthetic works.

The valorization of freedom as a radical self-creation demonstrates a postmodern hubris. The postmodern aesthete appears as a vastly ambitious Oedipus who would solve the riddle of the Sphinx not merely by disclosing "man," but by creating him anew. The postmodernist effectively engages in what might be called an alchemy of the self. Rather than turning lead into gold, however, the equally elusive goal is to transform the sticky webs of power into springboards of individual free-

[22] Michel Foucault, "About the Beginning of the Hermeneutics of the Self: Two Lectures at Dartmouth," *Political Theory* 21 (1993): 224.

[23] Judith Butler, *Gender Trouble: Feminism and the Subversion of Identity* (New York: Routledge, 1990), 140; Nietzshe, *Gay Science*, 232.

dom defined as a sort of sovereignty. Admittedly, Foucault denies that this alchemy ever produces a purified element. The invented self can never gain complete control within the webs of power. Contingency remains. Citing Nietzsche, Foucault acknowledges that one harbors "not an immortal soul but many mortal ones," and that these are "unable to be mastered by the powers of synthesis."[24] But as with Nietzsche, the tragico-heroic effort is to be made nevertheless. Foucault encourages us win our freedom by moving beyond the "subjected sovereignties" of humanism, beyond the "subject as pseudosovereign," to a self whose true sovereignty is marked by the absence of inhibitions in the artistic construction of identity.[25] In the face of the ubiquitous threat of normalization, the postmodernist retaliates with willful self-creation. Will to power takes on the persona of the self-creating master artist, even if in postmodern times the artist is a Picasso rather than a Rembrandt.

Despite the differences among postmodern liberty, positive liberty, and negative liberty—and there are many important differences indeed—the identification of freedom with mastery remains central to all. This mastery pertains to the higher self's control over the lower self, with positive liberty; to the empirically demonstrable self's control over its private domain, with negative liberty; and to the control of the artistic, agonistic self over its inevitably contested and protean constitution, with postmodern liberty. William Connolly correctly observes that "mastery is the route to freedom" for both "individualists" (negative libertarians) and "collectivists" (positive libertarians).[26] But Connolly fails to observe the residual pursuit of mastery, however subtly it is aestheticized, among the Nietzschean and Foucaultian postmodernists. Perhaps the reason is that Foucault, like most postmodernists, acknowledges his debt to Heidegger, who is acclaimed as the "essential philosopher" determining his "entire philosophical development." At the same time, Foucault insists that Nietzsche "outweighed" Heidegger in influence.[27] My sense is that Foucault's understanding of freedom evidences the burden of Nietzsche's weight.

[24] Foucault, *Foucault Reader,* 94.

[25] Michel Foucault, *Language, Counter-memory, Practice,* trans. D. F. Bouchard (Ithaca: Cornell University Press, 1977), 221–22.

[26] William, E. Connolly, *Identity\Difference,* 29. Connolly also worries that Heidegger might be taken prisoner by the members of the "communitarian" camp, who see freedom as an "attunement" to the world (225). My reassurance to Connolly in this regard is that Heidegger's talk of attunement *(Gestimmtsein)* refers not to a faith in the "higher direction" of nature or the cosmos, but to an openness to profound mystery.

[27] Michel Foucault, "Final Interview," *Raritan* 5 (1985): 8–9. See also William Spanos, "Heidegger and Foucault: The Politics of the Commanding Gaze," in *Heidegger and Criticism: Retrieving the Cultural Politics of Destruction* (Minneapolis: University of Minnesota Press, 1993); and Leslie Paul Thiele, "Reading Nietzsche and Foucault: A Hermeneutics of Suspicion?" *American Political Science Review* 85 (June 1991): 584–92.

What is wrong with the identification of freedom with mastery, whether of the positive, negative, or postmodern variety? The problem is that, like Nietzsche's identification of freedom with radical individuality, the identification of freedom with mastery is pathological. By pathological I mean something born of and nourished by existential resentment. When postmodern libertarians, like their positive and negative counterparts, completedly equate freedom with mastery, they are effectively striking out against an ambiguous and overpowering world. The mastery that is sought relieves the individual from fully acknowledging and hence authentically experiencing its thrownness in the world. The point is not that the pursuit of mastery or control is itself always pathological. Nor is the linkage of political freedom to control or mastery always pathological. Indeed, this linkage is often necessary, for the political liberties we enjoy are practically inseparable from the privileged jurisdiction individuals have over their lives. But the unrestricted identification of human freedom with the pursuit of mastery is pathological. It betrays a resentful unwillingness to acknowledge and affirm the limitations and contingencies that constitute Being-in-the-world. This resentfulness, I propose with (and against) Nietzsche, is philosophically suspect and politically destructive. Admittedly, the postmodern pursuit of freedom through artistic mastery may be extraordinarily creative, just as the modern pursuit of negative and positive liberties may be extraordinarily productive. But this does not vitiate my claim. As Nietzsche observes in the first essay of the *Genealogy of Morals,* the slave revolt in morality began when resentment turned creative, giving birth to values. Creativity and resentment frequently go hand in hand, though their alliance generally spells trouble. To eschew resentment, the creative self needs to mitigate its pursuit of sovereignty and discover its freedom elsewhere. Discovering this place of freedom is a task Heidegger came to set himself.

Heidegger on Freedom: Not Metaphysical

During his politically active career as rector of Freiburg University under the Nazi regime, Heidegger adopted a positive concept of liberty, locating freedom in the mastery of a self that prescribes its own law. In line with Nazi ideology, which he fervently propagated during his brief tenure, Heidegger situates the self within a Volk that circumscribes and defines its identity. Thus Heidegger bore out Heine's prediction that German romanticism would turn the nation against liberal culture. Addressing the question of academic freedom after the imposition of the Nazi *Gleichschaltung* (synchronization or coordination) which sought to organize students and faculty according to the *Führerprinzip* (leader principle) in an effort to integrate the university into the party and state, Rector Heidegger applauded the demise of negative liberty and the resuscitation of its positive counterpart. He asserted: "This will is a true will in that the German student body, through the new Student Law, places itself under the law of its own essence and in this way for the first time determines that essence. To give the law to oneself is the highest freedom. The much celebrated 'academic freedom' is being banished from the German university; for this freedom was not genuine, since it was only negative. It meant primarily freedom from concern, arbitrariness of intentions and inclinations, lack of restraint in what was done and left undone. The concept of the freedom of the German student is now brought back to its truth" (*SAG* 475–76). Here Heidegger proposes that freedom is found in subservience to a law of one's own making. But it is not the self as an individual that makes the law but the self as a member of an organic people. One wills the general will as it grows out of a people and is given voice through the party and the führer.

After his rectorate, Heidegger would scale back and eventually abandon his advocacy of a (nationalistic) positive liberty, without, however, moving in the direction of negative liberty. He rejected both the negative concept of liberty as "unfettered arbitrariness" and the positive concept of liberty as "the constraint of mere laws," including self-given laws (*QT* 25). Heidegger developed instead a new understanding of freedom that effectively extended and reworked his prerectorial approach. By the early 1940s, he would write: "Freedom is not what common sense is content to let pass under that name: the random ability to do as we please, to go this way or that in our choice. Freedom is not license in what we do or do not do. Nor, on the other hand, is freedom a mere readiness to do something requisite and necessary and thus in a sense 'actual'. Over and above all this ('negative' and 'positive' freedom) freedom is a participation in the revealment of what-is-as-such" (*EB* 307). In important respects, this understanding of freedom resembles those of Nietzsche and Foucault. Heidegger now posits freedom as an activity, event, or happening. However, he moves decisively beyond the notion of freedom as self-invention grounded in the mastery of a creative, artistic subject. Instead, freedom is proposed as a disclosive letting-be. Heidegger's development of this disclosive freedom presents us with more than yet another philosophic profile of a concept already overburdened with meanings. Heidegger's mature understanding of freedom is radically distinct from its modern, metaphysical forerunners and their postmodern derivations. It offers dignity in a freedom that celebrates caretaking rather than mastery.

The essence of human being is the provision of a place for Being to become disclosed. In this sense, human being may be posited, to employ

Heidegger's locution, as the "abode" of Being (N 244). Perhaps better said, human being is an abode in preparation for Being, what Heidegger calls a "site of openness" (IM 205). With this in mind, we might retrieve the image of human being as an illuminated circle whose radiuses represent its disclosive extension in time and space. Human being is a radiating finitude whose circumference is limited by a situated history. The illuminated circle of human being is largely defined by its horizon and its shadows. Heidegger understands human freedom to be inseparable from these limitations. Dissociating his understanding from a common notion of freedom as unrestricted movement, opportunity, or choice, Heidegger writes: "It is misguided to think one understands freedom most purely in its essence if one isolates it as a free-floating arbitrariness. Moreover, the task is precisely the reverse, to conceive freedom in its finitude and to see that, by proving boundedness, one has neither impaired freedom nor curtailed its essence" (MFL 196). Every act of freedom, in other words, is a foreclosing of alternatives and possibilities; illuminations only disclose in relation to darkened peripheries.

Freedom is not absolute liberty in the sense of an unbounded and ungrounded power to do, move, or create. Freedom is freedom to reveal what is. But what is, most fundamentally, is only insofar as it remains illuminated in contrast to what remains concealed. Heidegger writes: "Everyday opinion sees in the shadow only the lack of light, if not light's complete denial. In truth, however, the shadow is a manifest, though impenetrable, testimony to the concealed emitting of light. In keeping with this concept of shadow, we experience the incalculable as that which, withdrawn from representation, is nevertheless manifest in whatever is, pointing to Being, which remains concealed" (QT 154). In other words, only the no-thingness of Being allows human being to disclose beings as things. In this disclosing, Heidegger states, freedom pertains: "Without the original manifest character of Nothing there is no self-hood and no freedom. . . . Nothing is that which makes the revelation of what-is as such possible for our human existence" (EB 339–40). Human being, as a bounded circle of disclosure, displays its freedom to the extent that it remains open to the inexhaustible mystery of Being in its bounded disclosing of beings.

Traditionally, the organ of freedom has been located in the human will. As John Locke writes, expressing the common Western perspective: "We can scarce tell how to imagine any *Being* freer, than to be able to do what he *wills*."[28] Human beings have a free will, it is held, and they exercise their freedom when this will is active and unre-

---

[28] John Locke, *An Essay concerning Human Understanding*, ed. Peter Nidditch (Oxford: Clarendon Press, 1975), 244.

strained. Heidegger, by and large, does not deny that the faculty of will plays host to freedom. But as the host of freedom, the will is not its cause, merely its place of residence (*QT* 25). Moreover, the will plays host to freedom not by securing for the self dominion *over* the world but by securing the self *in* its world. Will, Heidegger writes, "is never encapsulation of the ego from its surroundings. Will is, in our terms, resolute openness, in which he who wills stations himself abroad among beings in order to keep them firmly within his field of action" (*WPA* 48). Free will is always a willing of openness.

Heidegger's commentators have often taken his concern with resoluteness, and his description of willing in terms of resoluteness, to imply a "decisionistic" orientation, a Nietzschean or existentialist notion of the heroic power to create the self anew. Here, as Sartre observes, one is "condemned to be free" because of the burden of total responsibility for the self one shoulders through willful choosing. Yet the notion of resoluteness, Heidegger maintains, does not imply such Promethean choices. Indeed, Heidegger disparages pretentious talk of grand decision making as all too prevalent in his time and as a mark of inauthentic speech (*HCT* 272).[29] Resoluteness is the very renouncing of subjective willfulness and, by implication, the renouncing of willful decision making. Heidegger explains that "the resoluteness intended in *Being and Time* is not the deliberate action of a subject, but the opening up of human being, out of its captivity in that which is, to the openness of Being" (*PLT* 67). Resoluteness or *Entschlossenheit,* which literally means unclosedness, is an opening of the self to the questioning, not the controlling, of (its) Being.

Resolute openness manifests human freedom; to be resolutely occupied with the question of one's own Being means "to understand oneself in one's own factual freedom" (*BP* 276). We are speaking here of the concern for oneself as a Being-in-the-world-with-others: "To be free is to understand oneself from out of one's own capacity-to-be; but 'oneself' and 'one's own' are not understood individually or egoistically. . . . They are understood in the basic possibilities of transcending Dasein, in the capacity-to-be-with with others, in the capacity-to-be by extant things" (*MFL* 214). In making its own Being an issue, then, human being opens itself to the question of beings as a whole, which entails opening itself to a populated world. Only in the midst of and as a concern for this world is freedom found.

Being is brought to light (or pushed back into the shadows) by way of human (ir)resoluteness, as a willing openness (or closedness) to the

---

[29] Those who criticize Heidegger for advocating "decisionism" often miss this point. See Wolin, *Politics of Being.*

world at large. And here we see why Heideggerian freedom and the pursuit of mastery are opposed, for the open and fundamental interrogation of one's world demands a forgoing of its mastery. Fundamental questioning ceases the moment the presumptions that necessarily precede efforts at domination arise. To be sure, the disclosure of Being occurs in all human activities and experiences, including human efforts at attaining various forms of control. And for many of life's affairs, efforts at gaining control or mastery are appropriate. But such efforts remain forgetful of Being. In these instances, being is revealed only as forgotten, as a watch is revealed in its absence on a tanned arm.

To reveal something as forgotten is to reveal it as no longer in question, as no longer fundamentally questionable. Freedom proper is truly manifest only in those thoughts, words, and deeds that evidence human being's "openness to the mystery" (*Offenheit für das Geheimnis*). And openness to the mysterious Being of beings recedes from us to the extent that we think, speak, and act in a manner that precludes profound (self-)interrogation. Summing up Schelling's thesis, Heidegger remarks that freedom demands pantheism (*ST* 85). That is, freedom demands openness to the impenetrable immanence of Being in beings. It also demands what Heidegger calls "releasement toward things" (*Gelassenheit zu den Dingen*). Heidegger borrows the term *Gelassenheit* from Meister Eckhardt. It literally means a letting-be. The dispositions that best prepare human being for the visitations of freedom, then, are an ontological openness to no-thingness (Being) combined with a receptive releasement toward things (beings). Human freedom for Heidegger, particularly after his "turning" of the mid-1930s, is fundamentally and foremost an openness and letting-be.[30] Freedom is a letting-be of things,

---

[30] Heidegger's "turning" is often understood as a turning away from existential concerns such as anxiety and resoluteness and a turning toward mystical concerns with releasement. However, David Krell is right to maintain "that *Gelassenheit* is already at work in the analysis of anxious Dasein in *Being and Time* (1927), and that anxiety in the face of death remains central to *Gelassenheit* (1959)." David Farrell Krell, *Intimations of Mortality: Time, Truth, and Finitude in Heidegger's Thinking of Being* (University Park: Pennsylvania State University Press, 1986), 155. John Caputo agrees, writing that "*Gelassenheit* is not the counter-concept to anxiety; it is its further refinement." John Caputo, *The Mystical Element in Heidegger's Thought* (n.p.: Oberlin Printing, 1978), 26. In turn, resoluteness is described by Heidegger as a willing of openness. Some find this position absurd. Maurice Cranston parodies Heidegger with the story of one of Heidegger's students who knew the importance of being resolved, but did not know what he was resolved to do, exclaiming: "Ich bin entschlossen, ich weiss nur nicht wozu!" Cited in Maurice Cranston, *Freedom* (New York: Basic Books, 1967), 3. The student was probably a confused acolyte, or as Karl Löwith recalls the situation, the maker of a "far from innocent joke." Karl Löwith, "Political Implications of Heidegger's Existentialism," *New German Critique* 45 (Fall 1988): 121. Yet some of the confusion is shared by Cranston, and perhaps Löwith. For Heidegger, one is never *resolved* "to do" anything in particular.

as they come to presence, and an openness to Being, as it remains hidden.

How are we to understand this letting-be? The teacher in Heidegger's "Conversation on a Country Path about Thinking" indicates that "when we let ourselves into releasement . . . we will non-willing," to which the scientist responds: "Releasement is indeed the release of oneself from transcendental re-presentation and so a relinquishing of the willing of a horizon. Such relinquishing no longer stems from a willing, except that the occasion for releasing oneself . . . requires a trace of willing. This trace, however, vanishes while releasing oneself and is completely extinguished in releasement" (*DT* 79–80). The teacher does not proceed to contradict the scientist in his interpretation of releasement. Neither, however, are the scientist's words those of the teacher. Effectively, the teacher needs the scientist, just as Heidegger needs representational locutions, to limn the ineffable. To describe how one might "will non-willing" in temporal terms, as a trace of willing that evaporates with the emergence of nonwilling, is perhaps as good an approximation as conceptual language will permit. The description is acceptable to the scientist, and to us, because, in its temporal separation of willing and nonwilling and its notion of evaporating traces of will it neither contradicts common sense nor flouts the logic that would reject the simultaneous existence of willing and will-lessness. Ultimately, however, the rules of logic and representational thought must be placed in abeyance if we are to experience the "unharnessed" will.[31] *Re*-presenting is to be abandoned because only the direct experience of releasement offers a sufficient base for its understanding.

The attempt to overcome willful mastery, like the attempt to over-

---

In resolute openness to Being, one disengages from willful doing. Heidegger writes, "He who wills, he who puts his whole existence into a will, *is* resolved. . . . but the essence of resolve lies in the opening, the coming-out-of-cover of human Being-there into the clearing of Being, and not in a storing up of energy for 'action.' . . . its relation to Being is one of letting-be" (*IM* 20–21).

[31] The term belongs to Nietzsche, for whom the heroic power of will displayed by "higher types" eventually yields its opposite. The lion metamorphoses into the child and the sublime man "must unlearn his heroic will, too: he should be an exalted man and not only a sublime one—the ether itself should raise him up, the will-less one! . . . To stand with relaxed muscles and unharnessed wills: that is the most difficult thing for all of you, you sublime men!" Nietzsche, *Thus Spoke Zarathustra,* 140–41. Nietzsche's understanding of a will-lessness emerging from will approaches that of Heidegger. However, Heidegger tends to focus on Nietzsche's radical subjectivism, neglecting other, less prevalent tendencies. Citing Nietzsche's definition of freedom (from *The Twilight of the Idols*) as the will to take responsibility for oneself, Heidegger identifies this with the Kantian notion of positive liberty as self-legislation. In each case, Heidegger tells us, "it all comes down to what is meant by 'self.'" And the "self" for Nietzsche, Heidegger too rigidly determines, is always the sovereign subject suffused by will to power (*G* 51:47).

come metaphysics, confronts us with a paradox in its pursuit. The will-fulness required for the overcoming of will is precisely that which we are trying to escape. The proposed resolution should come as no surprise. Willfulness, like metaphysics, is to be left alone. But having abandoned willfulness one might wonder what remains to be done. Heidegger's answer probably infuriated as many as it baffled. We are admonished to wait. The conversation between the teacher and the scientist again is illuminating. The teacher declares that "on our own we do not awaken releasement in ourselves" and therefore "we are to do nothing but wait." The scientist, as the reader's spokesperson, naturally asks: "Then what are we to wait for? And where are we to wait? I hardly know anymore who and where I am." The teacher responds: "None of us knows that, as soon as we stop fooling ourselves," and eventually concludes, "Waiting, all right; but never awaiting, for awaiting already links itself with re-presenting and what is re-presented. . . . In waiting we leave open what we are waiting for" (DT 59, 61, 62, 68).[32]

Waiting, it seems, is a good antidote for the technological hyperactivity to which we are prone. But there is more here. Once we stop "fooling ourselves" and escape the seductive powers of calculative thought, we realize that our most basic existential situation, our who and where, remains every bit a mystery. This realization is, minimally, the prerequisite for releasement. Life, after all, *is* waiting. Existentially speaking, it is a waiting for death. Life is not an *a*waiting because no one knows what death is. But waiting for death is not simply waiting for one's demise—that is, for one's annihilation or physical absence from the world. Rather, waiting for death is fully apprehending human being in its finitude. Human being is defined by Heidegger as that for which its own being is an issue. Consequently, the limits of human being, in particular its horizon of nonbeing, its death, are equally issues. Acknowledging, understanding, and accepting the finitude of human being constitutes wisdom. Thus philosophy, the love of wisdom, has from ancient times been identified with learning how to die.

Human being exercises its freedom waiting upon the disclosure of Being, yet this waiting is not an awaiting or a waiting for. We wait less in anticipation of an answer that might satisfy our will to knowledge than we wait in acceptance of our task to live questioningly. For Heidegger the "essence [of a human being] is to be the one who waits,

[32] "The *Thou* meets me through grace," Martin Buber writes in like fashion, "it is not found by seeking. . . . everything that has ever been devised and contrived . . . as precept, alleged preparation, or meditation, has nothing whatsoever to do with the primal, simple fact of the meeting." Martin Buber, *I and Thou*, trans. R. G. Smith (Edinburgh: T. and T. Clark, 1944), 11, 77.

the one who attends upon the coming to presence of Being in that in thinking he guards it. Only when man, as the shepherd of Being, attends upon the truth of Being can he expect an arrival of a destining of Being and not sink to the level of a mere wanting to know" (*QT* 41–42). Released from wanting to possess or control, conceptually or physically, human being exercises freedom in an interrogative thinking that Heidegger equates with gratitude. In thinking one becomes grateful for the gift of Being's mystery. Thinking becomes a thanking. Importantly, we are speaking of a "thanking which does not have to thank for something, but only thanks for being allowed to thank" (*DT* 85). We might substitute "think(ing)," "will(ing)," or "wait(ing)" for "thank(ing)" here; in all cases the activity is not justified by the achievement of a goal, but is, in itself, both summons and reward.[33] Means and ends merge in the exercise of freedom.

As such, freedom is not merely one value among others, nor even a *meta*value, the "value of all values"[34] that allows one to choose between and secure other values. Freedom goes to the essence of, and thus points beyond, human being. "Freedom," Heidegger writes, "is not a particular thing among others, not something lined up as part of a row, but rather it prescribes and permeates the totality of beings as a whole. If we are to investigate freedom as the ground of possibility of human being, then its essence is more primordial than man. Man is only a guardian of freedom ... human freedom signifies now no longer: freedom as a property of man, but the reverse: *man as a possibility of freedom*. Human freedom is the freedom which invades and sustains man, thereby rendering man possible" (*G* 31:134–35; see also *ST* 9). Traditional Western thinking posits freedom as the autonomous subject's most valued asset, as its capacity to comprehend and control what it confronts. Heidegger understands freedom as that which exposes human being to the incomprehensible and intractable: to Being. What is beyond one's power to master and possess, conceptually or otherwise, is beyond one's power to assess. Freedom, therefore, allows a reaching beyond calculation and valuation, beyond human jurisdiction.

---

[33] Reiner Schürmann writes: "But if it is true that the event of presencing founds nothing, that it cannot even be understood as long as the very search for a foundation is not renounced, the critique of grounds and reasons amounts indeed to deconstructing action: taking it out of its seemingly natural embeddedness in doctrine and meaningful order, and examining it *as one site where presencing occurs*. To the question "What ought we to do?" the answer is, then, the same as to the question "How ought we to think?" Love the flux and thank its economic confluences." Reiner Schürmann, *Heidegger on Being and Acting: From Principles to Anarchy* (Bloomington: Indiana University Press, 1987), 81.

[34] This is Herbert Read's formulation in *Existentialism, Anarchism, and Marxism* (London, 1949), 23, cited in Cranston, *Freedom*, 42.

Heidegger observes that "through the characterization of something as 'a value' what is so valued is robbed of its worth. That is to say, by the assessment of something as a value what is valued is admitted only as an object for man's estimation. But what a thing is in its Being is not exhausted by its being an object. . . . Every valuing, even where it values positively, is a subjectivizing. It does not let beings: be. Rather, valuing lets beings: be valid—solely as the objects of its doing" (*BW* 228). To proclaim God the "highest value," it follows, "is a degradation of God's essence. Here as elsewhere thinking in values is the greatest blasphemy imaginable against Being" (*BW* 228). Everything Heidegger says here of God or Being might also be said of freedom. Once freedom becomes a value, even the highest value, it ceases to identify that which enables us to partake of the mystery of Being. For this reason Heidegger would affirm that "Dasein's transcendence and freedom are identical" (*MFL* 185). Subjecting freedom to representational and conceptual thought, allowing its designation as a value, is an effective assertion of the self's capacity to assess and estimate (its relation to) Being. For Heidegger, however, "freedom's incomprehensibility consists in the fact that it resists comprehension," and this is so "because freedom transposes us into the occurrence of Being, not in the mere representation of it" (*ST* 162). Freedom, in short, is the gift that allows human being to glance beyond the self, beyond beings, and beyond their possession and mastery in thought, word, or deed.

That we are, as Heidegger states, called upon to be the shepherds of Being indicates that we find our freedom in caretaking, in concernfully letting the Being of beings be. In other words, freedom is not so much a property of our will as it is a reflection of our worldliness. Freedom is manifest in the care-full being of one's there. We shall have to look to the East, not elsewhere in the West (with the exception of Meister Eckhardt), to find resonance with this understanding. For Heidegger, and in stark contrast to the Western metaphysical tradition, freedom is not a value, but beyond valuation; freedom is evidenced not in willfulness but in a "waitfulness"; freedom is not an unbounded power or choice but a discovery and acknowledgment of one's place within bounds; freedom is not an obtaining or controlling but a letting-be.

Heidegger on Freedom: Political

"Real freedom," Bronislaw Malinowski writes, "is always an increase in control, in efficiency, and in the power to dominate one's own organism and the environment, as well as artifacts and the supply of natural resources. . . . To scour the universe for possibilities of freedom other than . . . [these] "is an idle philosophic pastime."[35] Heidegger proposes an antipodal understanding of freedom. The pursuit of this freedom is neither idle nor solely philosophical. It is significantly political. But that is not to say that there is a direct, unavoidable, and obvious translation of Heidegger's ontological perspective on freedom into political theory and practice. At the same time, our self-understandings, as individuals and members of collectivities, have political implications and repercussions. In attempting to answer the question "What is to be done?" the discovery and maintenance of an individual and a collective identity become essential parts of the doing. Alasdair MacIntyre argues that to answer the question "What ought I to do?" one must first answer the question "Who am I?" The latter question will involve locating oneself in "a nexus of social relationships, and it is within these and the possibilities which they make available that ends in the light of which actions may be criticized are discovered."[36] But determining who one is is not solely a matter of social location: it is also a question of existential and philosophic location, which, though never completely separable from a social context, is not reducible to it. The link between the ontology of freedom and its political manifestations is indirect but firm. Our actions in the world reflect our most fundamental sense of self. What we do rests in large part on who we think we are, ontologically no less than culturally, socially, and politically.

A Cartesian orientation that objectifies the world fuses our who and our how, our identity and our behavior, in a specific way. The world becomes the raw material for representation, acquisition, control, and domination by the subject. The dangerous self-confidence expressed in humanity's unsustainable exploitation of the earth is the fruit of this equation of freedom and sovereign power. The result is that humanity is now threatened by the ecological limits of a world it has unceasingly sought to possess and master.

On the other hand, if we discover our dignity in a freedom that is not equated with acquisitive control, then our politics and our lives will be transformed accordingly. If we accept with Heidegger that "the highest dignity of [human] essence . . . lies in keeping watch over the unconcealment—and with it, from the first, the concealment—of all coming to presence on this earth" (QT 32), then we might expect our comportment to reflect a distinct worldly solicitude. My argument is that

[35] Bronislaw Malinowski, *Freedom and Civilization* (London, 1947), 59, 65. Quoted in Bernard Crick, *In Defense of Politics*, 4th ed. (Chicago: University of Chicago Press, 1992), 217–18.

[36] Alasdair MacIntyre, *A Short History of Ethics* (New York: Macmillan, 1966), 187.

Heidegger's philosophy has ramifications, if not prognostications, for the public realm. Were human freedom exercised chiefly as an interrogative disclosure of the world rather than a possessive mastery of it,[37] significant changes in political culture might be expected.

Hegel claims, with typical aplomb, that "the history of the world is none other than the progress of the consciousness of freedom."[38] More recently, A. J. Carlyle wrote "it seems evident that the history of civilization during the last two thousand years is primarily the history of the development of liberty."[39] Indeed, the centrality of freedom to the Western political and philosophical tradition is evident. Freedom, despite its widely contested meanings—Hegel found it "indefinite, ambiguous, and open to the greatest misconceptions"[40]—is the Western world's most cherished prize. Any change on that score seems unlikely. The political relevance of Heidegger's philosophic contribution is that it allows us to maintain our love of freedom while reining in its most pernicious effects.

Still, the Heideggerian alternative may appear all too passive. Does disclosive freedom not reduce us to impotent observers of fate? Is disclosive freedom not a recipe for existential lassitude? Does it not mark the end of humanity's turbulent history of ingenuity, creativity, and destruction? If so, then disclosive freedom would be (as the ballad says)

[37] I choose the term *possessive mastery* because of its historical resonance. Philosophically, it recalls the effects of Cartesian subjectivism. In his *Discourse on Method,* Descartes proposes that "instead of that speculative philosophy which is taught in the Schools, we may find a practical philosophy by means of which, knowing the force and the action of fire, water, air, the stars, heavens and all other bodies that environ us, as distinctly as we know the different crafts of our artisans, we can in the same way employ them in all those uses to which they are adapted, and thus render ourselves the *masters* and *possessors* of nature." René Descartes, *A Discourse on Method* (New York: Washington Square Press, 1965), 117 (emphasis added). Politically, the term recalls C. B. Macpherson's use of *possessive individualism* to identify the liberal political theory deriving from John Locke and his immediate forerunners. By the seventeenth century, and increasingly so thereafter, Macpherson writes, "The individual was seen neither as a moral whole, nor as part of a larger social whole, but as an owner of himself.... The individual, it was thought, is free inasmuch as he is proprietor of his person and capacities. The human essence is freedom from dependence on the wills of others, and freedom is a function of possession." C. B. Macpherson, *The Political Theory of Possessive Individualism: Hobbes to Locke* (London: Oxford University Press, 1962), 3. Finally, the term recalls Nietzsche, who flirted with the idea of consolidating the philosophical quest for self-possession and the political quest for mastery.

[38] G. W. F. Hegel, *The Philosophy of History,* trans. J. Sibree (New York: Dover, 1956), 19.

[39] A. J. Carlyle, *Political Liberty: A History of the Conception in the Middle Ages and Modern Times* (Westport, Conn.: Greenwood Press, 1941), vii.

[40] G. W. F. Hegel, *Hegel's Philosophy of Mind,* trans. William Wallace and A. V. Miller (Oxford: Clarendon Press, 1971), 239.

"just another word for nothing left to lose," and nothing to be done. Heidegger suggests otherwise. First, he generally distinguishes between fate *(Schicksal)* and destiny *(Geschick):* fate compels us to the "inevitableness of an unalterable course," but nothing in this world, including the dominance of modern technology, is a fate for human being. Rather, the historical disclosure of Being, including its current technological form, is a destining *(QT* 25). Destiny does not compel, it calls. Human freedom is evidenced in listening to the destining of Being and responding actively. There is no question of blind obedience to fate, or resignation to an appointed lot. And the reason, Heidegger states, is that we are fundamentally free.

The problem before us is not that disclosive freedom amounts to fatalistic resignation and the diminution of our creative forces as a species. The problem is that historically these forces have consistently been shackled to the struggle for possessive mastery. This, I believe, is the proper response to critics who interpret Heidegger as promoting a sort of political quietism. The typical objection is that we cannot "think of democracy without imputing to man the minimal will and mastery that Heidegger denies him because will and mastery in some sense already contain the seeds of the world of technology conceived of as the 'will to will.' "[41] Yet Heidegger does not deny human being a "minimal" will and mastery. He simply prompts us to question its "unconditional character" and unbridled hegemony in the contemporary world *(PLT* 116). The disclosure of the Being of beings, which for Heidegger delimited the realm of human freedom, should frame our disposition neither pessimistically nor optimistically. Most fundamentally, it is a classically tragic experience—that is, an experience of resolute action tempered by the wise recognition of limits *(EGT* 44).

Saint Augustine declared it a great liberty to be able not to sin, and a greater liberty to be unable to sin. Heidegger believes that there is indeed freedom evidenced in being able not to will. But he insists that there is no freedom gained in being unable to will. To escape willfulness, a resolute will is necessary. Great effort is required (to prepare the self) to let beings and Being be. Just as freedom in resoluteness is not arbitrary willfulness, so freedom in letting-be is not a doing nothing.[42]

---

[41] Luc Ferry and Alain Renaut, *Heidegger and Modernity,* trans. Franklin Philip (Chicago: University of Chicago Press, 1990), 17.

[42] As Fred Dallmayr attests, there has been no dearth of confusion on this point, with contrary opinions in abundance: "No theoretical aspect of [Heidegger's] work has occasioned more controversy and heated debate than his attitude toward freedom. On the one hand, he is reproached for having carried the modern concept of freedom to an absurd point and thus for having promoted a blind and arbitrary decisionism. On the other hand,

Disclosive freedom is always the freedom resolutely to will openness to Being and releasement to beings. Openness and releasement do not preclude, but rather invite, activity and thought. In turn, letting-be is not tantamount to a retreat from the world. Quite the opposite: it entails the formation of worldly relationships made all the more dynamic because they are no longer constrained by the habits of possessive mastery. Heidegger writes: "The freedom to reveal something overt lets whatever 'is' at the moment *be* what it is. Freedom reveals itself as the 'letting-be' of what-is. . . . The phrase we are now using, namely the 'letting-be' of what-is, does not, however, refer to indifference and neglect, but to the very opposite of them. To let something be is in fact to have something to do with it. . . . To let what-is *be* what it is means participating in something overt and its overtness in which everything that 'is' takes up its position" (*EB* 305–6). "To free," Heidegger observes elsewhere, "really means to spare. The sparing itself consists not only in the fact that we do not harm the one whom we spare. Real sparing is something *positive* and takes place when we leave something beforehand in its own nature, when we return it specifically to its being, when we 'free' it in the real sense of the word into a preserve of peace" (*PLT* 149). To be free is to set free, is to let be. Heidegger identifies this effort of dynamic guardianship within the faculties of thought, speech, and action. Far from a fatalistic retreat, disclosive freedom launches us into an invigorated participation in worldly life.[43]

Still, the politics of Heidegger's philosophy of freedom is not programmatic. Nevertheless, our understanding of disclosive freedom may be deployed meaningfully, though not univocally, to inform important political concerns. Part 3 takes on this task at length. For now, I shall briefly illustrate its possibilities by examining the support Heidegger's notion of disclosive freedom finds in, and gives to, two efforts at political theorizing.

---

his writings sometimes are claimed to endorse a complete dismantling or eradication of human freedom and willing, and thus to sanction a deterministic fatalism." Fred Dallmayr, "Ontology of Freedom: Heidegger and Political Philosophy," *Political Theory* 12 (1984): 208.

[43] In an insightful examination, Michel Haar suggests that human freedom becomes enveloped and overpowered by the "narcissism of Being" that burgeons in Heidegger's later writings. Michel Haar, "The Question of Human Freedom in the Later Heidegger," *Southern Journal of Philosophy* 28 (1989): suppl. 1–16. Haar's worry, however, is based on the assumed equivalence of human autonomy and human freedom. Once we accept that freedom is better described as a contextual participation rather than an exercise of individual sovereignty, Haar's concern that Being has "dispossessed" us of freedom appears misplaced.

Sovereignty and the Politics of Public and Private

In one of her most difficult essays, "What Is Freedom?" Hannah Arendt takes issue with common Western concepts of liberty.[44] For Arendt, the nature of freedom has been obscured by the prevailing philosophical notions on which the political realm has been modeled. These notions identify freedom as a function of (the mastery of) will. Arendt maintains that freedom is far from being the (will) power to achieve or control one's desires or world. She indicates, in all probability to most readers' confusion, that to be truly free action "must be free from motive on one side, [and] from its intended goal as a predictable effect on the other."[45] In direct opposition to the traditional Western notion of freedom as the opportunity or power to attain one's wants or fulfill desires, Arendt strips from freedom both the final achievement of a goal and the initial motivations for its pursuit. The reason is that freedom for Arendt is less an individual achievement than a public event.

Freedom is manifest in the open spaces of the political realm wherein the actions of citizens intersect. But action and interaction (as opposed to behavior) are inherently unstable and unpredictable. What humans discover when they act in concert is that freedom is manifest in the very novelty of the results. Far from being controllable and predictable, Arendt states, action is closer to the nature of a miracle. Freedom is evidenced in the capacity "to begin something new and . . . not being able to control or even foretell its consequences."[46] In action, by way of freedom, the new and the unforeseen occurs.

The theme of sovereignty largely orients Western political thinking about individuals and states. Sovereignty is defined as control over the initiation and outcome of action. In the "eyes of the tradition," Arendt writes, freedom is consistently identified with sovereignty—that is, with the individual's remaining "master of his acts."[47] Arendt insists, how-

[44] Hannah Arendt, "What Is Freedom?" in *Between Past and Future* (New York: Penguin, 1968).

[45] Ibid., 151.

[46] Hannah Arendt, *The Human Condition* (Chicago: University of Chicago Press, 1958), 235. Jean-Luc Nancy offers the same understanding of those actions that we retrospectively observe: "History is perhaps not so much that which unwinds and links itself, like the time of a causality, as that which *surprises itself*. 'Surprising itself,' we will see, is the mark proper to freedom. History in this sense is the freedom of being—or being in its freedom. Thought is placed today—by history and by its own history—before the necessity of thinking this unforeseeability, this im-providence and surprise that give rise to freedom." Jean-Luc Nancy, *The Experience of Freedom*, trans. Bridget McDonald (Stanford: Stanford University Press, 1993), 15.

[47] Arendt, *Human Condition*, 235.

ever, that far from being the prerequisite for freedom, sovereignty signals its demise: "Under human conditions, which are determined by the fact that not man but men live on the earth, freedom and sovereignty are so little identical that they cannot even exist simultaneously. Where men wish to be sovereign, as individuals or as organized groups, they must submit to the oppression of the will, be this the individual will with which I force myself, or the 'general will' of an organized group. If men wish to be free, it is precisely sovereignty they must renounce."[48] Arendt's discussion of freedom is nothing if not shocking for the Western mind. I believe it is best viewed as a political reconstruction of Heidegger's understanding. Arendt insists, in words that might have been Heidegger's, that the "abyss of freedom" is the "*abyss* of nothingness that opens up before any deed that cannot be accounted for by a reliable chain of cause and effect and is inexplicable in Aristotelian categories of potentiality and actuality."[49] Arendt, like Heidegger, insists that freedom evaporates once it is possessed by a sovereign power. Indeed, freedom is not freedom until it possesses us. Like Heidegger's disclosive freedom, Arendt's conception of political freedom is antipodal to sovereignty and unpredictable. It is revealing of the world and of the new.

Perhaps the aspect of Arendt's theory most criticized is her distinction between the public and the private realms. For Arendt the public realm is the birthplace of freedom. Only in the public space devoted to the initiation and preservation of action is freedom to be found and safeguarded. The private realm, on the other hand, is the realm of necessity. It is devoted to satisfying human needs. Freedom lies in stark and unbridgeable contrast to the continuing and unavoidable processes that sustain life in the darkness of privacy. Arendt claims that the divorce between freedom and necessity, between the public and the private, is irreconcilable and complete. The provision of services and goods, the maintenance of households and the exercise of administration, are cut from the whole cloth of necessity. The public speaking of great words and the public doing of great deeds claim a monopoly on freedom. The novelty of birth that Arendt celebrates with such originality is here revived in the freedom humans exercise in political beginnings. This is a stunning vision of politics. The consequence of Arendt's position, however, is that everything that falls between the novelty of birth and the sporadic explosions of freedom evidenced in great speeches and deeds— that is, the vast bulk of human life—is relegated to the unredeemable realm of necessity.

[48] Arendt, "What Is Freedom?" 165.

[49] Hannah Arendt, *The Life of the Mind,* vol. 2, *Willing* (New York: Harcourt Brace Jovanovitch, 1978), 207.

In the "1844 Manuscripts," Marx states that humanity separates itself from the beasts by finding its freedom in production beyond physical need.[50] Arendt, despite her virulent attack on Marx's understanding
of a human being as an *animal laborans*, effectively extends his Enlightenment position. Freedom, however, is now found not in the realm of
surplus production, but in what might be called the realm of surplus
speech and action. Politics and freedom, for Arendt, are manifest only
in the human capacity for novelty and creation in word and deed
ungrounded in and distinct from the demands of everyday life. Maintenance and preservation—through labor, administration, and general
caretaking—are the sorry if necessary tasks of the unfree.

Arendt writes that "the appearance of freedom . . . coincides with the
performing act. Men *are* free—as distinguished from their possessing
the gift for freedom—as long as they act, neither before nor after; for
to *be* free and to act are the same."[51] Thus we see that Arendt, with
Heidegger and like Foucault, insists that freedom is an exercise. And
Arendt, with Heidegger but more explicitly and consistently than Foucault, dismisses sovereignty and attests to contingency in the exercise of
freedom. However, unlike Heidegger but with Foucault, Arendt insists
on the heroic nature of political life and the practice of freedom. Her
standards of heroism, notably, come directly from the Greeks rather
than through Nietzsche's labyrinth. Hence Arendt's heroic criteria for
freedom, in contrast to Foucault's, shift from self-creative to world-cre-
ative engagements. Nevertheless, her dismissal of the possibility of
a freedom exercised in mundane acts of caretaking is even more unrelenting.

Heidegger's notion of disclosive freedom philosophically buttresses
Arendt's dissociation of freedom from sovereignty. At the same time, it
critically addresses, and may be employed to emend, her overly constricted understanding of politics and its practices. Arendt wishes to
claim that the divorce of freedom and necessity, of the public and the
private, is irreconcilable and complete. Anything that speaks to the demanding necessities of life—daily physical or household concerns, for
example—does not partake of freedom and hence cannot be considered
the stuff of politics. As Heidegger demonstrates, however, freedom is
evidenced whenever and wherever human beings resolutely open themselves to Being and disclosively let the world of beings be. Political freedom, then, would be evidenced whenever speech and action disclose the
world of beings, and in particular our Being-with, publicly. There is no

[50] Karl Marx, *The Marx-Engels Reader*, ed. Robert C. Tucker, 2d ed. (New York:
W. W. Norton, 1978), 76.
[51] Arendt, "What Is Freedom?" 152–53.

reason to exclude from this category, as Arendt unfortunately does, many aspects of worldly and social life simply because they pertain to the unheroic realm of cultural, economic, or physical need.

Changing a baby's diapers or the oil in one's car, going to the marketplace or out of town for a holiday, do not in themselves evidence much political freedom, to be sure. But the provision of day-care facilities and parental leave from work, the promulgation of laws for the mandatory recycling of motor oil, the regulation of the sales of goods according to health and environmental standards, and the maintenance of the transportation infrastructure are important political concerns. The point is: what makes something political, in these cases and in general, has less to do with whether it pertains to our (basic) needs than whether and how these needs are collectively addressed and fulfilled. Politics and political freedom, in other words, may be in evidence or evidence their effects whenever the world of beings and the with-world of human beings are open to public disclosure. Political freedom, then, emerges most fundamentally in the caretaking of a public realm. And this caretaking, accomplished in words and deeds, is both preservative and creative in nature.

Arendt teaches us that sovereignty of either a personal or a national nature is antagonistic to freedom. In the same vein, Heidegger teaches us that grand, heroic words and deeds, if carried out in the willful and forgetful pursuit of possessive mastery, also preclude freedom's greatest exercise. Our political freedom is primarily discovered in the collective creation *and* preservation of a public realm. In today's world of consolidated bureaucracies and fragmenting states, this public caretaking is increasingly threatened.

Being, Doing, and Gender Identity

The boundary between private and public realms is permeable, and its navigation remains a political issue. With this in mind, feminist theorists have frequently criticized the ideological foundations of liberalism. Grounded in the concept of negative liberty, liberalism evidences an overriding concern for establishing boundaries between individuals in order to proscribe illegitimate intrusions. Consequently, liberals are primarily occupied with protecting individual independence and securing individual rights. Many feminists claim that these concerns reveal liberalism's masculinist biases, which are most evident in its neglect of the predominantly (though not uniquely) feminine concern with establishing and maintaining relationships and community.

Nancy Chodorow, relying on the work of feminist anthropologists,

psychoanalysts, and object-relations theorists, offers an explanation of
this disjunction based on the early socialization of children. A girl's
sexuality and sense of self, Chodorow theorizes, is "ascribed" to her
through her identification with her caretaker mother. She comes to understand her identity as expressive of her nature rather than explicitly
dependent on a performative act. A boy, on the other hand, grows up in
most societies with his same-sex parent much absent and infrequently in
the caretaker's role. His sexuality and sense of self are therefore much
less the product of an identification with a nurturing parent. In contrast,
a boy's identity must be "achieved" in distinction from—and perhaps
in opposition to—the mother as caretaker. Achieving a stable male
identity becomes a matter of asserting independence from the mother in
a defensive establishing of ego boundaries. Moreover, boys' socialization accentuates the performative character of the sexual act. Thus feminine identity tends to be socialized as a *being,* Chodorow observes,
while male identity, constantly in need of demonstration, is socialized as
a *doing.* The social and political ramifications of this psychological development are not difficult to divine. The marked differences in the development of male and female identities in early childhood produce a
disjunctive and hierarchical social and political structure. Male values
of independence, competitive achievement, and aggressiveness oppose,
dominate, and reinforce female values of dependence, caretaking, and
passivity. Chodorow concludes that "until masculine identity does not
depend on men's proving themselves, their *doing* will be a reaction to
insecurity rather than a creative exercise of their humanity, and
woman's *being,* far from being an easy and positive acceptance of self,
will be a resignation to inferiority."[52]

The empirical evidence for Chodorow's thesis is weak, and her research is rather insensitive to the roles potentially played by culture,
race, and class, not to mention the differences in individual psycho-
logies. But her work has stimulated many other feminist attempts to
question the cognitive and emotional predispositions that structure our
social and political lives.[53] Without affirming the suspect generalizations
of these efforts, I would submit that their resonance with such a wide
audience speaks to the increasing instability of liberal and patriarchal
formulations of political and social identity. The prevalent notions of
(negative) liberty that ground these identities are evidencing their limits.

[52] Nancy Chodorow, "Being and Doing: A Cross-Cultural Examination of the Socialization of Males and Females," in *Feminism and Psychoanalytic Theory* (New Haven:
Yale University Press, 1989), 44.

[53] See, for example, Carol Gilligan, *In a Different Voice: Psychological Theory and
Women's Development* (Cambridge, Mass.: Harvard University Press, 1982), and Mary
Belenky et al., *Women's Ways of Knowing: The Development of Self, Voice, and Mind*
(New York: Basic Books, 1986).

Heidegger's understanding of freedom as a disclosive letting-be informs and buttresses this feminist psychology and political theorizing. In a patriarchal world that conceives of freedom as independence and sovereignty, relations of possessive mastery will continue to structure human identity and define human dignity. I am not suggesting that disclosive freedom could obviate the interminable and unavoidable struggles of identity to which human beings are heir. The point is only that these struggles need not be conducted in a singular fashion. They may be waged interpretively, for understanding, rather than solely competitively, for self-assertion. According to Heidegger, "*interpretation* in the broadest sense" refers to those concern-full concrete relations we may establish that abjure control while recognizing the nature of our worldly embeddedness (*BT* 89). The self engaged in interpretive struggle, then, necessarily acknowledges its relationship to others as constitutive of its own being. Identities grounded in interpretive struggle are founded on an understanding of a situated self *and* other. The struggle for mastery and possession, on the other hand, need not entail an understanding of the self, and seldom entails an understanding of the other, except insofar as it proves useful for her exploitation.[54] Only the interpretive struggle for contextual understanding rests on the disclosure of a shared world. Disclosive freedom, the medium of this interpretive struggle, entails rather than curtails in its own actualization the participation in freedom of that which lies beyond the self.

As long as freedom is restricted to mean the control of a private realm, or, as with positive liberty, the control of oneself and one's world, politics will remain a domain in which the individual meets the world and the other in a singular struggle for self-assertion. Alternatively, if precisely our relatedness to the world and to others begets our freedom, then the struggle for understanding comes to the fore. Again, the question of the (trans)formation of identity is key. At this juncture philosophy, politics, and psychology most clearly cross paths, and the cultural and political implications of our understandings of freedom and dignity emerge. Patriarchal culture will likely infect politics whenever freedom is understood and exercised solely as a masterful doing rather than a disclosive, interpretive way of being. The discovery of disclosive freedom facilitates the evolution (or retrieval)[55] of gender-harmo-

[54] The best account of this dynamic that I am aware of is Tzvetan Todorov's *Conquest of America: The Question of the Other* (New York: Harper and Row, 1984).

[55] I do not know whether in fact more gender-balanced societies existed in our primeval past. But the first recorded use of the word *freedom*, appearing on a Sumerian clay document from 2350 B.C.E., suggests as much. The cuneiform tablet describes a sweeping popular revolt against regal abuse. Here the word *amargi*, which literally means "return to the mother," designates the liberty sought and gained. Samuel Noah Kramer, *The Sumerians* (Chicago: University of Chicago Press, 1963), 79.

nized personalities and societies. The political signficance of Heidegger's philosophy of freedom, in this light, is not that it inverts the traditional hierarchy of doing and being, but that it seeks to establish their balance.

Conclusion

Twenty-five hundred years ago, Pericles urged his fellow Athenians to take on the burden of freedom. "Make up your minds that happiness depends on being free," he said in his funeral oration, "and freedom depends on being courageous."[56] In fifth-century Athens, freedom was already the most cherished value. The pursuit of this value, however, became a mask for imperial domination. Euripides would thus have Iphigenia justify her own murder by her father, Agamemnon, for the sake of a freedom called mastery. The young heroine lectures the reluctant Clytemnestra: "Sacrifice me, sack Troy. That will be my monument for long ages, that will be my children, my marriage, my good name. It is natural for Hellenes to rule barbarians, and not, mother, for barbarians to rule Hellenes. They are a slave race, Hellenes are free."[57] The development of Western freedom has evinced numerous variations on this theme.

From its inception, freedom in the Western world has remained predominantly in the service of possessive mastery. Only the historical subjects and objects change: from the domination of master over slave (and man over woman) in imperial Greece; to the rule of the higher over the lower self with Plato, Aristotle, the Stoics, and Augustine; to Rousseau's and Marx's romantic collectivization of command in the rule of the general will and proletarian consciousness; to liberalism's assertion of the individual's sovereign control of a private realm; and finally, to postmodernism's aesthetic attempt to translate the Stoic ideal of self-control into a full-fledged self-creation.

Hegel was not wrong in his assessment of history as the progress of the consciousness of freedom. He correctly discerned its origins in the

---

[56] Thucydides, *The Peloponnesian War* (New York: Penguin, 1954), 149–50.

[57] Euripides, *Iphigenia at Aulis,* in *Ten Plays by Euripides,* trans. Moses Hadas and John McLean (New York: Bantam, 1960), 348. As Simon Hornblower writes: "It would be wrong to be too sentimental about what 'freedom' [*eleutheria*] meant to Greeks; Thucydides (iii.45.6) makes a speaker use the phrase 'freedom, or rule over others', and similar uses can be found in Greek authors from Herodotus (i.210) to Polybius (v.106). In modern times Sir Isaiah Berlin has distinguished between two 'kinds of freedom', freedom from something and freedom to do something. Greeks valued the second kind, which included freedom to oppress and dominate, at least as much as the first." Simon Hornblower, *The Greek World, 479–323 B.C.* (London: Methuen, 1983), 69.

intricate dynamics of the master/slave relationship.[58] And yet, firmly situated within the Western metaphysical tradition, Hegel could not see beyond its perimeter. Even at the height of the progress in consciousness, freedom retains its defining relationship with mastery. Hegel argues, therefore, that modern freedom is gained only by exchanging the mastery of some over the lives of others for humankind's mastery over history itself. At this point a "full-blown liberty" of "uncontrollable strength" appears.[59] Pondering this freedom in light of the unsustainable domination of the earth it promotes, one is of reminded of Edmund Burke's observation that "the effect of liberty to individuals is, that they may do what they please: We ought to see what it will please them to do, before we risque congratulations, which may be soon turned into complaints."[60] Before offering congratulations for the monumental achievement of modern freedom, we ought to investigate, with Burke, what it has pleased humankind to do with it. Or rather, pace Burke, we ought to investigate how the persistent Western idea that freedom means willfully doing whatever one pleases has itself caused much of the mischief.

I am not suggesting that disclosive freedom is without its own dangers. Negative liberty is apt to degenerate into license and the disintegration of community; positive liberty into tyranny and totalitarian control; postmodern liberty into apathy and despair in the face of an inescapable and normalizing web of power, or alternatively into the anarchic self-aggrandizement of one who, in the face of this power, embraces an unbounded self-creation. Disclosive freedom, no doubt, has its own susceptibilities and pathologies. Openness to the mystery of Being might degenerate into fatalism, and releasement toward things might deteriorate into passivity. I am not proposing, then, that we should turn our backs on hard-won and still insufficiently propagated freedoms—negative, positive, or postmodern—that benefit women and men and do not unsustainably exploit the earth. Rather, the task is one of critically engaging, supplementing, and perhaps sublimating their

[58] Nietzsche makes a similar point with a psychological intent. Recently, Orlando Patterson has also argued that our concept of "freedom was generated from the experience of slavery." Orlando Patterson, *Freedom*, vol. 1, *Freedom in the Making of Western Culture* (New York: Basic Books, 1991), xiii. Patterson's basic argument is hardly novel, and his explanation of why the valorization of freedom in non-Western slaveholding societies did not occur is thin. But Patterson's historical breadth and sociological insights are remarkable. And I am sympathetic to the corollary of his thesis: that Western notions of freedom are inextricably bound, perhaps mostly vicariously, to the yearning for and experience of mastery.

[59] Hegel, *Hegel's Philosophy of Mind*, 239.

[60] Edmund Burke, *Reflections on the Revolution in France* (Garden City, N.Y.: Doubleday, 1961), 20.

practice. The pursuit of any freedom, including disclosive freedom, most fruitfully occurs not as a crusade against competitors but as an invitation to expand horizons. The task at hand is not to bury the past and its achievements, but to prepare to receive the future. And our future as a species appears doubtful indeed if human dignity can be experienced in nothing other than possessive mastery.

Berlin argues that positive liberty (as self-government) should be fostered to the extent that it serves to protect negative liberty. My argument is that negative, positive, and postmodern liberties should be protected to the extent that they serve to foster disclosive freedom. What Berlin at one point concedes of positive liberty, I would unbegrudgingly affirm for negative and postmodern liberties as well: their exercise easily leads to abuse and perversion, yet held in balance they remain "essential for a decent existence."[61] Heidegger, unfortunately, was too reluctant to make such an affirmation. Still, he does not completely impugn the practical worth of prevalent notions of freedom. Rather, he observes their pathologies and notes specifically regarding negative and positive liberty and their Nietzschean alternative that disclosive freedom stands over and above them from a philosophic perspective.

I have insufficiently demonstrated the political implications of disclosive freedom. My sense is that they remain ambiguous. This ambiguity is, to be sure, unsettling. But we should not be dissuaded from the exploration and practice of disclosive freedom for that reason alone. Isaiah Berlin, in closing his essay on the two concepts of liberty, asserts that the principle underlying negative liberty, perhaps only the "late fruit of our declining capitalist civilization," is no less valid because the duration of its historical ascendency cannot be guaranteed.[62] The "relative validity" of our convictions, Berlin argues, should not dissuade us from upholding them. Indeed, he maintains that it would be the sign of a dangerous political immaturity to demur in the face of such uncertainty. I submit that the decaying fruits of postmodern civilization bear the seeds of disclosive freedom. This freedom, properly cultivated, offers us dignity and stamina in the political struggle against the

---

[61] In a recent interview Berlin stated, "The only reason for which I have been suspected of defending negative liberty against positive and saying that it is more civilized is that I do think that the concept of positive liberty, which is of course essential to a decent existence, has been more often abused or perverted than that of negative liberty. . . . Certainly the weak must be protected against the strong. . . . Negative liberty must be curtailed if positive liberty is to be sufficiently realized; there must be a balance between the two, about which no clear principles can be enunciated." Isaiah Berlin, "Philosophy and Life: An Interview," *New York Review of Books,* May 28, 1992, 52–53.

[62] Berlin, *Four Essays on Liberty,* 172.

"unchecked momentum" and "irresistible power" of a technologically driven way of life. Whether and how disclosive freedom will find a foothold in the postmodern world, and if it does just what its historical role and longevity might be, remain beyond our power to determine. But, like Berlin, I believe that the convictions and principles that arise from our philosophic and worldly experience of freedom are on this count no less valid.

Four

Freedom in Thought

> To think and to be fully alive are the same,
> and this implies that thinking must always
> begin afresh.
> (Hannah Arendt, *The Life of the Mind*)

DISCLOSIVE FREEDOM is facilitated by releasement toward things and openness to the mystery of Being. But this is not to say that freedom is achieved without effort and enjoyed in passivity. Heidegger insists that "releasement toward things and openness to the mystery never happen of themselves. They do not befall us accidentally. Both flourish only through persistent, courageous thinking" (*DT* 56). Persistent, courageous thinking provides the foundation on which disclosive freedom gains its foothold in the world. Indeed, there is a unique and original freedom to be practiced in thought itself.

The practice of thinking, for Heidegger, is something quite distinct from that which is commonly understood by the term. And the disclosive freedom evidenced in thought is something quite distinct from the freedom of thought commonly championed in contemporary society. Freedom of thought was politically instituted in the West, first as a response to the disasters visited upon states by religious intolerance and subsequently and more thoroughly as a basic right parallelling the rise of economic liberalism. Freedom of thought has us ponder that which religious doctrine, social mores, or political tradition might otherwise forbid or depreciate. The courage for and safeguarding of such freedom of thought is crucial to democratic political life. But strictly speaking, it is mislabeled. Freedom of opinion better suits the aforementioned right, as it is generally invoked today, for it pertains to the important prerogative of holding and justifying opinions in the face of opposing and competing beliefs. Heidegger too often depreciates this important political right. The reason is that he is less concerned with safeguarding (the right to) convictions in the face of opposition than with an activity that consistently undermines convictions. His concern is with the freedom *in* thought that the event of thinking manifests.

A different sort of courage is required for freedom in thought than for freedom of opinion: not the courage to persist in the face of manifest opposition, but the courage to persist in the face of nothingness. Thinking demands the courage to break away from habitual cognition and belief, and, more fundamentally, from their modes of representation and conceptualization. In turn, courage is needed to challenge our self-understandings as conceptual and representational cogitators. Thinking proper always finds itself questioning the Being of being, and hence is confronted with the nonrepresentable no-thing that Being is.

Heidegger writes, "We stubbornly misunderstand this prevailing *belonging* together of man and Being as long as we represent everything only in categories and mediations, be it with or without dialectic. . . . Only the entry into the realm of this mutual appropriation determines and defines the experience of thinking" (*ID* 32–33). Before attempting to describe further just what this experience of thinking entails, it will be helpful to prepare the ground by detailing what the experience of thinking is not. To foreshadow this *via negativa* we may observe Heidegger's succinct description of what thinking does not achieve. He writes: "1. Thinking does not bring knowledge as do the sciences. 2. Thinking does not produce usable practical wisdom. 3. Thinking solves no cosmic riddles. 4. Thinking does not endow us directly with the power to act" (*WCT* 159). One might well wonder what is left for thinking to do after these much-valued achievements are forsworn. The answer Heidegger supplies is unsettling.

Philosophy, Common Sense, Science, and Logic

Thinking, first of all, is not a preoccupation with philosophic systems or their creators. To be sure, philosophic thought always leads us into "conversation with the philosophers of earlier times."[1] But as genuine conversation, it constitutes a cooperative voyage to unknown lands rather than a chronicle of journeys already made. Philosophic icons are only a means of access to the enduring questions and their historical manifestations. "The point," Heidegger stipulates, "is not to gain some knowledge about philosophy but to be able to philosophize" (*BP* 2). Hence it would be "fatal" for philosophy if, "lacking the resolve for genuine questioning," we would simply "busy" ourselves with the stories of philosophers for intellectual stimulation (*WPK* 9). The important thing is to ground oneself directly in the questioning of Being. Familiarization with another's work necessarily comes up short.

True philosophy, Heidegger insists, reaches to what remains "unsaid"

[1] Martin Heidegger, "From the Last Marburg Lecture Course," in *The Future of Our Religious Past: Essays in Honour of Rudolf Bultmann*, ed. James Robinson (New York: Harper and Row, 1971), 312.

in the works of philosophy, to their source of inspiration and animating force. "It is one thing to determine and describe the opinions of philosophers," Heidegger writes. "It is an entirely different thing to talk through with them what they are saying, and that means, that of which they speak. Thus, if we assume that the Being of being addresses itself to philosophers to the extent that they state what being is, in so far as it is, then our discussion with philosophers must also be addressed by the Being of being. We must then ourselves, through our thinking, go to meet philosophy on the path it is traveling" (WP 67–68). Philosophers, in other words, may point us in the right (or wrong) direction. But we should never confuse their outstretched arms with the journey demanded.

Thinking is necessarily open-ended; hence systematic philosophy, strictly speaking, is a contradiction in terms. Philosophic writing, in this respect, is effectively "for show." As Heidegger bluntly puts the point, "philosophy is always necessarily a bit of sophistry" (HCT 301). Philosophic treatises do not in themselves necessarily evidence thinking. In an exaggerated generalization, Heidegger goes so far as to say that "the things which we conceive and assert to be the results of thinking, are the misunderstandings to which thinking ineluctably falls victim. Only they achieve publication as alleged thought, and occupy those who do *not* think." Socrates is consequently designated the purest thinker of the West, for he wrote nothing, refusing "refuge" from thinking in literature (WCT 169, 17). Socrates maintained himself within the "draft" of thought that carries one where it will. Its unpredictable course is anathema to the systematicity demanded by philosophic texts. Still, this is not to condemn written philosophy out of hand. It is only to acknowledge its necessary limitations, necessary not simply because words require pen lest they become forgotten or confused, but also because the thought of Being is only approachable through words. We necessarily philosophize out of our linguistic embeddedness, an embeddedness that is at once our fortune and our limitation.

We also philosophize, and think, unavoidably embedded in history and culture. This is not to deny that philosophic thought pertains to the enduring question of Being. The historically and culturally mediated relation of human being to Being is, in fact, the fundamental subject of thought. But thinking always only understands itself "within the limits set for it" (WL 39), and these limits are both temporal and spatial. Heidegger writes, "We philosophize only when the position of our human being becomes the real need of the question about Being as a whole. Since, however, our human being is historical, it remains so in philosophizing, too" (ST 11). Any attempt to escape to an ahistorical, acultural thinking is vain, an enterprise as futile as the attempt to jump over one's own shadow (*IM* 199). Worse, the effort belies a fundamental misunderstanding of the nature of thought. Our historically situated being is not simply an attribute that we might set aside for investigation and subsequently overcome, as life with or without clothes or hair might be entertained. We are our historically situated being. Thinking is always thinking about Being as it finds its place of disclosure in the particularities of time and space.

Heidegger goes further. He insists that "talking about thinking in general makes sense only if we experience thinking everywhere and exclusively as that which determines our historical human existence" (*PT* 58). This is not to say that history, the actual events of worldly life, are produced by sheer thought. Thinking produces nothing per se, nor does it, as scientific inquiry might, bring about historically significant change. Rather, thinking determines our historical existence in the sense that thinking situates human being most fundamentally in its historical context, as a discloser of Being. For Heidegger, "the question 'What is called thinking?' is—if it is at all permissible to put this into words—a world-historical question." World history, Heidegger goes on to say, signifies "the *fatum* that there *is* world, and that man *is* as its inhabitant" (*WCT* 136). To think is to question the nature of Being as it comes to be revealed in the opening of human being. Historical Being-in-the-world is therefore determined by thinking in the sense that the meaning of human being, as the place of Being's historical disclosure, comes to the fore in thought. Thought brings us toward "a historical sojourning" (*QT* 180–81). Thinking is historical because our historical worldly dwelling is the province of thought and because we come to be at home in this world by way of thought.

Despite its worldliness, thinking does not help us shift in our historical or cultural milieu. The opposite is closer to the mark. Thinking challenges the common sense that allows us to cope with quotidian affairs. Common sense, the cognitive analysis and synthesis of experience that facilitates our competence in the everyday world, is a crucial and quite irreplaceable faculty. Without this practical know–how, we might despair of ever making it through our daily affairs. Indeed, without common sense, we might even despair of ever being able to think. The leisure that philosophic thought requires, leisure in the Aristotelian sense of time devoted neither to work nor to play but to contemplation, is only attained by way of our more or less successful navigation through the everyday world. In thinking, however, navigational responsibilities and habits cease. A more elemental—that is, more radical—activity takes place.

Heidegger acknowledges the importance of common sense, but in large part he does so in order to stem its colonization of thought. "We respect sound common sense," he affirms, "but there are realms that it does not penetrate, and they are the most essential ones" (WPK 27). The thinker needs common sense in order to survive, as a ballerina needs to be able to walk flat-footedly. Despite its indispensable utility, however, walking is not dancing, and a ballerina must continually struggle against its habituations. Likewise, thinking is not common sense, and the former must continually expose and overcome the plodding utility of the latter. Philosophic thought "remains a constant attack on man's common sense; not with the intention of generally removing the latter or even of putting philosophy in the place of everyday thinking, but in order to make this thinking constantly uneasy so that it might lose its trust in its own self-importance" (ST 81). Common sense allows the stabilization of our beliefs about the world and ourselves that we might find practical footholds for our actions and identities. Thinking undermines these beliefs, exposing our contingency and undermining our competence.

The self-importance of common sense is surely deserved in its own right. Thought, however, operates with different standards. Heidegger makes the following distinction: "Hegel once expressed the point as follows, though only in a purely metaphysical respect and dimension: 'Better a mended sock than a torn one—not so with self-consciousness.' Sound common sense, bent on utility, sides with the 'mended' sock" (WCT 89). Thinking, on the other hand, knows its concern to be the torn sock. Not that a torn sock is more useful if we wish to walk from A to B. But precisely its nonfunctionality frees us to ponder many questions: Where are we now? Where are we going? And, ultimately, what is the meaning of our journey?

To put things rather too simply: philosophic thought is concerned with the question "why?" while common sense orients itself to the question "how?" or "what?" This "how" or "what" is presented by common sense not only as a utilitarian orientation to means, asking "What are the necessary means for achieving given ends and how are we to employ them?" but also as a utilitarian orientation to ends, asking "What, in the end, is to be done?" Philosophic thought, on the other hand, is decidedly not a tool that facilitates the achievement of one's goals. Nor is it even a theoretical orientation that might determine the end of action itself. If anything, philosophic thought undoes the work that went into establishing and justifying one's means and ends. Thinking gives us pause. In asking "Why?" it renders us less, not more, competent and efficient in mundane affairs. Because our identities largely hinge on the struggles and goals we regularly set ourselves, philosophic thought also challenges the identities we have appropriated, including that identity we all share as utility-minded, rational pursuers of means and ends. Heidegger puts the point well: "It is absolutely correct and proper to say that "You can't do anything with philosophy." It is only wrong to suppose that this is the last word on philosophy. For the rejoinder imposes itself: granted that *we* cannot do anything with philosophy, might not philosophy, if we concern ourselves with it, do something *with us?*" (*IM* 12). What philosophy might do with us, however, is mostly an undoing.

The uselessness of philosophic thought not only distinguishes it from common sense, but from science as well. Philosophic thought is concerned with Being while scientific thought is concerned with beings (*BP* 11, 15). The scientific purpose of investigating beings is to discover enduring answers to straightforward questions. The philosophic point of investigating Being is to formulate enduring questions that defy straightforward answers. Science, even science not designed for practical application, remains eminently utilitarian. "Pure" science no less than applied science seeks answers that are terminal and constructive. The answers, even if they do not address the material needs of life, are intended as lasting contributions to the edifice of knowledge. Thinking, on the other hand, contributes nothing lasting except the propensity to question anew. As Heidegger writes: "The scientific researcher inquires in order to reach useful answers; the thinker inquires in order to ground the *questionableness* of beings as a whole" (*WPK* 6). Science, it has been said, attempts to maximize explanatory power with a minimal expenditure of thought.[2] Philosophy, conversely, is engaged in a maximization of thought that achieves minimal power of explanation.

The measuring rod of science is utility, that is, the utility of contributions to the construction of systems of (practical or pure) knowledge. Hence science can speak in terms of its progress. Measurements of success pertain to its endeavor. In philosophy, however, there is no progress (*ERS* 63). Indeed, Heidegger goes so far as to say that the pursuit of progress in thinking is fatal for philosophy. "If there is something like catastrophe in the creative work of great thinkers," Heidegger writes, "then it consists not in being stymied and in failing to go farther, but precisely in advancing farther—that is to say, in their letting themselves be determined by the initial impact of their thought, an impact

---

[2] Edward O. Wilson writes: "The heart of the scientific method is the reduction of perceived phenomena to fundamental, testable principles. The elegance, we can fairly say the beauty, of any particular scientific generalization is measured by its simplicity relative to the number of phenomena it can explain. Ernst Mach, a physicist and forerunner of the logical positivists, captured the idea with a definition: 'Science may be regarded as a minimal problem consisting of the completest presentation of facts with the least possible expenditure of thought.'" Edward O. Wilson, *On Human Nature* (Cambridge, Mass.: Harvard University Press, 1978), 11.

that always deflects them. Such going 'farther' is always fatal, for it prevents one from abiding by the source of one's own commencement" (*ERS* 81). If the origin of one's thinking is abandoned in order to produce some concrete achievement, then that thinking is moribund. For the enduring source of thought is the indefatigable questionableness of Being. To leave this questionableness behind in order to advance down the road toward some specific answer, however useful this answer might be, is to abandon the project of thinking itself. While the borders of science are unanswered questions, those obstacles lying before the scientist that future research and discovery might one day overcome, the borders of philosophy are unanswerable questions, contemplative banquets lying before the philosopher that will forever solicit digestion. Philosophic thinking does not progress because, unlike science, it constitutes an ongoing refinement of questions, not answers. The world of thought is one of exploration and rediscovery. There is little attempt to build lasting colonies.

There are many good reasons to make advances toward answering specific questions with finality. But the benefits of these scientific journeys should not be confused with the waywardness of thinking itself. Heidegger writes: "With the term *thinker* we name those exceptional human beings who are destined to think one single thought, a thought that is always 'about' *beings as a whole*. Each thinker thinks only one *single* thought. It needs neither renown nor impact in order to gain dominance. In contrast, writers and researchers, as opposed to a thinker, 'have' lots and lots of thoughts, that is, ideas that can be converted into much-prized 'reality' and that are also evaluated solely in accord with this conversion-ability" (*WPK* 4). Here Heidegger leaves the false impression that philosophic thought is monomaniacally fixated while creative, practical thought should be disdained. The "conversion-ability" of scientific ideas is, within its own realm, a fine and indispensable thing. But it is not philosophy. In turn, abiding attachment to the source of a single thought does not indicate in philosophy, as it might in science, a stubborn refusal to broaden one's perspective. Thinking the single thought of Being is no philosophic limitation as it continually uncovers an unmanageable plenitude of problems and wonders, spanning the breadth of historical time and space. As Heidegger observes, "The finitude of philosophy consists not in the fact that it comes up against limits and cannot proceed further. It rather consists in this: in the singleness and simplicity of its central problematic, philosophy conceals a richness that again and again demands a renewed awakening" (*MFL* 156). The disclosure of Being is inexhaustible.

Without the measure of progress to gauge its success, philosophic thought also abides without a measure to gauge its failures. Here we observe yet another key distinction between philosophy and science. Scientific theories expose themselves to refutation. Indeed, their potential refutability is crucial to their scientific status. Not only does a science explain an aspect of the world by means of its theories, but its theories designate what the world would have to be like in order to falsify its claims. Philosophic thought, on the other hand, does not supply its own criteria of falsification. Indeed, the very attempt to refute philosophic thought marks a misunderstanding of its nature (*BW* 216). Invoking Aristotle, Heidegger insists that wisdom begins with knowing the distinction between what is available for proof and falsification and what is not (*PT* 29). Only the ignorant would attempt to prove or disprove art, even though it invites judgment. The same is true for philosophy. According to Heidegger, "to think critically means to distinguish (*krinein*) constantly between that which requires proof for its justification and that which, to confirm its truth, demands a simple catching sight of and taking in" (*PT* 26). The thinking of Being solicits vision, not verification.

Being irrefutable is not the same as being without error. Indeed, Heidegger admits that to think greatly is necessarily to err greatly (*PLT* 9). With this in mind, Heidegger would place his entire work under the proviso "I can provide no credentials for what I have said. . . . Everything here is the path of responding that examines as it listens. . . . Stay on the path, in genuine need, and learn the craft of thinking, unswerving, yet erring" (*PLT* 186). Heidegger does not speak here out of personal humility (which, it turns out, was not his characteristic virtue). Rather, he speaks directly to the nature of philosophic thought. The impossibility of refutation in philosophy does not attest to its perfection, but rather marks its inherent imperfectibility. Thinking is a falling short.

Despite having no quarter for refutation, the philosophic abode is hardly one marked by accord. Many disagreements erupt between its guests. Heidegger calls these lovers' quarrels (*BW* 216), but we know that these sorts of quarrels are often the fiercest. Philosophy is fundamentally contestable and contested. And in the end, "agreement prevails only about pseudo-philosophy" (*MFL* 71). To say, then, that thinkers always think the Same, the Being of being, is not to say that they have identical or even compatible thoughts. Though attempts at refutation in philosophy amount to labor lost, the alternative is not passive accord. Vigilant contestation that takes the form of more profound questioning is required. In this effort to unsettle and probe deeper, dogmatic assertion is forbidden. Philosophy stands without authorities. "In the domain of thinking," Heidegger insists, "there are no authoritative statements. The only measure for thought comes from the thing itself to be thought. But this is, above all, the [eminently] Questionable" (*OGS* 64). Philosophy is a decidedly lawless endeavor.

If thinking will not be structured by external standards such as utility, progress, or falsifiability, must it then not structure itself by internal standards? Philosophy, we might suppose, must at least remain internally coherent, which is to say logically rigorous, even if empirically defiant. Heidegger strongly opposes this restriction as well. Philosophic thought is not an exercise in deduction or induction. "Logic is an invention of schoolteachers, not of philosophers," Heidegger tersely remarks. Logic, like common sense, fails to meet the criterion for philosophic thought. It is not free enough for fundamental questioning. Thinking only truly happens once logic and reason are left behind.

Rationality is actually thinking's vehement opponent, "the most stiff-necked adversary of thought" (*QT* 112). But would it not be enough to say that thinking goes beyond the narrow boundaries that define logical reasoning, much as art escapes but does not oppose the calculations of science? Unfortunately, this will not do. Thinking and logic are adversaries in that these two enterprises are founded on mutually exclusive grounds. Rational formulation is always a metaphysical, representational venture (*WBG* 209). The absence of logic (and common sense) from philosophic activity, however, does not indicate a vacuum to be filled by "sheer feeling." Rather, a "more radical, stricter thinking" emerges (*IM* 121–22).

Logic ensures that relations between mental constructs remain consistent. To do so, logic situates itself most fundamentally within the boundaries of the proposition that *A* and *not-A* cannot coincide. For the logician, this law of negation is fundamental. But what happens when we investigate the foundation for this law, when we question the Being of this negation? Here logic can supply no answer (no more than the intrinsic value of knowledge or the usefulness of utility are demonstrable by science or common sense). Philosophic thinking, unlike logic, does not "calculate" consistent relations between things. It is actuated "by what is 'other' than what-is" (*EB* 357). And the no-thing that is Being is prior to and more fundamental than the law of negation that would deny it. Heidegger writes, "Nothing is the source of negation, not the other way about. If this breaks the sovereignty of reason in the field of enquiry into Nothing and Being, then the fate of the rule of 'logic' in philosophy is also decided. The very idea of 'logic' disintegrates in the vortex of a more original questioning" (*EB* 342). The Being of negation is a question of the "other than what is." The no-thingness of Being grounds negation itself just as it grounds assertion.

Heidegger most clearly explains this position in a provocative rearrangement of the groundwork of reason. Rationality is grounded in the basic assumption that nothing occurs without a reason or cause. The Leibnizian formula for this rational truth is known as the principle of ground, which states simply: "Nothing is without ground." After examining the proposition at length, Heidegger suggests a change in emphasis: "Contemporary man constantly pays heed to [*hören auf*] the principle of ground in that he progressively becomes a slave [*höriger wird*] to the principle [of ground]. . . . [But] if we listen to, that is, if we freely give ourselves to, what is genuinely spoken in the principle, then the principle will suddenly sound differently. The principle will no longer read: *Nothing* is *without* ground, but rather: Nothing *is* without ground."[3] A few rereadings may be necessary to hear what is "genuinely spoken" here. "*Nothing* is *without* ground," the principle of ground that grounds rationality, posits that without a ground, without a reason, nothing can come to be. In short, everything has a cause. Heidegger's ontological reformulation posits something quite different. "Nothing *is* without *ground*" speaks to the priority, and therefore the groundlessness or causelessness, of nothing, of the no-thing that Being is. "Nothing *is* without *ground*" means that, indeed, Being *is* without ground. Causality cannot ground Being because Being already grounds causality. The primordial nothingness of Being, however, is neither the emptiness of space nor the negation of logic. Rather, the nothingness of Being is pure potentiality, that hiddenness that comes to presence in all things, in emptiness and negation no less than in being and affirmation.

The search for the ground of being(s), with ground here identified as an enduring essence, is the quintessential metaphysical pursuit. Logic, Heidegger worries, prompts such metaphysical thinking and in so doing abets in the refusal to think Being. To experience the Being of beings as a nothingness that is not, at the same time, a simple negativity or emptiness: this is the core of philosophic thought. "The most durable and unfailing touchstone of genuineness and forcefulness of thought in a philosopher," Heidegger stipulates, "is the question as to whether or not he or she experiences in a direct and fundamental manner the nearness of the nothing in the Being of beings. Whoever fails to experience it remains forever outside the realm of philosophy, without hope of entry" (*ERS* 95). The fundamental logical contradiction of the nothingness of Being—its being both *A* and *not-A*—is the unstable foundation that ensures that philosophic thinking, unlike rational calculation, will always discover the impetus for further questioning in its own answers.

[3] Martin Heidegger, "The Principle of Ground," *Man and World* 7 (August 1974): 216–17.

Heidegger writes: "Only because of wonder, that is to say, the revelation of Nothing, does the 'Why?' spring to our lips. . . . Why is there any Being at all—why not far rather Nothing? . . . All questions that do justice to the subject are themselves bridges to their own answering. Essential answers are always but the last step in our questioning. . . . The essential answer gathers its motive power from the inwardness of the asking and is only the beginning of a responsibility where the asking arises with renewed originality. Hence even the most genuine question is never stilled by the answer found" (*EB* 348–49, 351, 352). In taking on the burden of thinking, the thinker always begins afresh, with "renewed originality," because the "why" that springs to her lips, grounded in the enigma of Being, never loses its resistance to resolution or its capacity to inspire.

Unlike logical deduction, whose success is measured by the respite found at the conclusion of its labors, the success of philosophic thought may only be gestured at by the profundity of its exertion. As Heidegger explains: "We do get into a strange position in our task, that is, in every philosophical lecture—for there *is* something incomprehensible in what we have to discuss. And we would thus go against our task if we even tried to dissolve everything into a flat comprehensibility and thus get rid of the incomprehensible element" (*ST* 134). The incomprehensible is, as Heidegger puts it, what remains unthought in any thinking. It is that which thought approaches and glimpses, but, because veiled, forever solicits further inquiry. The unthought is a limitation to thinking, but a limitation that does not mark a capitulation: "What is unthought in a thinker's thought is not a lack inherent in his thought. What is *un*-thought is there in each case only as the un-*thought*. The more original the thinking, the richer will be what is unthought in it. The unthought is the greatest gift that thinking can bestow" (*WCT* 76). The unthought, incomprehensible element of thinking, then, signals not thinking's failure but its potential for success; success in thinking is always a measure of the depth to which the hiddenness of Being becomes questionable.

The Flight from Thinking

Humans are conventionally defined as rational animals. Heidegger disagrees. Reasoning, understood as deductive or inductive calculation, does not go to the essence of human being. Indeed, the triumph of the human calculator may signal the demise of the truly human. In exploring this point Heidegger asks the following questions, and proposes that the manner in which they are answered is far from an obscure philosophic concern:

Does the definition of man as the rational animal exhaust the essence of man? . . . Or does not the essence of man remain, does not his relationship to Being remain, does not the essence of Being still remain, and more and more dazzling, remain what is worthy of thought? May we, if this should be the case, abandon what is worthy of thought in favor of the madness of exclusively calculative thinking and its immense success? Or are we obliged to find paths upon which thinking may be capable of cor-responding to what is worthy of thought, instead of remaining bewitched by calculative thinking, and thus overlooking what is worthy of thought? That is the question. It is the world-question of thinking. Our reply to it will decide what will become of the earth and what will become of the existence of man upon the earth.[4]

The stakes in the game are certainly high. Heidegger suggests that our very humanity stands threatened by the cogitation that robs us of the disposition to ponder the Being of being. This abandonment of Being takes place while we stand mesmerized by the immense productivity of reason. The danger, as Heidegger observes, is that "there might go hand in hand with the greatest ingenuity in calculative planning and inventing indifference toward meditative thinking, total thoughtlessness. And then? Then man would have denied and thrown away his own special nature—that he is a meditative being. Therefore the issue is the saving of man's essential nature. Therefore, the issue is keeping meditative thinking alive" (*DT* 56).[5] In comparison to the accomplishments of calculative thinking, the uselessness of philosophic thinking leaves it ripe for neglect. The questionable Being of being threatens to become an idiosyncratic and dated curiosity in a technologically oriented world. Any reawakening to philosophic thought, Heidegger states, will demand great effort. The task of becoming at home with what is most worthy of questioning, he forewarns, "becomes more difficult as time goes on."[6]

The metaphor of reawakening is apt. The task is not so much to keep though alive as to prevent its dormancy. Philosophic thought is not moribund, nor could it ever be eradicated. Heidegger acknowledges that as long as there are human beings, philosophizing of some sort will exist (*EB* 349). Contemporary humanity is not incapable of thought,

---

[4] Ibid., 222.

[5] The charge has been leveled that Heidegger's own prose has distracted his readers from meditative thinking. Adorno warned: "Whoever is versed in the jargon [of authenticity] does not have to say what he thinks, does not even have to think it properly. The jargon takes over this task and devaluates thought." Theodor Adorno, *The Jargon of Authenticity*, trans. K. Tarnowski and F. Will (Evanston: Northwestern University Press, 1973), 9. For certain readers, Heidegger's language has indeed had this effect. This danger will be addressed in the following chapter.

[6] Martin Heidegger, "A Letter from Martin Heidegger," in *Heidegger and the Quest for Truth*, ed. Manfred Frings (Chicago: Quadrangle, 1968), 19.

just neglectful of it. But "even while we are thoughtless, we do not give up our capacity to think," Heidegger reassures us, "in thoughtlessness we let it lie fallow. . . . man today is in *flight from thinking*" (*DT* 45). The human capacity for philosophic thought threatens to become dormant. We are witnessing a "collapse" of thinking in the face of calculation (*EGT* 40). What might the stimulant to renewed philosophic thinking be, given that we are already overstimulated with the demands of reason and technology and the abundant spoils of their triumphs? The answer Heidegger supplies seems unpersuasive. He writes that "the poverty of reflection is the promise of a wealth whose treasures glow in the resplendence of that uselessness which can never be included in any reckoning" (*QT* 181). Thinking, in other words, must be its own reward. Nothing we bring to bear in its support from the arsenals of common sense, science, or logic holds sway. The answer is unpersuasive, but it is not meant to persuade. Thinking must redeem itself; nothing else can or will.

At this point the reader might be inclined to reject a thinking that has no utility, exhibits no progress, answers no questions, fails to direct our action, and spurns rationality. Does such philosophic thought not reduce itself to a radical doubt whose obsessive confrontation with Being's nothingness preempts every opportunity or inclination to say or do anything (about beings)? Is such philosophic thought not simply a paralyzing skepticism? The answer is a qualified no. Philosophic thought is indeed a skepticism in the original Greek sense of the word *skepsis*, meaning inquiry. But the fundamental point is this: thought inquires not that it may sustain doubt, but doubts that it may sustain inquiry. The difference is crucial. Heidegger writes: "We thus recover the original meaning of the word 'skepsis'; σκεψις means seeing, watching, scrutinizing, to see what and how beings as beings. Skepsis in this sense pursues the Being of beings with its gaze. . . . Thinkers are innately skeptical about beings—because of this skepsis into Being. . . . [T]hat skepticism which in all knowing and conduct ends up with the conclusion that the knowledge supposedly attained always amounts to nothing . . . i.e., a sheer addiction to doubt, is absolute sophistry. . . . [S]kepsis of this kind is merely the semblance of skepsis, and thus a flight from thinking into the system of opinion."[7] Essential philosophic thinking is inquiry into the nature of Being. But Being remains "*the enigma*" demanding unflagging inquiry (*N* 228). Its mystery does not justify an addiction to doubt. Addictive doubt actually inhibits inquiry through agnostic complacency. Heidegger wishes to distinguish philosophic

[7] Martin Heidegger, *Hegel's Concept of Experience* (San Francisco: Harper and Row, 1970), 65–66, 73, 110.

thinking from the metaphysical disposition that either inhibits profound doubt, allowing calculative reason to go its way unhindered, or fetishizes doubt, allowing profound inquiry to grind to a halt.

Heidegger marks this distinction between metaphysical cogitation and philosophy proper by focusing not so much on the object of thought as on its unique manner or way. How one thinks, for Heidegger, is at least as important as what one thinks: "Our reflections make it clear that in thinking the most burdensome thought *what* is thought cannot be detached from the *way in which* it is thought. The *what* is itself defined by the *how*, and, reciprocally, the *how* by the *what*" (*ERS* 119). Training in philosophy, in this regard, is literally a learning how to think. "We are introduced to and become acquainted with what philosophy is," Heidegger maintains, "only when we learn how, in what manner, it is" (*WP* 91). Heidegger's most basic claim for himself—often neglected by his commentators—is that unlike the metaphysicians, he asks the question of Being "in a more questioning manner."[8] The problem with metaphysics, then, is not that it asks the wrong questions, but that it asks its questions wrongly. Heidegger writes: "The guiding question of Western philosophy is, 'What is being?' To *treat* this question as stated and posed is simply to look for an answer. To *develop* the question as it is formulated, however, is to pose the question more essentially. . . . [It is] a more original form of inquiry, one which does not crave an answer. . . . An answer is no more than the final step of the very asking; and an answer that bids adieu to the inquiry annihilates itself as an answer" (*ERS* 192). Many approach a truly philosophic mode of thinking, but most eventually succumb to the metaphysical seduction of seeking an answer that might then be put to good use (*WPA* 20). Only thinking proper sustains inquiry for its own sake, as a deepening of one's questioning. From Plato and Aristotle onward, Heidegger insists, philosophy has operated under a "technical interpretation of thinking" wherein thinking increasingly becomes "a process of reflection in service to doing and making" (*BW* 194). The present supremacy of calculative thought, as evidenced in the modern triumph of science and technology, was preceded by a long history of metaphysical explorations that bore a similar utilitarian focus.

Heidegger states that "thirst for knowledge and greed for explanations never lead to a thinking inquiry" (*WL* 13). This is the sense in which thinking remains a form of skepticism. One thinks skeptically when one inquires not in order to construct an answer about beings, but in order to establish an interrogative relationship with Being (cf. *N*

---

[8] Martin Heidegger, "Modern Natural Science and Technology," *Research in Phenomenology* 1 (1977): 3.

201). It follows that "thinking is not grasping or prehending . . . thinking knows nothing of the grasping concept" (*WCT* 211). Yet the legacy
of the metaphysical tradition beginning with Plato has been the triumph
of conceptual thought (*EGT* 29). The English word *concept* derives
from the Latin *concipio*, which means to grasp or take hold of. The
etymology is no less revealing in German, where *Begriff* stems from
greifen, which also means to grasp hold of. Conceptual thinking attempts to capture what it stalks. It is an indispensable tool for humankind. But truly philosophic thought is not a grasping conceptualization
that seeks terminological or representational closure. Thinking solicits;
it does not seize. Heidegger observes the common trope of having a
thought *come to us*. The thinker awaits the arrival of thoughts (*PLT* 6).
"To know how to question," Heidegger concludes, "means to know
how to wait, even a whole lifetime" (*IM* 206).

Thinking Being is a waitful questioning that forgoes the mastery of
conceptual representation. Heidegger therefore proposes that questioning is the piety of thought. He explains: " 'Piety' is meant here in the
ancient sense: obedient, or submissive, and in this case submitting to
what thinking has to think about" (*WL* 72). But to what, precisely, do
pious thinkers submit? Piety constitutes a "surrender to that which is
worthy of questioning" (*QT* 180). Piety submits one questioningly to
the mysterious relation between Being and being. But this "waitful"
way of thinking, pious thinking, is in decline. For Heidegger it follows
that "*Most thought-provoking is that we are still not thinking*—not
even yet, although the state of the world is becoming constantly more
thought-provoking" (*WCT* 4). Most thought-provoking is a world in
which human submission to pious thought is waning, though its decline
is hardly noticed amidst the flurry and flourishing of our intellectual
capture of the world.

The Caretaking of Difference

Thinking, Heidegger straightforwardly admits, "has no result. It has no
effect." Yet the "material relevance" of thinking "is essentially higher
than the validity of the sciences"—and, we may also add, higher than
the validity of logic, rationality, or common sense. It is higher, Heidegger insists, for one reason: "because it is freer. For it lets Being—be"
(*BW* 236). Freedom *in* thought does not pertain to the mastery of ideas
nor to the possession of opinions or beliefs. Freedom in thought is not
found in the power and productivity of logic, science, or common sense.
It is distinct from and opposed to calcutative reason, whose tremendous

growth in power largely defines the modern world.[9] However, because forgoing conceptual control in order to let Being be evidences freedom, thinking preserves the essential dignity of human being.

Heidegger insists that in the end "*every* philosophy fails," never arriving at its final destination. Yet philosophy is not for that reason in vain: "Philosophy is always completed when its end becomes and remains what its beginning is, the question. For only by truly remaining in questioning does it force what is worthy of question to appear. . . . Being is the ether in which man breathes. Without this ether, he would descend to the mere beast and his whole activity to the breeding of beasts" (*ST* 98). To the extent thinking brings us to dwell in the mystery of Being, it brings human being into its uniqueness and grandeur. Human being achieves its greatest heights, Heidegger submits, in its shepherding of Being. As befits a thoughtful caretaking, the shepherding of Being begets no proprietary rights. There is no possessive mastery here. Ontological guardianship denotes rather a bringing into harmony, an attunement with the mysterious (*WPK* 183). Heidegger writes that thinkers are actuated by a single task, already well described by one of the Seven Sages, Periander of Corinth, when he said, "Take into care beings as a whole [*Meleta to pan*]" (*WPK* 5). Freedom in thought is this holistic caretaking.

In taking beings as a whole into care, Dasein is also cared for. Human being cannot be defined apart from its questioning relation to Being, nor Being apart from its thoughtful disclosure by human being. Philosophy forever plies these waters. For Heidegger, "Every philosophical—that is, thoughtful—doctrine of man's essential nature is *in itself alone* a doctrine of the Being of beings. Every doctrine of Being is *in itself alone* a doctrine of man's essential nature. But neither doctrine can be obtained by merely turning the other one around. . . . every way of thinking *takes its way* already *within* the total relation of Being and man's nature, or else it is not thinking at all" (*WCT* 79–80). The matter most worthy of thought, it follows, is "the relation of Being to that living being, man" (*ERS* 232). Heidegger is contemptuous of any attempt to define human being in a way that does not account for its questioning relationship to Being or does not do so in a questioning manner. "To be sure, there are books today entitled: 'What is man?' " Heidegger observes, "but the title merely stands in letters on the cover.

[9] Weber understands increasing rationalization to mean "that principally there are no mysterious incalculable forces that come into play, but rather that one can, in principle, master all things by calculation. This means that the world is disenchanted." Max Weber, *From Max Weber: Essays in Sociology*, trans. H. H. Gerth and C. Wright Mills (New York: Oxford University Press, 1958), 139.

There is no questioning. Not only because people have been so busy writing books that they have forgotten how to question, but because the writers already possess an answer and what is more an answer that forbids questioning" (*IM* 142). The problem with any scientific identification of human being is that, philosophically speaking, its method betrays its substance. Ruled by a utilitarian reason and representational logic, science cannot mediate what remains most essential to human being: the capacity for a thinking that erupts out of conceptual confines and interrogatively consumes the thinker. It cannot mediate the human capacity for freedom in thought.[10]

Scientific writings on the nature of human being are distinct from truly philosophical quests, which always bear the form, as Wittgenstein observes, "I don't know my way about."[11] In thinking one necessarily proceeds without clear direction or identifiable markers. Unlike calculative thinking, which maintains its field of vision within substantive strictures and methodological conventions, philosophic thinking "demands of us not to cling one-sidedly to a single idea, nor to run down a one-track course of ideas" but instead to "venture" after the meaning that "reigns in everything that is" (*DT* 53, 46). In thinking we "deal seriously with whatever is as the latter is brought into the light of its Being" and "make everything we do answer to whatever essentials address themselves to us at a given moment" (*QT* 137–38; *WCT* 8).[12] The thinker inquires into the meaning of everything that is as it presents itself, for regardless of what (particular being) presents itself, its Being solicits a questioning disclosure. Thinking occurs at the moment of our being swept up in a questioning of the whole that infuses each of the parts.

---

[10] Jean-Luc Nancy states the issue well: "Every thinking is therefore a thinking about freedom at the same time that it thinks *by* freedom and thinks *in* freedom. . . . Thinking is always thinking on the limit. The limit of comprehending defines thinking. Thus thinking is always thinking about the incomprehensible—about this incomprehensible that 'belongs' to every comprehending, as its own limit." Freedom, therefore, can never truly be appropriated by thinking, only temporarily "pirated." Nancy, *Experience of Freedom*, 54, 20.

[11] Ludwig Wittgenstein, *Philosophical Investigations*, trans. G. Anscombe (New York: Macmillan, 1953), 49, par. 123. Making this same point in distinction to science and its method, Isaiah Berlin recently stated: "Not to know where to look for the answer is the surest symptom of a philosophical problem. . . . Philosophy consists of trying to move toward resolving problems where prima facie there appears to exist no obvious technique for finding the answers." Berlin, "Philosophy and Life," 50–51.

[12] One is reminded of Hannah Arendt's statement that the activity of thinking is "the habit of examining and reflecting upon whatever happens to come to pass, regardless of specific content and quite independent of results." Hannah Arendt, "Thinking and Moral Considerations: A Lecture," *Social Research* 38 (1971): 418. Arendt makes a similar statement in *The Life of the Mind*, whose section called "Thinking" begins with a quotation from Heidegger.

Heidegger writes that "the matter of thinking is . . . Being—but Being with respect to its difference from beings. . . . For us, formulated in a preliminary fashion, the matter of thinking is the difference *as* difference [*Differenz*]" (*ID* 47). Thinking is a guardianship of ontological difference. That is, thinking is an "appropriation" or letting belong together of Being and being (*ID* 39). It is within this appropriated difference [*Unterscheidung*] of beings and Being that human being dwells (*G* 51:47). Thoughtful guardianship is only ever initiated or sustained by a particular state of mind: wonder or astonishment. According to Heidegger, "Astonishment, as *pathos*, is the *archē* [the beginning] of philosophy. . . . The *pathos* of astonishment thus does not simply stand at the beginning of philosophy, as, for example, the washing of his hands precedes the surgeon's operation. Astonishment carries and pervades philosophy. . . . Thus, astonishment is disposition in which and for which the Being of being unfolds" (*WP* 80, 85). Philosophic wonder is not the achievement of a systematic procedure. It is more likely the sudden result of being stymied in the midst of a sustained query. Wonder at the Being of beings involves a leap (*ERS* 129). On the other side of this leap, Heidegger observes, "everything . . . strikes us as strange" (*WCT* 12). In thinking the Being of beings, struck by wonder, the philosopher comes to dwell in the uncanny luminosity of difference.

The wonder of thinking defies easy categorization only because it remains a uniquely philosophical experience. We might be tempted to understand this strange and newly won relationship to existence as religious, for it appears to escape any other characterization. Heidegger firmly maintains that it is anything but religious. The leap of thinking is decidedly not a leap of faith. "The unconditional character of faith, and the problematic character of thinking," Heidegger emphasizes, "are two spheres separated by an abyss" (*WCT* 177). Religious thought terminates in faith, while philosophic thought, on the other side of the abyss, remains an interminable questioning. Hence thinking embraces what religion attempts to circumvent: groundless inquiry. The most eminent contradiction, that of Being's nothingness corresponding to its very pervasiveness, is the source of philosophic wonder. Thus the "feast of thinking," a feast whose nourishment is the contradictory and the questionable, is never a religious event (*WPA* 5).

Despite Heidegger's talk of dwelling in difference, philosophic inquiry forbids ensconcing oneself in a comfortable haven. It is a rather anxious affair. Anxiety (*Angst*) is the inseparable twin mood of philosophic wonder. Thinking Being brings one face-to-face with a profound nothingness lying at the heart of all that is. This is the nothingness "which alone touches man to the quick. Man alone of all beings, when addressed by the voice of Being, experiences the marvel of all marvels:

that what-is *is*. . . . The clear courage for essential anxiety guarantees that most mysterious of all possibilities: the experience of Being. For hard by essential anxiety, in the terror of the abyss, there dwells awe [*Scheu*]. Awe clears and enfolds that region of human being within which man endures, as at home, in the enduring" (*EB 355*; translation emended). One needs courage to think because thinking plumbs the abyss. Wonder and anxiety join hands before it, separated by a heart-beat.

What transforms anxiety into wonder is our capacity to welcome the unknown and unknowable, to let Being be. Anxiety becomes wonder when the pursuit of conceptual control and cognitive mastery is abandoned such that freedom in thought may be engaged. Anxiety, in this sense, is to be overcome but never suppressed or denied. There is to be no whistling in the dark while navigating thought's path. Rather than shielding oneself from the awesome mystery of Being by rehearsing the melodies of science, reason, religion, or common sense, one learns to be at home with anxiety itself.

The task of making thinking one's abode is particularly difficult today. The interminableness of questioning, the uselessness of inquiry, and the anxiety of nothingness all serve to magnify the seductive power and productivity of calculation and conceptualization. The world has become too complex to allow us easily to find our dignity in the inexhaustible simplicity of thought. Heidegger warns of this danger: "We know too much and believe too readily ever to feel at home in a questioning which is powerfully experienced. For that we need the ability to wonder at what is simple, and to take up that wonder as our abode" (*EGT* 104). In short, there are moods far more comforting and alluring than wonder and anxiety. Seeking the constant security of these moods might well become irresistible were it not for the exuberance of freedom in the affirmation of Being that lies at the heart of all thinking as questioning.

Heidegger approvingly cites Hölderlin's poem *Socrates and Alcibiades*, which reads: "Who has most deeply thought, loves what is most alive" (*WCT* 20). Thinking is essentially a loving thanks for what is, that it is. "Original thanking is the thanks owed for being," Heidegger writes. "The supreme thanks, then, would be thinking? And the profoundest thanklessness, thoughtlessness? . . . As we give thought to what is most thought-provoking, we give thanks" (*WCT* 141, 143, 146). Thinking, as questioning, becomes thanking, as affirming, in its witnessing of difference. Yet thinking, Heidegger explicitly states, is not a simple yea-saying. He writes that "Dasein is the inquirer into the why. The human being is not primarily the nay-sayer . . . but just as little is the human being a yea-sayer. The human is rather the why-questioner.

But only because man is in this way, can he and must he, in each case, say, not only yes or no, but essentially yes and no" (*MFL* 216). Human beings are unique among the earth's creatures because they question the ground of their being. But this questioning is not to be understood as the cynicism or "sheer addiction to doubt" of the naysayer. Nor, however, is it to be understood as either the heroic self-assertion or the religious faith of the yea-sayers. Rather, it is defined by an anxious wonder. Pious questioning is both a yes and a no: yes to an openness to the mystery and yes to the letting-be of what is; no to calculative reason that would shield us from the nothingness lying at the heart of everything and the contingency lying at the heart of our Being, and no to answers that would terminate fundamental questioning in religious faith or pragmatic concerns.

The truth shall make you free, Heidegger might have said, echoing Saint John. But the truth Heidegger is concerned with makes us free only by way of fundamental inquiry. Human being is the why-questioner, a thinking being. In thought we are offered a home, a place where we may come into our own, which is to say, a place where our most basic freedom becomes manifest. At home in thought, our thinking becomes an interrogative affirmation, a questioning thankfulness, simple yet inexhaustible.[13] Parmenides formulated as a dictim this expression of philosophic wonder: "One should both say and think that Being is." Thinking renders its affirmative witnessing of Being (as hiddenness) into a thankful saying of what is. Freedom in thought cultivates freedom in speech. The latter will not germinate and cannot grow without the former. "Thinking cuts furrows into the soil of Being," Heidegger writes (*WL* 70; cf. *BW* 242). Language is that soil—and freedom in speech its harvest.

[13] Jean-Luc Nancy maintains that "*freedom cannot be the object of a question*, but is 'only' the *putting into question of an affirmation*." Unfortunately, Nancy vitiates this understanding by suggesting that "thinking must be in search of a nonquestioning mode of thinking." Nancy, *Experience of Freedom*, 23, 165. This is a serious mistake, probably brought on by Nancy's false equation of questioning with answer-finding. As Nietzsche observed in *Untimely Meditations* (9), it is a grave error to confuse a seeker with a finder.

Five

Freedom in Speech

> The name that can be named is not the
> enduring and unchanging name.
>   (Lao Tzu, *Tao Te Ching*)

THE COMING to presence of Being is, from a philosophical point of view, all there is to think about. But this is no restriction, for the worldly manifestations of Being's presencing are as diverse as life itself—indeed, more so. Examining how we may participate in this presencing goes to the core of Heidegger's project. Despite the unmanageable plenitude of difference and the numerous modes of its disclosure, a unifying feature may be discerned. Most essentially, we disclose the Being of being through language. As Heidegger writes, "Thinking attends to the lighting of Being in that it puts its saying of Being into language as the home of existence" (*BW* 239). Elsewhere we read: "All ways of thinking, more or less perceptibly, lead through language in a manner that is extraordinary" (*QT* 3). Heidegger also affirms that all ways of acting are led through language in a manner that is extraordinary. What is extraordinary about the way language serves as the medium of our thoughtful and active Being-in-the-world is the concern of this chapter.

Homo Faber versus *Zoon Logon Echon*

Heidegger differentiates thinking from the application of "calculative" reason, whether in the service of common sense, science, or logic. The distinction may jar our common presumptions, but the nature of thinking is ephemeral enough that its isolation from instrumental service and practical application retains an intrinsic appeal. More shocking, perhaps, is Heidegger's insistence that language is equally divorced from instrumentality. Language, we generally assume, is the most powerful tool humankind has ever developed. We assume that *Homo faber*, the toolmaking human, reaches the greatest heights, rising above the mute beasts, by the skillful use of speech and writing. The development of civilization itself appears to rest on this linguistic foundation. Heidegger disputes this received wisdom. It is not that he finds the greatness of human being to be tied to something other than language. Rather, he denies that language is essentially and primarily an instrument available for our use. "Language," Heidegger bluntly states, "is not a tool at [our] disposal, rather it is that event which disposes of the supreme possibility of human existence" (EB 276–77). Rather than an invention we employ, language more closely resembles a happening in which we participate. If Aristotle's definition of human being as the *zoon logon echon*, the animal with speech, is correct, then the reason for this is that through language human beings experience a freedom unknown to the beasts.

Heidegger offers a singular understanding of language. He is not blind to the many roles language may play, and the manifold tasks it may derive therefrom. Still, he insists that most essentially language is not something that human subjects instrumentally employ for the purpose of gaining (conceptual) control over their world. Rather, language is what displays us—to ourselves and to others—as always, already in the world. We disclose our Being-in-the-world, often quite unintentionally, whenever we speak. In addition to its instrumental purposes, language reveals human being's worldliness through its disclosure and mediation of moods and comportment. Heidegger explains that our "way of speaking," including our intonation, modulation, and tempo, reveal the particular manner in which we find ourselves in the world (BT 205). Speech, regardless of specific content, already displays our worldliness through its manner.

Through poetry our (way of) Being-in-the-world is consciously brought to the fore. By "poetry" Heidegger generally means to indicate both philosophic and poetic speech. He affirms, with Hölderlin, that human being dwells poetically on the earth. We are, first and foremost, linguistically in the world, not simply because language allows us to define our world, but because we come to be defined as worldly dwellers through our language. The point is not that we linguistically reveal a world that somehow previously existed in muteness, nor that we are worldly dwellers who happen to be capable of speech. Rather, to be worldly inhabitants is to dwell in language. Language is the ubiquitous medium in which human being steeps.

Heidegger's position is surely not that our social and worldly existence is made available to us only when we vocalize or exchange words. Human being constitutes and persists in its worldliness through language despite any silence or solitude. Heidegger would insist that "we are always speaking, even when we do not utter a single word aloud, but merely listen or read, and even when we are not particularly listening or speaking but are attending to some work or taking a rest" (PLT 189). At any particular moment we may not participate in conversation with ourselves or others. But we do not, on that count, cease to dwell in language, for as human beings we exist linguistically in a more thorough sense. Our mute actions, no less than our silent thoughts, emerge and constitute themselves "more or less perceptibly" through language. Heidegger explains: "When we go to the well, when we go through the woods, we are always already going through the word 'well,' through the word 'woods,' even if we do not speak the words and do not think of anything relating to language" (*PLT* 132). In short, we mediate ourselves and our world through speech.

Language brings the world into Being, and brings us into the world's Being. If it is true that as representatives of *Homo faber* we have made language, then it is equally true that as worldly beings language has made us. Heidegger writes: "Since language really became actual as conversation, the gods have acquired names and a world has appeared. But again it should be noticed: the presence of the gods and the appearance of the world are not merely a consequence of the actualization of language, they are contemporaneous with it. And this to the extent that it is precisely in the naming of the gods, and in the transmutation of the world into word, that the real conversation, which we ourselves are, consists" (*EB* 279). Human being is an ongoing historical conversation. Language writes the text of our Being-in-the-world, spelling out our limitations and possibilities. Language, Heidegger writes, is "the house of Being and the home of human beings" (*BW* 239). Language fosters interactive participation in what is manifest, the world and the with-world, and brings into question that which escapes manifestation in its hiddenness, Being. As such, language constitutes our primordial abode.

The main threat to human being's discovery of this abode is the assumption that language serves a purely instrumental function. In a technologically structured world, this view gains increasing currency. Heidegger insists that today's "unrestrained technological objectification" deforms language "into an instrument of reportage and calculable information . . . a manipulatable object, to which our manner of thinking must conform" (*PT* 29). Technological objectification reduces all words to terms, in the sense of instrumental designations for specific objects. This reduction is furthered by the neologisms, abbreviations, and acronyms that proliferate in technological societies. Herein, words become sheer signs, ciphers that no longer evoke a historic worldliness. One might watch a movie on TV, or send a fax through one's modem. The language involved here conveys information efficiently. And, to be sure, such efficiency has its place and purpose. But there are costs involved. Lost in the abbreviations, acronyms, and neologisms is the fuller evocation of the physical and historical, which is to say, the worldly nature of speech and speakers. In speaking of TV we lose the sense of *tele-vision*, being vision at a distance; in speaking of movies we lose the sense of *pictures in motion*; in speaking of faxes we lose sight of the nature of *facsimiles*, and in speaking of a modem we would lose sight of the nature of a *modulator demodulator*, if we ever had a sense of what that meant. Lost here is part of the relation between human beings and their world. That worrying about such losses strikes many as rather absurd is, for Heidegger, indicative that technological thought is already hegemonic. It is, for Heidegger, a "symptom" of the "one-track thinking" that technological life begets (*WCT* 34).[1]

When words become mere signs for speedy communication, they become one-dimensional. They may serve an instrumental purpose very well, but they cease to resonate with the multiple chords inherent in language. Indeed, were language successfully reduced to unequivocal signs, philosophic thought, sustained as it is by the *difference* speech evokes, would become nearly impossible.[2] Heidegger vehemently opposes this reduction: "Words are not terms, and thus are not like buckets and kegs from which we scoop a content that is there. Words are wellsprings that are found and dug up in the telling, wellsprings that must be found and dug up again and again, that easily cave in, but that at times also well up when least expected. If we do not go to the spring again and again, the buckets and kegs stay empty, or their content stays stale" (*WCT* 130). When we speak most essentially, we do so not as toolmakers. But the technological colonization of language threatens to preclude our being cast in any other role.

To insist that language is not reducible to utilitarian signs is not to say that language is somehow divorced from practical concerns and concrete life. Indeed, language continually makes available our fundamental relation to the world in a way that purely instrumental communication cannot. Language, in this sense, is eminently practical. For our Being-in-the-world is always a historical being, and language constantly retrieves and preserves our historical embeddedness. Moreover, dwelling in the medium of language is not without practical effect. Those who pay attention to language are inevitably transformed by it. Lan-

---

[1] Heidegger's phrase recalls Herbert Marcuse's thesis that "functionalized, abridged and unified language is the language of one-dimensional thought." It follows for Marcuse that in an age of technology, "syntax, grammar, and vocabulary become moral and political acts." Herbert Marcuse, *One-Dimensional Man: Studies in the Ideology of Advanced Industrial Society* (Boston: Beacon Press, 1964), 95, 196.

[2] Plato's *Republic* gave the first theoretical indication that the total state could not abide the fecundity of poetic speech. Modern totalitarian regimes also understood this threat. After thirty hours of interrogation, poet Reiner Kunze of the former East German state was warned by a Stasi officer: "I forbid you to write lines of poetry with double meanings. We have experts who decode everything!" Amos Elon, "East Germany: Crime and Punishment," *New York Review of Books*, May 14, 1992, 8.

guage "roots us to our earth and transports and ties us to our world," Heidegger writes. "Meditation on language and its historical dominion is always the action that gives shape to Dasein itself. The will to originality, rigor, and measure in words is therefore no mere aesthetic pleasantry; it is the work that goes on in the essential nucleus of our Dasein, which is historical existence" (WPA 145). What we do largely depends on who we think we are, and who we think we are largely depends upon the language by which we define or describe ourselves and others. Shelley asserts that "poets are the unacknowledged legislators of the world." Powerful language given to us by poets (or politicians, makers of motion pictures, or sound-bite advertisers) does indeed often assume a legislative role. But equally important, the will to originality, rigor, and measure that each experiences in any authentic attempt to bring words to bear on his or her historical existence makes language the legislator of the self. We become what and how we speak.

With this in mind, we may understand Heidegger's rather obsessive (and sometimes fanciful) preoccupation with etymology. Attention to etymology fosters a critical awareness that instrumental speech is but the veneer of language. Instrumental speech facilitates communicative transactions, yet hides the layers of meaning below. At the deepest level, resting on a mute foundation, we may glimpse language's flirtation with difference itself, its housing of Being. Yet from the perspective of *Homo faber*, concern for this reclusive aspect of language seems a fruitless distraction. Ahistorically, technically, words do not resonate. They simply indicate. In a world wherein language is largely reduced to a box of implements in the service of utilitarian ends, ontological questioning itself seems quite beside the point. Heidegger was aware of this threat, lamenting that "not only is man unacquainted with the truth of Being, but wherever 'Being' crops up he proclaims it the specter of sheer abstraction, thus mistakes it and repudiates it as vacuous nothingness. By surrendering all remembrance, instead of ceaselessly recollecting the essential historical fullness of the *words* 'Being' and 'to be,' he hears mere *terms,* whose empty reverberations he rightly finds irritating" (N 249). Irritation may be the sentiment many experience when approaching Heidegger's own etymological musings and poetic speech, for words that previously were familiar tools put to fruitful tasks now confront one with a startling unruliness. Heidegger's words, like Daedelus's sculptures, appear to have gained lives of their own. Indeed, Heidegger does not refrain from shocking his readers by delivering language to us in the guise of destiny itself. He writes that "in the duality of the participial significance of ὄν the distinction between 'to be' and 'a being' lies concealed. What is here set forth, which at first may be taken for grammatical hair-splitting, is in truth the riddle of Being. . . . We might assert in an exaggerated way, which nevertheless bears on the truth, that the fate of the West hangs on the translation of the word ἐόν, assuming that the translation consists in *crossing over* to the truth of what comes to language in ἐόν" (*EGT* 32–33).[3] Language has indeed escaped the toolbox and come to life with a vengeance.

Linguistic Chauvinism, Terminological Totemism, and Postmodern Language Games

Heidegger speaks of the fate of the West rather than the fate of the world bearing on the translation of a few Greek words. The importance of the Greek language to the West, though it sounds trite to say so, is historical. Were Western languages not developed out of Greek and its cognate tongues, ontological resonances would have to be sought elsewhere. That is to say, the historical roots of all languages bear ontological riches. At times, however, Heidegger allowed historical contingency an undue veneration. His nostalgic attempt to find a primordiality and purity at the roots of language remains suspect. Heidegger insists that the Greeks "in a unique way thought out of their language, i.e., received from it their human existence" (*QT* 164). We may concede such uniqueness to the Greeks. But we may do so only because it does not impinge on the uniqueness of other linguistic peoples, the singular way in which they, too, think out of their language. However, Heidegger goes too far when he claims that "in the Greek language what is said in it is at the same time in an excellent way what it is called. . . . What it presents is what lies immediately before us. Through the audible Greek word we are directly in the presence of the thing itself, not first in the presence of a mere word sign" (*WP* 45). To be sure, language is always more than mere word signs. But it never completely escapes this role, either in Greek antiquity or the present day. Indeed, language allows the disclosure of difference precisely because it balances between Being and beings without ever reducing itself to the pure invocation of the former or the solely instrumental designation of the latter.

Heidegger also went too far, and much less innocently so, when extolling "the special inner kinship between the German language and the language of the Greeks and their thought" (*OGS* 62). He would declare German to be, along with the Greek language, "at once the most powerful and most spiritual of all languages" (*IM* 57). Graced with such a

---

[3] Jacques Derrida has reminded us of the seriousness of this position, quoting Heidegger, who states: "Tell me what you think about translation and I will tell you who you are." Jacques Derrida, *Of Spirit: Heidegger and the Question*, trans. G. Bennington and R. Bowlby (Chicago: University of Chicago Press, 1989), 4. See also *G* 53:74ff.

philosophical language, Germany might rightfully assert its status, Heidegger would declare in the mid-1930s with unintentional irony, as "the most metaphysical of nations" (*IM* 37–38). Heidegger would admit that every true language is philosophic to some degree. But this fact is often obscured by a nationalistic fervor. He could not resist declaring that the philosophic capacity of a language rests on the "depth and power of the existence of a people and race" and that only the German language rivaled Greek in this respect (*G* 31:51).

To salvage the profound core of Heidegger's insights on language, we must deny him this linguistic chauvinism. Our relation to Being is dependent on our saying of Being, to be sure, for the saying and thinking of Being are the same. But this thoughtful saying is made possible, indeed inevitable at some level, in the historical and linguistic development of all peoples. The experience of difference is not essentially determined by the particularities of a language, but by the human faculty and experience of language as such.[4] Human being, not national being, is the shepherd of Being. And this shepherding takes place by way of words that summon ontological rather than ethnic difference.

Heidegger insists that "the differentiation of beings and Being makes possible every naming, experience, and conceiving of a being as such" (*N* 154). In speaking we are not solely affixing labels to things. We are also giving utterance to "isness." We are saying what is, and thus participating in its presencing. Unfortunately, Heidegger occasionally asserts a temporal priority to the disclosure of Being over the naming and conceiving of beings. This, too, we must resist. He writes: "Naming does not come afterward, providing an already manifest being with a designation and a hallmark known as a word; it is the other way around: originally an act of violence that discloses Being, the word sinks from this height to become a mere sign, and this sign proceeds to thrust itself before the being" (*IM* 172). Though Heidegger is correct to dismiss the temporal priority of representative or utilitarian speech, his reversal is nonetheless unwarranted. The ontologically disclosive nature of language and its instrumental character, we may presume, have always coexisted, just as they simultaneously manifest themselves today. Heidegger himself came to admit that his romantic assumption about the deterioration of speech from an original, premetaphysical purity among the early Greeks was "untenable" (*TB* 70). Our access to Being is only given through beings. Ontological signification rests on human

---

[4] Heidegger would come close to accepting this position after the war, declaring that "'German' is not spoken to the world so that the world might be reformed through the German essence; rather, it is spoken to the Germans so that from a fateful belongingness to the nations they might become world-historical along with them. The homeland of this historical dwelling is nearness to Being" (*BW* 218).

being's historical and concrete worldliness, which necessarily includes its purposeful, utilitarian coping with the ready-to-hand and its conceptual isolation of the present-at-hand. Any linguistic disclosure of Being, therefore, requires beings to bear out difference. It is not that Being precedes being(s), or vice versa. Being grounds being, to be sure, but not in the sense of a cause preceding or producing an effect. Rather, Being stands implicit in being, awaiting its unconcealment in the illuminated circle of human being. It follows that language houses Being not at some original time, previous to the advent of beings, but always and only in the actual disclosure of beings.

The wonder of language is not that it manifests the (temporal) priority of Being in its poeticizing, but that it testifies to difference and hence resists its reduction to a system of signs efficiently trafficking in beings. Nevertheless, the prevailing tendency, which Heidegger attempted to resist with his unwarranted reversal, is for language to be depreciated to a set of tools for naming, conceiving, and manipulating things. This tendency is evident even in contemporary philosophical discourse. As philosophy becomes increasingly analytic in orientation, it evidences a methodical attempt to assign singular names to things. But this attempt unequivocally to catalogue the universe in the pursuit of cognitive control runs afoul of the inexhaustibility of difference. We may understand Heidegger's concern for this reduction of language to a systematic semiotics when he writes: "The life of actual language consists in multiplicity of meaning. To relegate the animated, vigorous word to the immobility of a univocal, mechanically programmed sequence of signs would mean the death of language and the petrification and devastation of Dasein" (*WPA* 144). Elsewhere he writes: "Essential words are not artificially invented signs and marks which are pasted on things merely to identify them. Essential words are deeds which happen in those moments where the lightning flash of a great enlightenment goes through the universe" (*ST* 25). Though overly dramatic in presentation, Heidegger's understanding of the ontological power of language is defensible. But essential words, one must reaffirm, do not appear on the scene in the absence of words that have application as conceptual tags or instrumental markers. The historical origin of language is, in the end, obscure and unretrievable. What we may observe is the enduring capacity of language to escape the univocality thrust on it by analytic systems. Language safeguards ontological difference by straddling the ontic world of beings and the ontological world of Being. The point is not to deprecate the symbolic and utilitarian use of language but to acknowledge that it forever rests in tension with its poetic counterpart.

Heidegger's opposition to utilitarian and representational language is occasionally misconstrued as an embrace of postmodern language games. Having relieved language of its charge of representing an objective reality, certain postmodernists tout language as ungrounded play, a linguistic romp in a playground of signs. Adopting this view, Richard Rorty argues that language levitates, disconnected from anything like Being, infinitely available and malleable to speech retailers. Rorty, developing the work of the later Wittgenstein and Donald Davidson, equates speaking with "trading" in a free-market system defined by its currency of words. Here language is reduced to "the exchange of marks and noises among human beings for particular purposes."[5] Such linguistic consumerism, an identifiably postmodern pastime, actually marks the completion of a metaphysics that enframes the world within a utilitarian drive. No longer tied to truth by way of its representational accuracy, language becomes a free-floating construction of technological humankind.

Language, Richard Rorty rightly insists following Heidegger, should not be understood as the verbal organization of symbols that mirror an objective world in the human mind. Language is not reducible to a system of representations limning eternal ideas, concrete entities, or analytic abstractions. But neither, pace Rorty, is it a reservoir of surplus symbols available for artistic or pragmatic consumption. Speech is more than the use and exchange of signs and symbols in a linguistic trade fair. Language, Heidegger states, measures the breadth of our being (*PLT* 222). It can do this only because of its capacity to carry us beyond ourselves, into the enigma of Being. This is "the promise of language" (*WL* 90). Language is the house of Being in which human being finds its home. But the task at hand is not to take inventory, affix linguistic tags, and have a garage sale. The task is to preserve language's capacity to shelter profound mystery. What is brought to the fore in philosophic speech are not things in need of unequivocal names, but that which ultimately escapes naming. The no-thing that is Being is badly served by ordinary speech philosophy. Heidegger's understanding of language, then, must be distinguished from postmodern language games no less than from modern representationalism. Heidegger rejects all efforts to master language, regardless of whether this mastery is perpetrated by the practical toolmaker or the playful aesthete.

---

[5] Richard Rorty, "Wittgenstein, Heidegger, and the Reification of Language," in *The Cambridge Companion to Heidegger*, ed. Charles Guignon (New York: Cambridge University Press, 1993), 350. John Caputo offers an apposite criticism of Rorty: "But Heidegger has nothing to do with Rorty's remedy against ocularism, which is to sever the bonds between Being and thought in favor of purely intra-linguistic relations. . . . Rorty's deconstruction of the visual metaphor results in a blind-folded language game." John Caputo, "The Thought of Being and the Conversation of Mankind: The Case of Heidegger and Rorty," in *Hermeneutics and Praxis*, ed. Robert Hollinger (Notre Dame: University of Notre Dame Press, 1985), 255.

Through his account of the technological deformation of language, Heidegger may be distinguished from most other critics of technology. Lewis Mumford, for instance, rejects the common notion that the fabrication of tools serves as the best indicator of human development. He gives a sustained historical account of how the struggle for individual and cultural self-expression, not the struggle for technological power, best accounts for the distinctive rise of humanity from bestiality to civilization.[6] But Mumford depreciates the importance of the development of material tools in order to emphasize the importance of the development of symbolic tools, namely the symbolic instruments of art, play, ritual, and most importantly, expressive language. He argues that creative self-expression via the use of symbols, not material enhancement via technological development, was most fundamental to the development of human nature and most essential to its genius. Mumford's critical stance toward technology is laudable. Implicit in Mumford's account, however, is a residual subjectivism and utilitarianism that Heidegger would reject. According to Mumford (and postmodernists such as Foucault), the antidote for technological domination is the resurrection of artistic expression and its attendant self-invention. Herein Mumford retains the notion that the essence of human freedom is found in a form of mastery and appropriation. He simply substitutes the artistic mastery of symbols for the technological mastery of objects, the controlled work of tongues for the controlled work of hands.

Heidegger, on the other hand, depreciates the use of language as an artistic tool almost as much as he does its use as a technical one. "That we retain a concern for care in speaking is all to the good," Heidegger warns, "but it is of no help to us as long as language still serves us even then only as a means of expression" (*PLT* 146). Language is primarily neither an artistic instrument of self-expression nor a utilitarian instrument of material production. Language is not something that we unproblematically put to work, as any tool, symbolic or otherwise, decidedly is. Rather, language must be left to do its work upon us. It is metaphorical in the etymological sense of something that carries us over and beyond. In language we are transported into the realm of Being. Neither the manner of transport nor the destination is completely within our jurisdiction. To attempt to make it so, by way of artistic no less than technical control, is to misunderstand the potential of language.

Language, Heidegger rightly insists, is simply not to be mastered—at least not if we are to experience freedom in speech. But forgoing mastery is not tantamount to accepting servitude. In reestablishing a rela-

[6] See Lewis Mumford, *The Myth of the Machine: Technics and Human Development* (San Diego: Harcourt Brace Jovanovich, 1967).

tionship to language, one should not exchange a master morality for a slave morality. Heidegger overcompensates in this regard, falling prey to his own rhetoric. He writes, for instance, "Man acts as though *he* were the shaper and master of language, while in fact *language* remains the master of man" (*PLT* 146). But language does not master human being any more than human being ever truly masters language. To speak with Heidegger of language's mastery (of humans) is to reify and anthropomorphize language, and thereby to betray its capacity to carry human being beyond itself. Heidegger is mistaken in stating that in using language man subverts a "relation of dominance." Language does not establish a relation of dominance over humans in the first place. Language is less a despotic ruler that we overthrow to our detriment than a gift we are given that we frequently abuse. Like all gifts, language is to be given and received in freedom.

By seeking a (pragmatic or artistic) mastery of words, we jeopardize our sheltering of Being. In playing this "high and dangerous game and gamble," Heidegger warns, we are apt to forget that "we are the stakes" (*WCT* 119). We become the stakes because our freedom in speech lies in the balance. However, in avoiding the Circe of possessive mastery that threatens our freedom, we become vulnerable to another enchantress. This is the Siren that lies in wait for those who celebrate the power of language to escape instrumentality. As words cease to become mere tools of a trade, they threaten to take on magical powers. In escaping the toolbox, language may become totemized. Heidegger's writings remain susceptible to such reification. Indeed, Heidegger himself was tempted by the power of poetic speech to escape its symbolic function and incarnate the (no)thing-in-itself. In his effort to shun any merely representational role for "Being," the word itself is occasionally imagined magically and immediately to incarnate "isness."

The temptation is to equate "Being" with Being. In becoming totemized, Being becomes an obstacle to disclosure rather than its vehicle. Freedom in speech is overpowered by a mantric anesthesia. Heidegger, despite his flirtation with terminological totemism, became aware of this threat. He cautions that the effort to gain access to Being through language must relinquish "the wish to define in so far as this must be established on assertions in which thinking dies out. . . . Accordingly, a thoughtful glance ahead into this realm of 'Being' can only write it as B̶e̶i̶n̶g̶" (*QB* 81). Heidegger's crossing-out or erasure of "Being" is intended to hinder its metaphysical reduction to a mere representation no less than its transubstantiation into the actual thing-in-itself. Writing B̶e̶i̶n̶g̶ though cumbersome and susceptible to its own reification, militates against conceptual mastery and mindless incantation. It aims at restricting the power of language over thought whenever the former becomes an obstacle to the latter. To this same end, Heidegger would discontinue labeling his work hermeneutics and phenomenology. These words, originally resonant with ontological significance, had hardened into tools through overhandling. They would be dropped, Heidegger explains, "in order to abandon my own path of thinking to nameless-ness" (*WL* 29). Words always court deformation. Linguistic wellsprings may be reduced to linguistic buckets, no longer secretory of thought. Equally dangerous, language may be reified into a totemistic force. The ambiguous freedom to which human beings are privileged by their ca-pacity for speech is then exhanged for a servitude to pragmatic affairs or rituals of incantation.

Invocation, Idle Talk, and the Right of Free Speech

Whenever language is asked to do too little (serve as a mere tool) or too much (not only invoke but actually incarnate Being), its relationship to thought is corrupted. Yet in a certain sense, the distinction between thought and language does not exist. Thinking, as a witnessing of Being's disclosure, necessarily takes linguistic form, as an affirmative saying of what is. And language, as the house of being, is always a thoughtful dwelling. "Language is not the expression of thinking," Hei-degger insists, "but is thinking itself, its stride and its voice" (*QB* 105). Thinking only comes into its own through language: "only when man speaks, does he think—not the other way around, as metaphysics still believes" (*WCT* 16). It is mistaken to suppose that language is employed by thought to make explicit and concrete what previously existed in some prelinguistic form. This is generally the case with every-day language and with cognition, which, as Heidegger writes, "merely employs language" but does not truly "speak language" (*WCT* 128). With regard to philosophic speech, however, the experiential saying of Being—that Being is—*is* its thinking. In short, "Thinking of Being is the original way of poeticizing. . . . Thinking is primordial poetry" (*EGT* 19).

When Heidegger refers to language, then, he is referring to something closer to a thoughtful invocation than to an everyday conversation, a scientific statement, or a metaphysical discourse. The repetitious and poetic nature of Heidegger's writings is perhaps best understood in this light. Words, properly spoken, disclose Being. To say "that Being is" is less to make a propositional statement about the nature of reality than to participate in this reality as its witness. Heidegger insists that "lan-guage is not an agglomeration of words used to designate sundry famil-iar things but *the original resonance of the truth of a world*" (*ERS* 105).

Speaking language rather than merely employing words produces a sympathetic vibration. Repetition and poetic formulations may foster such resonance by breaking us free from conventional usages and their instrumental purposes. As noted above, however, this pious invocation of Being forever threatens to become a narcotic chant. But Heidegger's intent is that it remain a stimulant to ontological interrogation. Speaking language is an invocation of Being that questions while it affirms.

Best equipped for this task of interrogative invocation is poetry, which is the form of speech most akin to thinking. Indeed, Heidegger could never decide "whether poetry is really a kind of thinking, or thinking really a kind of poetry" (*WL* 83). Even the "most rigorous" philosophic work is necessarily poetic: indeed "the distinction between 'theoretical' and 'poetical' cannot be applied to philosophical texts" (*ERS* 73). To say that one comes to think only through poetic speech is not to suggest that poetry says, and can say, all there is to be thought. Quite the opposite is true. What gives poetry its philosophic power is that it is able to say what remains *un*thought by leaving *un*said yet beckoning what is to be thought. Goethe suggested that poetry brings the universal to appearance in the particular. One might add that poetry speaks the unspoken, and the unspeakable, by way of thoughtful speech (*WL* 188). *"Language speaks as the peal of stillness,"* Heidegger observes. "Only as men belong within the peal of stillness are mortals able to speak in *their own* way in sounds" (*PLT* 207–8). By sheltering the unspoken and hidden, poetic-philosophic language allows us to appropriate the difference of Being and beings. It is expressive of truth not by way of a logic, nor by way of the causality implicit in its syntax, nor even by way of the (representational) accuracy of its semantics. Rather, poetic-philosophic language constitutes both the physical vibration that evidences what is and, by way of the unbridgeable chasm separating words and things, the abstract symbol that gestures at the nothingness (Being) that infuses being.

Language, physical yet abstract, resonant yet symbolic, discloses difference by way of this twofold nature. "For language," Heidegger writes, "is the most delicate and thus most susceptible vibration holding everything within the suspended structure of the appropriation. We dwell in the appropriation inasmuch as our active nature is given over to language" (*ID* 38). To give oneself over to art or science or music or love is to dwell in its capacity for truth. Philosophy, most fundamentally, gives itself over to language. And to be given over to language is to let language speak us, as witnesses to difference, at least as much as we speak language.

Poetic-philosophic discourse cannot guarantee the invocation of difference, for philosophy is never self-sufficient. "In order to exist, everything genuine needs semblance," Heidegger observes. "There is neither a philosophy, in all its purity, nor a sophistry with a complete monopoly. Both belong together in a particular historical 'culture' which is possible in many diverse ways" (*MFL* 212). All ontological invocation inevitably rides on the coattails of metaphors and representational concepts. Philosophy is the amalgam of ontological and common speech as it exists within particular cultures. Common speech does not reach beyond the instrumental use of language. Because common speech does not question profoundly, it cannot affirm the profoundly questionable. Because common speech does not acknowledge the Being of beings, it cannot utter difference. Common speech is philosophy's foil.

Still, there is nothing wrong with common speech per se. It is an intricate and indispensable part of human life. What is dangerous is the tendency of common speech to mold and constrain thought as a whole. The threat is not only that language would become overtly constrained by a restricted lexicon or syntax, which, like Orwellian Newspeak, would make philosophical inquiry difficult or impossible. More insidious is the deprivation mediated through the moods or states of mind that common speech induces. That is, the manner in which we are in the world is largely regulated by language. Referring to common speech as "idle talk" (*Gerede*), Heidegger illustrates this relationship among one's speech, mood, and world. He writes: "Idle talk is the possibility of understanding everything without previously making the thing one's own. . . . The fact that something has been said groundlessly, and then gets passed along in further retelling, amounts to perverting the act of disclosing. . . . Thus, by its very nature, idle talk is a closing-off, since to go back to the ground of what is talked about is something which it *leaves undone*. . . . The dominance of the public way in which things have been interpreted has already been decisive even for the possibilities of having a mood—that is, for the basic way in which Dasein lets the world 'matter' to it. The 'they' prescribes one's state-of-mind, and determines what and how one 'sees'" (*BT* 213). To speak is to elicit a particular way of Being-in-the-world. To speak is to summon a mood. One's mood, in turn, will restrict the way in which the world comes to be experienced, linguistically and otherwise. Language discloses who and how we are in the world, primarily by way of the moods it summons and sustains. "Anemic" speech, Heidegger observes, will yield anemic thoughts, eventually leaving one in a state of ontological enervation.

The philosophical invocation of difference, Heidegger acknowledges, emerges in the midst of a pervasive culture of common speech. Hence philosophic speech is forever in danger of being colonized by it. Unfortunately, Heidegger would not readily admit the obverse, and equally evident, relation: common speech is always susceptible to the outbreak of ontological insight. Everyday speech may escape its own strictures of instrumental communication to invoke difference. Idle talk, defined by its unwillingness to ground itself in the questionableness of Being, retains the potential to deconstruct itself. This unpredictable and uncontrollable aspect of common speech is largely ignored by Heidegger. To be sure, the (self-)interrogation of *das Man* occurs in limited fashion. And when it does erupt, utilitarian language generally reestablishes itself quickly enough on the firm ground of opinion and belief. But language's capacity to witness difference is thereby neither eradicated nor exhausted. It simply has slipped away, temporarily overpowered by common speech and thought, only to reassert itself at a later time and place. Words are wellsprings, and their instrumental use cannot completely contain their ontological seepage.

The rich and unpredictable potential of language to invoke the Being of being precludes its neat bifurcation into the philosophic and the nonphilosophic. Freedom in speech may be exercised wherever and whenever words are spoken. There are no generic discriminations that might justify ontological dismissal of entire genres of speech. One can only listen intently for the echo of difference, whether in the novel or the poem, the philosophic text or the sidewalk conversation. Despite Heidegger's reluctance to acknowledge this point, his admonition that we nurture an openness to Being implicitly solicits from us an openness to (others') speech wherever and whenever it occurs. "Listening to," Heidegger affirms, "is Dasein's existential way of Being-open as Being-with for Others" (*BT* 206). With this in mind, the unpredictable potential of freedom in speech may provide a defense for freedom of speech. The justly hallowed right to free speech might be grounded not only in the speaker's prerogative to utter opinions and beliefs, but also in the listener's duty to remain open to, even solicitous of, the ontological difference these opinions and beliefs may harbor. Additionally grounded in this duty, the political right to free speech would be less likely to degenerate into a mere license for noisemaking. For the limitations to the duty of listening (though not to the prerogative of speaking) become evident whenever speech refuses to interrogate the foundations of opinion and belief.

This refusal of self-interrogation is often based on the assumption that the important thing is to have opinions rather than remain open to their questioning. Herein opinions effectively become a form of private property, chattels whose possession, control, and proliferation become ends in themselves. Freedom of speech reduces itself to another form of the possessive mastery of language: the right to say whatever one wants, how one wants, whenever and wherever one wants. The point is not that this right should be forsworn. Our right to make willful use of language is not the danger, nor is our valuing language for its usefulness. The danger arises when we identify the freedom experienced in speech solely with the power to vocalize and manipulate sundry opinions and beliefs, for at this point we become deaf to language that is beyond use and valuation.

Heideggerese and the Gift of Language

A mystic is someone who considers language and communication not only insufficient but generally a hindrance to the unmediated perception of truth. Given Heidegger's depreciation of common speech, his celebration of the poetry of silence, and his criticism of linguistic pragmatism, the charge of mysticism looms large.[7] In the end, however, Heidegger's devotion to the shared, worldly nature of language saves him from this charge.

Truth, for Heidegger, always occurs within the context of worldly disclosure. And this disclosure is grounded in an extraordinary way by the human capacity for speech. Speech, in turn, is always shared. Therefore the perception of truth is for Heidegger facilitated rather than hindered by speech and communication. We may at any particular time converse only with ourselves, as we do in silent thought. But that is not to deny the shared nature of language. Rather, it is to acknowledge our capacity to extend this sharing to ourselves. Heidegger writes that "the very sense of any discourse is *discourse to others and with others*. It therefore makes no difference for the essential structure of discourse whether a fixed address directed to a specific other is of current interest or not" (*HCT* 263). In speaking, regardless of its purpose or form, we silently acknowledge our worldly Being-with. Being-in-the-world-with-others is the unavoidable subtext of any traffic with words. For Heidegger, we may share in truth only because we share in language.

Despite these indications that Heidegger does not deprecate the linguistic access to truth, one cannot ignore the mystic-poetic nature of Heidegger's own writings. John Caputo describes the problem, observing that the difference between Heidegger and certain other philosophers, such as Kant and Wittgenstein, is that "instead of merely talking about the limits of philosophy, Heidegger has in fact attempted to *traverse* these limits. He has not merely described certain limits on philosophical discourse; he has indeed undertaken to create and speak

[7] Bernd Magnus writes, in a not uncommon judgment, that "the author of *Being and Time* yields to mysticism in the end." Magnus, *Heidegger's Metahistory of Philosophy*, 141.

a non-philosophical, or post-philosophical, language, a language which borrows much from the poets, mystics, and mystic-poets."[8] Caputo's account is accurate enough, given a crucial emendation: we must substitute "experience" for "traverse" in reference to Heidegger's philosophic effort. Heidegger's project is to philosophize in a way that allows one to experience, but not traverse or transgress, human horizons.[9] Still, an important point remains: Heidegger is not interested in conceptually describing these philosophic limits, as Kant and Wittgenstein do, but in experiencing them directly. In turn, he is interested in describing this experience, and in so doing Heidegger necessarily pushes his philosophic discourse into what might fairly be called mystic-poetic forms.

Heidegger acknowledges the affinity of his writings to those of the mystics, particularly to the works of Meister Eckhardt. This affinity is in itself unproblematic so long as the worldly and shared nature of language, and the linguistically mediated access to truth, are maintained. The difficulty arises if the attempt to escape conceptual and representational language results in the endowment of particular words such as *Being* with totemistic powers. Heidegger was not immune to this enchantment, but he did advocate its resistance. His writing of Being as ~~Being~~ was an attempt to defuse the linguistic totemism that threatens to usurp the philosophical effort to speak questioningly. Heidegger himself explicitly warns that "we must avoid uninhibited word-mysticism." But any specific defense against accusations of mysticism, he admits, would be "both superfluous and useless" (*HPS* 99). In ridding oneself of a particular locution in order to deny its magical powers, one is faced with the need to supply another, equally indefensible locution to do its work. Meanwhile, as this semantic cat-and-mouse game proceeds, the fundamental questioning that philosophic language fosters would lapse. Heidegger's alternative is to acknowledge the threat of totemism with the gesture of erasure and proceed apace. Heidegger is known well enough for his creation of an idiosyncratic philosophical vocabulary. More significant, however, is his ongoing retrieval from ordinary words of their profound and manifold resonances. For Heidegger "the ultimate business of philosophy is to preserve the *force of the most elemental words* in which Dasein expresses itself" (*BT* 262). *Being* is such a word, and, in some form or other, it proves indispensable.[10]

---

[8] Caputo, *Mystical Element in Heidegger's Thought*, 260.

[9] For a general discussion of this theme, see Joan Stambaugh, *The Finitude of Being* (Albany: State University of New York Press, 1992).

[10] In an attempt to avoid Heidegger's linguistic totemism, Thomas Sheehan suggests that "Being" (*Sein*) simply be removed from our lexicon and "forgotten" (in a paper and discussion at the annual meeting of the American Political Science Association, Chicago, 1992). Unfortunately, Sheehan could offer no viable substitute. Nor could he escape Hei-

Richard Rorty describes Heidegger's tenacious effort to identify language with the disclosure of Being as a religious retreat into revelation and thus as a "failure of nerve" in the face of postmodern life. "Heideggerese is only Heidegger's gift to us," Rorty quips, "not Being's gift to Heidegger."[11] On the contrary, Heideggerese, idiosyncratic as it certainly is, may fairly be described as Being's gift to Heidegger. But this is only to say that each person, in his or her own way and time, may receive such a gift. This gift is given whenever one speaks with that "originality, rigor, and measure in words" that testifies to one's historical being as a discloser of Being. To acknowledge that difference erupts in language is not to retreat into religous revelation. Rather, it is to advance past the constricted perspective that finds no means to describe the experience of the transcendent otherwise than as theistic.

Abandoning resonant ontological speech in order to escape accusations of religious mysticism constitutes the true "failure of nerve." In avoiding this speech, we might indeed produce a uniformly accessible language. Our language, as a reservoir of word-signs, would then make itself wholly available for transactions and trade of the greatest efficiency. We would have achieved a technological ordering of language befitting our technological ordering of the world. But the cost of such an enterprise would be high indeed. "Man has already begun to overwhelm the entire earth and its atmosphere, to arrogate to himself in forms of energy the concealed powers of nature, and to submit future history to the planning and ordering of a world government," Heidegger writes ominously. He continues, "This same defiant man is utterly at a loss simply to say what *is;* to say *what* this *is*—that a thing *is*" (*EGT* 57). Excusing ourselves from participation in the enigma of Being, we court the danger of leaving ourselves nothing but technological means to accomplish philosophical ends. The loss Heidegger observes amounts to the loss of human dignity, for human dignity consists in the full exercise of human freedom, and a crucial element of this freedom is manifest in speech that discloses what is. Only in exercising this freedom, which constitutes a "bearing witness," do we truly undertake "the affirmation of human existence" (*EB* 274–75). The gift of language is the gift of freedom. The tragic irony is that our attempt to possess and master this gift signals its loss.

---

degger's charge that all such attempts ultimately come to neglect fundamental questioning.

[11] Rorty, "Wittgenstein," 353.

Six

Freedom in Deed

> Andrea: Unhappy the land that has no heroes.
> Galileo: No, unhappy the land that needs
> heroes.
> (Bertolt Brecht, *Leben des Galilei*)

THE RELATIONSHIP of philosophy to politics poses a perennial problem. Max Weber, who approached the issue with much insight, aptly described politics as the "slow boring of hard boards." Throughout history, efforts to transform philosophic theory into practice would be turned awry by the resistant and exacting nature of political reality. Aristophanes portrays philosophy (suspended in the clouds with Socrates) as having little to do with politics, except perhaps to endanger it. Plato's ill-fated trips to Syracuse in the early fourth century appear as one of the first direct rebuffs of a philosopher who would attempt to foist ideals on the world. Perhaps the most infamous recent example of the unlucky marriage of philosophy and politics is Martin Heidegger's stint as a university rector under National Socialism. The historical continuity of the problem itself is best illustrated by a Freiburg colleague who, coming across Heidegger in a streetcar shortly after he resigned his post, remarked sarcastically: "Back from Syracuse, Herr Heidegger?"[1] In light of this problem and its historical persistence, the purpose of this chapter is twofold. First, it reiterates a historically demonstrable truth in the context of Heidegger's life—that philosophy cannot serve as an immunization against undesirable politics. Second, and more importantly, it demonstrates that Heidegger's philosophy neither leads inevitably to fascism nor remains politically impotent. Indeed, Heidegger's philosophic work offers support for an original theorization of a postmodern politics with democratic import. This theorization will be structured by an examination of the relation of politics to art, a relation that was of key concern to Heidegger and, since antiquity, has largely defined the association of philosophy and politics. The relationship between politics and art has always been a treacherous one. But the dan-

---

[1] See Hans-Georg Gadamer, "Zurück von Syrakus?" in *Die Heidegger Kontroverse*, ed. Jürg Altwegg (Frankfurt am Main: Athenaeum, 1988), 179.

ger chiefly arises out of the philosophic misconstrual of the meaning of art, a misconstrual already apparent in Platonic thought, and one temporarily embraced by Heidegger.

Philosophy and Political Biography

At the outset of any attempt to relate Heidegger's philosophy to questions of politics, certain features of Heidegger's life demand voice. My intent here is not to save Heidegger from his own biography, or to exonerate him in spite of it, but to think through him into an explicitly political realm. Biographical discussion serves simply to prepare the reader so that she may approach the subsequent arguments with a fresh recollection of a historical background that should never be obscured, however one chooses to mesh its reality with a philosophic or political project.

In May 1933, Heidegger accepted the post of rector of Freiburg University and became one of the small number of university professors to join the Nazi Party. Heidegger claims (*OGS* 46), and his claim is largely supported by his former students and colleagues, that until he accepted the position of rector he had no involvement and little interest in political affairs. Then came his call to Syracuse. Heidegger appears to have been convinced that Hitler could bring social harmony and spiritual renewal to the German people.[2] His acceptance of an administrative role at the university within the Nazi regime is perhaps best understood as an expression of Heidegger's hope to lead the leader (*den Führer führen*) of the Third Reich. He wanted to provide Hitler and his political movement with a philosopher and a philosophic foundation.[3]

Heidegger contemptuously rejected the Nazis' biologically based racism, and he was critical of certain of the party's high-ranking ideologues such as Bäumler, Krieck, and Rosenberg. But these disagreements were downplayed, presumably because of Heidegger's belief that Nazism

---

[2] "In regard to 1933," Heidegger later wrote, "I expected from National Socialism a spiritual rejuvenation of all life, a reconciliation of social antagonisms, and the rescue of Western existence from the danger of communism." Quoted in Victor Farias, *Heidegger and Nazism* (Philadelphia: Temple University Press, 1989), 284.

[3] As Richard Rorty observes, "the sort of leader Heidegger had in mind in his constantly repeated invocation of 'the leaders and protectors of the destiny of the German people' was not Hitler, but himself. The rectorial address puts forward, in entire seriousness, the claim that only Heideggerian philosophy can bring the universities into the service of this destiny. One cannot exaggerate the degree to which Heidegger took philosophy, and himself, seriously." Richard Rorty, "Taking Philosophy Seriously," *New Republic*, April 11, 1988, 31.

would foster a needed national resurgence.[4] Hence during his short tenure as rector, Heidegger toed, with certain hedgings, the Nazi line. He
condemned academic freedom and attacked the university's liberal constitution. Though he resisted certain of its demands, he was for the most
part an avid spokesperson for the regime's Gleichschaltung, or stream-
lining of academic and cultural life to party and state purposes.[5] In this
role, he intrigued against and informed on certain of his colleagues,
imperiling their careers.[6] Many of his rectorial speeches read like so
much Nazi propaganda.[7] And some of his lectures from this period displayed a hybridization of philosophy and politics that, in the words of a

[4] As Philippe Lacoue-Labarthe writes, for Heidegger "it was worth putting up with a
little bit of racism to see the movement victorious: anti-semitism was simply regarded as
an incidental cost." Philippe Lacoue-Labarthe, *Heidegger, Art, and Politics: The Fiction
of the Political,* trans. Chris Turner (Oxford: Basil Blackwell, 1990), 33. Karl Moehling
identifies Heidegger's position in similar fashion: "Thus Heidegger was both attracted to
and repelled by Nazism. He was put in what he called 'a middle position' of believing in
the social and national ideas of the movement while rejecting its essential racism." Karl
Moehling, "Heidegger and the Nazis," in *Heidegger: The Man and the Thinker,* ed.
Thomas Sheehan (Chicago: Precedent, 1981), 36. Heidegger was not above opportunisti-
cally conspiring against Jews on occasion, though he reserved the most vicious slurs of his
political period for Catholics. See Hugo Ott, *Martin Heidegger: A Political Life,* trans.
Allan Blunden (New York: Basic Books, 1993), 246.

[5] Heidegger, in a speech delivered in 1933, spoke of the need for the university to be
"integrated again into the Volksgemeinschaft and be *joined together with the State."* Martin Heidegger, "Political Texts, 1933–34," *New German Critique* 45 (Fall 1988): 100.
He also expressed his eagerness to cooperate with the *Gleichschaltung* in a personal tele-
gram to Hitler. And Karl Löwith remembers that "the students in Berlin demanded that
all the other universities follow the example of '*Gleichschaltung*' practiced in Freiburg."
Löwith, "Political Implications of Heidegger's Existentialism," 124.

[6] Heidegger once commissioned a junior lecturer as a confidential agent to gather evidence needed to dismiss a fellow Freiburg professor. See Ott, *Martin Heidegger,* 219.

[7] In 1933, for example, Heidegger gave a number of impassioned speeches in support of
Hitler's proposal to withdraw from the League of Nations (not the United Nations, as
Michael Zimmerman anachronistically states. Michael Zimmerman, *Heidegger's Confrontation with Modernity: Technology, Politics, Art* (Bloomington: Indiana University
Press, 1990), 68. The tone and vocabulary of these speeches were thoroughly nazified, as
may be seen in the following example: "All faculties of will and thought, all strengths of
the heart and all skills of the body, must be unfolded through battle, heightened in battle,
and preserved as battle" (*SAG* 479). Notwithstanding the inflammatory rhetoric, I agree
with Frank Edler's argument that Heidegger's intent was not to mimic Nazi ideologues
but to manipulate their one-dimensional speech so as to infuse it with philosophic import.
"Heidegger appropriated certain Nazi street words," Edler writes, "in order to redefine
and transform the meaning of these terms. . . . Heidegger thought he could guide the
revolution by stealing the language out from under the noses of Nazi ideologues." Heidegger's aim, Edler concludes with some merit, was "to guide the revolution toward that
decision of reenacting the origin of Greek philosophy." Frank Edler, "Philosophy, Language, and Politics: Heidegger's Attempt to Steal the Language of the Revolution in
1933–34," *Social Research* 57 (1990): 205, 227, 238.

former student, left one wondering whether one was being encouraged to read the pre-Socratics or join the party. As the September 1945 report of the Denazification Commission states, "there can be no doubt that in the crucial year of 1933 Heidegger consciously placed the full weight of his academic reputation and the distinctive art of his oratory in the service of the National Socialist revolution, and thereby did a great deal to justify this revolution in the eyes of educated Germans, to raise the hopes people had placed in it, and to make it much more difficult for German science and scholarship to maintain its independence amidst the political upheaval."[8]

Unwilling to carry out the command of a government minister to remove two deans and make new appointments loyal to the party, Heidegger resigned the rectorate in the spring of 1934, less than a year after assuming the position. His judgment and decision were reinforced within months. The Night of Long Knives of June 30, 1934, which marked the demise of Ernst Röhm's storm troopers, constituted for Heidegger a turning point in the Nazi movement. The confusions, limitations, and dangers of Nazism were becoming apparent.[9] But Heidegger's resignation of the rectorate represents a double disillusionment. Heidegger had not only become suspicious of the Nazi regime by 1934, but had also become increasingly frustrated with his own failure to garner authority within the university, and perhaps within the party and the state.[10] Not only did the revolution appear to be taking a wrong turn, but Heidegger had also failed to secure a position from which philosophy might speak authoritatively to power.[11]

Heidegger would come to defend his actions and decisions as rector to the postwar French occupational forces, who nonetheless eventually barred him from teaching (until the winter semester of 1950–51) and whose inquisition landed him in a sanatorium with a nervous breakdown. Heidegger also defended himself to certain of his former students and colleagues, and occasionally to the media. In these apologies, Heidegger unwaveringly claims to have taken on the rectorate to protect

[8] Quoted in Ott, *Martin Heidegger*, 327.

[9] Heidegger wrote that "anyone who after that still assumed an administrative office in the university was in a position to know beyond the shadow of a doubt, with whom he was bargaining" (*SAG* 499).

[10] This failure was in part due to an anti-Heidegger faction that by the spring of 1934 had emerged within the Nazi Party. Led by Ernst Krieck and Heidegger's former Marburg colleague Erich Jaensch, this faction characterized Heidegger's philosophy as obsessed with "hairsplitting distinctions" and equated it with Talmudic thought. Ott, *Martin Heidegger*, 256–57.

[11] Reflecting on the situation in 1937, Heidegger laments that one of his "biggest mistakes" was his effort to approach a government ministry with truly "creative demands and ambitious goals." Ibid., 375.

the university from external control. This protection, he maintains, could only be offered from a position of authority, and therefore he was obliged to join the party. Much of what he said and wrote at the time, Heidegger insists, constituted only those "compromises" that needed to be made were he to retain the power and prerogative to safeguard the university.[12] Despite making such compromises, Heidegger claims never to have maintained any personal or political relations with party functionaries (*SAG* 486). Many of these aforementioned claims are justly disputed by Heidegger's critics and biographers. They are at most, beyond any interpretive generosity, half-truths. Some are flatly false. In any case, Heidegger continued, albeit less actively, to support the movement long after the spring of 1934, and he maintained his party membership until the dissolution of the Reich.[13] Many of his lectures well into the 1940s reaffirmed support, despite voiced misgivings, for Germany's historical effort at national resurgence. In short, Heidegger was an active and avid Nazi while rector, and a more passive supporter of the movement, if not the regime, until the end of the war. Even in his postwar writings, Heidegger maintains his attachment to what he had earlier (in 1935) called the "inner truth and greatness" of National Socialism, defined as "the encounter between global technology and modern man" (*IM* 199). In a 1966 interview (posthumously published), he stated: "I see the situation of man in the world of planetary technicity not as an inextricable and inescapable destiny, but I see the task of thought precisely in this, that within its own limits it helps man as such

[12] Heidegger claims that it was "only in the interest of the university" that he joined the Nazi Party: "What moved me especially was the possibility, pointed out by canon Sauer, that, should I refuse, outsiders would impose a rector" (*SAG* 493, 483). Moehling accepts this apology, and goes on to quote Heidegger from his letter to the denazification committee: "It was never my intention to deliver the university to the party doctrine but, conversely, to attempt from within National Socialism and while having a point of reference to it to bring about a spiritual change in its development" Moehling, "Heidegger and the Nazis," 33. An excerpt from Heidegger's 1966 interview illustrates these points: "Spiegel: You said in the fall of 1933: 'Let not doctrines and ideas be the rules of your Being. The Führer, himself and he alone, is today and for the future German actuality and its law.' Heidegger: . . . When I took over the rectorate, it was clear to me that I would not survive without compromises. The sentences you quote I would no longer write today. Such things as that I stopped saying by 1934" (*OGS* 49).

[13] For example, former student Karl Löwith reports that in a 1936 meeting, Heidegger "left no doubt about his belief in Hitler. . . . He was convinced now as before that National Socialism was the right course for Germany; one only had to 'hold out' long enough. The only aspect that troubled him was the ceaseless 'organization' at the expense of 'vital forces'." Karl Löwith, "My Last Meeting with Heidegger," *New German Critique* 45 (Fall 1988): 115–16. And in May 1938, local party officials in Freiburg, apart from noting his flagging financial contributions, recorded that Heidegger remained "an exemplary Party member." Ott, *Martin Heidegger*, 374.

achieve a satisfactory relationship to the essence of technicity. National Socialism did indeed go in this direction. Those people, however, were far too poorly equipped for thought to arrive at a really explicit relationship to what is happening today and has been underway for the past 300 years" (OGS 61). Heidegger never fully repudiated his involvement with Nazism, and stubbornly remained convinced of its erstwhile potential. He could not abandon the quixotic belief that he might have equipped for philosophic thought a movement that displayed the political power to mobilize an entire people.

Heidegger does make certain attempts in his philosophic writing, albeit indirect and irresolute ones, to distance himself from the regime that, by the mid-1930s, had largely displaced the movement in which he originally had placed his hopes. While admitting that he voiced no "specific attacks" on the Nazis after his resignation as rector, Heidegger suggests that such attacks were unnecessary. It sufficed, he claims, to express his "fundamental philosophical positions" against the "dogmatism and primitivism" of the Nazi ideologues: "Since National Socialist ideology became increasingly inflexible and increasingly less disposed to a purely philosophical interpretation, the fact that I was active as a philosopher was itself a sufficient expression of opposition."[14] Heidegger locates this philosophic opposition chiefly in the prewar years following his resignation as rector, claiming that already in his 1936 lectures on Nietzsche, "All who could hear at all heard this as a confrontation with National Socialism" (OGS 53). Heidegger's critical distance from the Nazis' racist and imperialist ambitions also appears, for example, couched in his 1938 lecture course, which resulted in the publication of "The Age of the World Picture." Here Heidegger attacks the subjectivism of Enlightenment rationalism no less than "the planetary imperialism of technologically organized man" who "grasps himself as a nation, wills himself as a people, fosters himself as a race, and, finally, empowers himself as lord of the earth" (QT 152). And again, in his 1939 lecture course on Nietzsche, Heidegger would implicitly criticize Nazism in his condemnation of the technological values propagated around him: " 'values,' utterly transformed into calculable items, are the only ideals that still function for machination: culture and cultural values as grist for the mill of propaganda, art products as serviceable objects—at exhibitions of our achievements and as decorations for parade floats" (WPK 182). Finally, we hear in his wartime lecture, veiled in a confrontation with Nietzsche, Heidegger's admission that National

[14] Martin Heidegger, "Letter to the Rector of Freiburg University, November 4, 1945," in *The Heidegger Controversy: A Critical Reader,* ed. Richard Wolin (New York: Columbia University Press, 1991), 64.

Socialism had radically betrayed his hopes through its crass celebration
of a workers' and soldiers' state. It had become the technological nem-
esis of his philosophic aspirations: "In Nietzsche's notes the terms
'worker' and 'soldier' and 'socialism' are already the designation for the
crucial agency of the chief forms of the execution of the Will to Power!
. . . But do the 'workers' and 'soldiers,' by virtue of their experience,
also know the Being of being? No; yet, perhaps they no longer need to
know this. Perhaps from time immemorial the Being of being has never
been experienced by those who directly shape, produce and represent
beings" (G 51:37, 39). There is, then, undoubtedly some truth to
Heidegger's claim that his "debate with Nietzsche's metaphysics is a
debate with *nihilism* as it manifests itself with increased clarity under
the political form of fascism."[15] Yet this debate is hardly an open contestation. It more closely resembles a muffled complaint of betrayal.

Heidegger's "confrontation" with National Socialism coincides with
the "turn," or Kehre, in his philosophy. His retreat from politicized
philosophy finds him increasingly rejecting, and securing substitutes for,
the voluntarism, decisionism, and willful subjectivism rife in fascist ideology, persistent in metaphysics and more complexly intrinsic to Nietzsche's thought. Heidegger would eventually come to equate the "total
state" as the height of technological dominance, while the "arbitrariness
of 'dictators' and 'authoritarian states'" would be identified as "the
most proximate impulse and staging ground for the realization of the
metaphysical will of modern world history" (G 51:18). We thus witness
his effective if not explicit acknowledgment that his earlier political adventures were symptomatic of the disease his philosophy seeks to cure.
Heidegger's postwar writings on technology generally substantiate this
claim.[16]

Yet Heidegger's debate with Nietzsche often also serves scandalously
to depreciate the significance of the Nazis' brutality. Writing in the
midst of the war, Heidegger suggests that "the value-thinking of the
metaphysics of the will to power is murderous in a most extreme sense,
because it absolutely does not let Being itself take its rise, i.e., come into

[15] Ibid., 65.

[16] Aware of this feature of Heidegger's corpus (but having Nietzsche play quite a different role than I have cast him in), Reiner Schürmann proposes that we derive our politics
by reading Heidegger in reverse, critically engaging his earlier writing through the lens of
his later work. If, for the sake of argument, we accept the legitimacy of Schürmann's
methodological tactic, we may then extract from Heidegger an argument for an "economy
of presencing" unconstrained by an overarching principle. The result, an anarchic praxis
in a "plural economy," is antipodal to fascism. Schürmann's thesis is not that Heidegger's
philosophy leaves us no alternative but anarchic praxis. But its derivation, he claims, is
born of a Heideggerian impulse. Schürmann, *Heidegger on Being and Acting*, esp. 13,
282, 290, 295.

the vitality of its essence" (QT 108). The phrase "murderous in a most extreme sense" cries out to be restricted to the totalitarian venture that Heidegger himself had once encouraged and that at the time was wreaking havoc in the world. When we read that "blindness in the face of the extreme need of Being, in the form of the needlessness that prevails in the midst of crowds of beings, is still more hazardous than the crass adventures of a merely brutal will to violence" (N 247), one cannot excuse the callousness of Heidegger's "merely" in the context of the Nazis' ruthless extermination of millions of innocent victims.

In light of Heidegger's initially avid support for Nazism and the irresoluteness of his subsequent criticisms and retractions, a significant number of Heidegger's critics insist that his fascistic tendencies cannot be separated from his philosophy, that indeed the former follows necessarily from the latter. This position has been rearticulated periodically since the end of the war, each time creating something of a controversy.[17] Karl Löwith's 1939 polemic, republished in 1946, served up the first installment of the "Heidegger debate." Löwith substantiates the claim that Heidegger's philosophy was essentially related to his politics with a recollection of Heidegger's own words. At a 1936 meeting in Rome, Löwith suggested to Heidegger that "his partisanship for National Socialism lay in the essence of his philosophy," and reports: "Heidegger agreed with me without reservation, and added that his concept of 'historicity' was the basis of his political 'engagement.'"[18] A quarter of a century later, Theodor Adorno would reaffirm that Heidegger's philosophy was "fascist right down to its innermost components."[19] For Adorno, the innermost components of Heidegger's philosophy included the very "language of authenticity" that structured it.[20] More recently, Victor Farias achieved some notoriety in France by instigating yet another outbreak of the controversy with the publication of Heidegger et le Nazism. Farias attempts to substantiate the rootedness of Heidegger's thought in Nazism with a twofold strategy. First, he details Heidegger's extensive dealings with the Nazi regime. Second, he argues that Heidegger exhibited a long-standing (philosophic) relation to fascist ideology from his earliest days, long before the Nazis rose to power. On the crest of this latest wave of accusation, Richard Wolin

[17] Emil Kettering identifies seven "phases" of the controversy from 1946 to the late 1980s. Guenther Neske and Emil Kettering, Martin Heidegger and National Socialism: Questions and Answers, trans. Lisa Harries (New York: Paragon House, 1990), 127–32.
[18] Löwith, "My Last Meeting with Heidegger," 115.
[19] Diskus, January 1963, cited in Richard Bernstein, The New Constellation: The Ethical-Political Horizons of Modernity/Postmodernity (Cambridge, Mass.: MIT Press, 1991), 81.
[20] Adorno, Jargon of Authenticity, 197.

reasserts that "Heidegger's Nazi experience stood in an 'essential' relation to his philosophical project as a whole," and that his "involvement
with National Socialism—which was of the order of deep-seated, existential commitment—was far from being an adventitious, merely biographical episode. Instead, it was *rooted in the innermost tendencies of
his thought.*"[21] None of these critics suggests that Heidegger's philosophy was merely a facade for his politics. But many argue that it
amounts to the other side of the coin. As Pierre Bourdieu maintains, the
"social unconscious" speaks through all philosophy and in Heidegger's
work the conservative revolution achieved its "structural equivalent."[22]

I believe these assertions to be mistaken. Heidegger's philosophy, to
be sure, remains susceptible to fascistic interpretation. And Heidegger,
one must acknowledge, failed or simply refused to rally his philosophy
for antifascistic purposes. Nevertheless, along with many of Heidegger's
most incisive readers, such as Hannah Arendt, Hans-Georg Gadamer,
Jacques Derrida, Phillipe Lacoue-Labarthe, Jean-François Lyotard, and
Richard Rorty, one ought not attempt to shackle Heidegger's philosophy to his Nazi past. No truly philosophic corpus is reducible to a singular politics. There are no necessary or straightforward political ramifications of writings as rich and deep as those of Heidegger. We do a
great disservice to philosophy and ourselves if our revulsion at Heidegger's speeches and actions of the 1930s and 1940s prevent us from exploring the full dimensions of his work. When all is said and done,
Heideggerian philosophy is importantly Socratic. Heidegger is a gadfly
worrying the steed of contemporary Western society. In this respect,
Heidegger is a cultural critic, and his philosophy, like Socrates', is an
interminable questioning that assails cognitive and behavioral conventions. But the worldly nature of his philosophy does not legitimate its
reduction to a specific political program—revolutionary, reactionary, or
otherwise.

Heidegger, in an essentially Socratic statement, insists that approaching an understanding of human being's relation to Being has as its prerequisite the abandonment of all beliefs, attitudes, and worldviews that
presume firm political knowledge (*KPM* 245). Yet Heidegger, in embracing Nazi dogma, escaped the burden of this philosophic skepsis.
Still, the attempt to bind Heidegger's general philosophy to Nazism is
only slightly less worrisome than the attempt to shackle Socrates'
thought to the despotic exploits of those with whom he fraternized,

---

[21] Wolin, *Politics of Being*, 8, 66.
[22] Pierre Bourdieu, *The Political Ontology of Martin Heidegger* (Stanford: Stanford
University Press, 1991), 104–5.

namely Alcibiades or the leaders of the Thirty Tyrants.[23] At the same time, we might say that Heidegger attempted to serve as his own Plato, putting into word and, for a brief period, into deed what by disposition he could only properly think. With this parallel in mind, Hannah Arendt writes rather apologetically of her former teacher: "Now we all know that Heidegger, too, once succumbed to the temptation to change his 'residence' [the abode of thinking] and to get involved in the world of human affairs. As to the world, he was served somewhat worse than Plato, because the tyrant and his victims were not located beyond the sea, but in his own country. . . . [But] the attraction to the tyrannical can be demonstrated theoretically in many of the great thinkers."[24] Arendt's Platonic comparison solicits further reflection. Heidegger's grave error may be traced, despite his unending attacks on metaphysics, to his adoption and historicization of a Platonic conception of art and his partaking of a rather un-Platonic, but typically Greek, chauvinism. More specifically, the "attraction to the tyrannical" that Arendt observes in philosophers in general, and in Heidegger in particular, may be traced back to the Platonic aestheticization of politics. This argument is best introduced not by examining more of the words and deeds that mark Heidegger's involvement in "the world of human affairs," but by investigating his effort to shirk the responsibility of its expiation.

Heidegger's Silence

Heidegger's work is saddled with a number of political liabilities. The charges most difficult to parry for his commentators, however, are perhaps not those that stem from Heidegger's political intrigues of the 1930s and 1940s. Many otherwise respectable Germans were swept up in the rise of Nazism. We may resolutely condemn and yet understand their error. In this light, it is not what Heidegger said, wrote and did during his twelve-month rectorate or his twelve-year party membership, but what he left unsaid, unwritten, and undone in the three decades following the fall of the Third Reich that remains most damning. Until the end of his days, Heidegger maintained an unconscionable public

[23] Socrates would eventually be put at risk by his falling out of favor with Critias and Charmides when they took their part in (and the former actually led) the Thirty Tyrants. One wonders whether Socrates' refusal as leader of the boule to carry out the executions ordered by the Tyrants was in Heidegger's mind when he resigned the rectorate because of his own unwillingness to carry out the academic dismissals demanded by the party.

[24] Hannah Arendt, "Martin Heidegger at Eighty," in Murray, *Heidegger and Modern Philosophy*, 301–3.

silence regarding Nazism and its atrocities. He adamantly refused to admit, let alone atone for, his complicity. Many would severely chastise Heidegger for this "unwavering practice of denial."[25] As David Krell wrote, reflecting an increasingly common perspective, "Heidegger consigned the horrors of the Holocaust to total silence. . . . The death camps cry for painstaking thinking and writing, though not overhasty speech. And Heidegger's silence is more deafening than all the noise of his rectorship."[26]

In explaining his continuing party membership after his resignation of the rectorate, Heidegger protested that any other behavior would have placed himself and his family in grave danger. This defense reveals a lack of courage, to be sure, though with both of Heidegger's sons stationed on the Russian front,[27] perhaps a forgivable one. However, no like excuse can justify Heidegger's postwar silence. Admitting only that his allegiance to Nazism constituted "the greatest stupidity" of his life, Heidegger shows remorse for an intellectual miscalculation more than a moral or political transgression. He informed Ernst Jünger that instead of apologizing for his error, he would rather wait for Hitler to rise from the dead and beg forgiveness for misleading him.[28] Heidegger's only other explanation of his unwillingness to repent is equally damning. In response to a letter from his former student Herbert Marcuse, Heidegger wrote in January 1948: "You are totally right that I have failed to offer a public and clear confession. . . . A confession after 1945 was impossible for me, because the Nazi partisans demonstrated their change of heart in a disgusting manner, and I have nothing in common with them."[29] In postwar Germany there were, for Heidegger's taste, too many too eager to voice their condemnation of past involvements as a relatively painless means of resuscitating present opportunities. Certainly one may share Heidegger's disgust at the self-serving motivations that prompted such confessions and denouncements. But to refrain from a needful and proper act of verbal restitution, carried out with true remorse and understanding, because similar actions are too commonly undertaken in disdainful pretense is the height of arrogance and inauthenticity.

Heidegger's public silence, it turns out, was not total. With regard to

---

[25] Jürgen Habermas, "Work and *Weltanschauung*: The Heidegger Controversy from a German Perspective," in *Heidegger: A Critical Reader*, ed. H. Dreyfus and H. Hall (Cambridge: Basil Blackwell, 1992), 189.

[26] Krell, in *WPA* xii.

[27] Ott, *Martin Heidegger*, 162.

[28] *Der Spiegel*, August 18, 1986, 167.

[29] Quoted in Farias, *Heidegger and Nazism*, 285.

the Holocaust it was broken on two occasions.[30] In both cases, however, silence was exchanged for an unsanctionable response. In the Club of Bremen Lectures, originally given in 1949, Heidegger twice announced the essential equivalence of the extermination camps and other phenomena—first the motorized food industry, the blockades of East Germany, and the manufacture of hydrogen bombs, and then the perishing of millions from hunger in China.[31] The effect of these comparisons, and probably their intent, was to diminish the significance of the Nazi atrocities. The Reich's premeditated annihilation of millions in an attempted genocide is equated with sundry modern technological developments, along with the wantonly destructive effects of ideologically based politics. On other occasions Heidegger did himself further damage. Placed against the all-encompassing problem of the global will to technological mastery, fascism, Heidegger declared, was essentially indistinguishable from modern democracy. Therefore his "mistakes" as a proponent of Nazism may be judged "so insignificant that they may not even be called tiny" (*SAG* 499).

Heidegger's equations are unsustainable: not because hydrogen bombs, military blockades, and the ravages of war and social upheaval beget less destruction of human life than do explicitly fascistic politics, for they have been and may prove still to be equally (if not more) destructive; nor because one can never compare a nonmurderous act (agribusiness) to a murderous one (genocide), because such comparisons, supplemented with proper distinctions, may shed much light on the cultural undercurrents of an age that give structure and support to its social and political phenomena; nor yet because modern (state and corporate) capitalism grounds itself in something other than many of the same technological dictates as fascism, for it does. The important difference comes down to one of intentions. And this difference—between the hateful, cruel, and genocidal intentions of the Nazis and the generally irresponsible and covetous ones of agribusiness, for example—remains a far from insignificant concern.

In the past, with Kant, we might have said that intentions make all the difference in the world. Then we could simply dismiss Heidegger's feeble attempts at apology out of hand. Today, however, with the tremendous power and development of technology, this would be a facile and dangerous course to take. Heidegger's comparisons, while certainly objectionable in the ways outlined, should not be dismissed. Nazism

---

[30] In a more general context, Heidegger also referred to incarceration in wartime Germany as the "annihilation of freedom" in a 1952 lecture. Quoted in Lacoue-Labarthe, *Heidegger, Art, and Politics*, 116.

[31] See Neske and Kettering, *Martin Heidegger and National Socialism*, xxix, xxx.

was a technologically driven enterprise in which concern for the world was denied so that the lust for domination might run rampant. Agribusiness, in turn, is a technologically driven enterprise in which concern for the world is subordinated so that the lust for profit may run rampant. In each case, technological mastery overwhelms the needful relations human beings might establish with the earth and with each other.[32] Still, intentionality is of the essence here, even if it retains no monopoly on the means of evaluating human action. Heidegger's moral obtuseness is most evident in this regard, for Heidegger rarely paid attention to the significance of pain and suffering and the pervasiveness of cruelty.[33] People often recognize their humanity by way of the injuries done to it. Heidegger remains oblivious to this fact, and his philosophy, no less than his politics, suffers for it.

In speaking of technology, Heidegger referred to the "saving power" inherent in danger when it is understood as danger (*QT* 42). Unfortunately, Heidegger refused to cast the Holocaust in this light. It is not enough to condemn Nazism and its atrocities; one must seek to understand it, including what made it possible. To lose sight of this imperative and remain deaf to its call, as Heidegger did, is inexcusable. Nor is the case mitigated on account of Heidegger's unsurpassed insight into other (technological) dangers to which we are now more prone and which deserve our most attentive thinking. For in grappling with the meaning of the Holocaust, we discover its sole and inadequate redemption: the saving power that emerges in the thoughtful confrontation of all grave dangers—this being among the gravest the world has known.

---

[32] A passage from Wendell Berry, who makes no mention of Heidegger in his work, may suffice to illustrate this point: "Our leaders have been for many years as oblivious to the realities and dangers of their time as were George III and Lord North. They believe that the difference between war and peace is still the overriding political difference—when, in fact, the difference has diminished to the point of insignificance. How would you describe the difference between modern war and modern industry—between, say, bombing and strip mining, or between chemical warfare and chemical manufacturing? The difference seems to be only that in war the victimization of humans is directly intentional and in industry it is "accepted" as a "trade-off." Were the catastrophes of Love Canal, Bhopal, Chernobyl, and the Exxon Valdez episodes of war or peace? They were, in fact, peacetime acts of aggression, intentional to the extent that the risks were known and ignored. . . . Our so-called industrial accidents should be looked upon as revenges of Nature. . . . Now she is plainly saying to us: 'If you put the fates of whole communities or cities or regions or ecosystems at risk in single ships or factories or power plants, then I will furnish the drunk or the fool or the imbecile who will make the necessary small mistake.'" Wendell Berry, *What Are People For?* (San Francisco: North Point Press, 1990), 202–3.

[33] See John D. Caputo, "Heidegger, Politics, and Pain: An Interpretation of Heidegger's Development" (paper delivered at the annual meeting of the American Political Science Association, Chicago, 1992); see also Caputo, *Demythologizing Heidegger*.

What is most reprehensible in Heidegger's silence is the attempt to obscure the severity and significance of perhaps the most vicious act of calculating, organized men in human history when underlining its severity and exploring its significance remains our necessary burden. As Jacques Derrida writes, "Heidegger's horrible, perhaps inexcusable silence . . . leaves us the commandment to think what he himself did not think."[34]

In grappling with Heidegger's silence, critics and commentators have offered rather uniform explanations. The general argument runs something like this: From the lofty heights of the thought of Being, Heidegger remains oblivious to the differences between beings, in particular to the various sorts of relations human beings might establish with other beings—with artifacts, with nature, and most importantly, with one another. Heidegger subsumes all such distinctions by way of two general and mutually exclusive categories: poetic-philosophic revelation of Being, and in its absence, technological "challenging-forth." Agribusiness and extermination camps, modern fascism and bourgeois democracy, all fall into the latter category. Possibilities of human being that are not poetic-philosophic but that remain nontechnological are consistently ignored. In particular, the category of collective ethical life, the notion of a political existence that incorporates a nontechnological mode of being with the other, is lost. Heidegger's hard-and-fast dichotomy between the poetic-philosophic and the technological neglects all other ways of human being.

In this vein, Richard Bernstein argues that there are two important silences in Heidegger. The first silence is the one frequently condemned: Heidegger remained mute on the Holocaust. The second silence effectively explains the first, and is more damning from a philosophic perspective because it more clearly demonstrates Heidegger's betrayal of philosophy. Bernstein speculates that Heidegger eventually rejected politics as a topic worthy of thought after his own embarrassing involvement with the Nazis.[35] In order to justify this apoliticism, and the silence it begets, Heidegger attempted to submerge a distinguished and long-standing philosophic tradition that highlights the indelibly political nature of human being.

Central to Heidegger's writing on the technological nature of modern times is his discussion of Aristotle's notion of truth as alētheia. In the

---

[34] Jacques Derrida, "Heidegger's Silence," in Neske and Kettering, *Martin Heidegger and National Socialism,* 147.

[35] One must remark, however, that Heidegger remained silent regarding politics long before the Nazis' rise to power or his involvement with them. Similarly, Heidegger derided biographical attempts to expound philosophic doctrines before his own biography would prove such an embarrassment to his philosophy.

Nicomachean Ethics, Aristotle observes a number of ways in which alētheia may present itself to human being. Key to this discussion is Aristotle's treatment of the human capacity for practical knowledge, or
phronēsis. But this political capacity is ignored and concealed by
Heidegger, who expounds on Aristotle as if *technē* and *poiēsis* were the
only objects of concern. Bernstein writes: "*Phronēsis* is the intellectual
virtue or 'state of the soul' that pertains to *praxis,* just as *technē* relates
to *poiēsis.* . . . Throughout his essay Heidegger speaks as if there are a
plurality of modes of revealing, but he only explicitly considers two
modes: *poiēsis* (bringing-forth) and *Gestell* (challenging-forth). . . . The
entire rhetorical construction of 'The Question Concerning Technology'
seduces us into thinking that the only alternative to the threatening danger of *Gestell* is *Poiēsis.* It excludes and conceals the possible response
of *phronēsis* and *praxis.*"[36] Heidegger's silence is thus revealed as a sub-
terfuge that attempts to conceal the political ways of revealing truth
inherent in the human condition and recognized as such since Aristotle.
With politics ignored as a unique mode of human being, Heidegger easily slots the remaining possibilities into the diametrically opposed categories of poetic-philosophic thought and technological mastery.

The Fictioning of the Political

We may deepen Bernstein's insights with Philippe Lacoue-Labarthe's
critical appraisal of Heidegger's politics. Though contemptuous of all
attempts to deny the importance of Heidegger's philosophy because of
his Nazism, Lacoue-Labarthe writes that Heidegger's "commitment of
1933 is neither an accident nor an error" but a "*doing wrong.*"[37] The
wrong done, specifically, was the "offense against thought" Heidegger
committed in affiliating himself with Nazism when he knew, or should
have known, that Nazism embodied a fundamental "misapprehension
. . . regarding the essence of *technē.*"[38] This misapprehension turned the
dangerous "dream of the City as a work of art" that has linked philosophy to politics since Plato into a nightmare ending in the Holocaust.
"Auschwitz is, very precisely," Lacoue-Labarthe concludes, "the useless
residue *(le déchet)* of the Western idea of art, that is to say, of *technē.*"[39]
As such, it is "the product of a pure metaphysical decision."[40]

Lacoue-Labarthe argues that in 1933 Heidegger persuaded himself to

[36] Bernstein, *New Constellation,* 120–22.
[37] Lacoue-Labarthe, *Heidegger, Art, and Politics,* 18, 22.
[38] Ibid., 128, 110.
[39] Ibid., 46.
[40] Ibid., 48.

toe the Nazi line (and even wave its flags) in an effort to save the university from degeneration into an institute organized around technological mandates. The intent was to save science from "technicism." With the failure of the university's *Selbstbehauptung* (self-assertion), Heidegger's effort to blaze the appropriate trail for knowledge gave way to the celebration of art. Lacoue-Labarthe's thesis is that in 1935, after breaking with the Nazis, Heidegger's real politics emerged in an effort to reassert what he held to be the movement's "inner truth and greatness." At this point, National Socialism was supplanted by a "national-aestheticism" that Lacoue-Labarthe locates in the "innermost 'political' recesses" of Heidegger's discourse and that, retrospectively, displays Heidegger's earlier political commitment as "entirely consistent with his thought."[41] Nazism was a crude and distinctively modern attempt at the "aestheticization of politics." Heidegger effectively sought to better this project by disavowing the Nazis' "technicist" misapprehension of technē and returning it to its Greek origins.

Plato was the first to dream the "dream of the City as a work of art." In this dream, the philosopher-king molds the polis according to a heavenly design, crafting it into an embodiment of the Forms. Politics, for Plato, is conceived as representative art that masterfully brings the transcendent Idea down to earth. Plato thus gives birth to what Lacoue-Labarthe calls "the fiction of the political." Herein "the political belongs to the sphere of *technē* in the highest sense of the term, that is to say in the sense in which *technē* is conceived as the accomplishment and revelation of *physis* itself."[42] Plato rejected the poets' and politicians' technē of mimicking tradition and custom in order to impose a new philosophic foundation for politics. But this philosophic foundation is also imitative. Its *mimēsis*, however, is self-grounding, in the sense of not having to step out of a charmed philosophic circle, into the empirical world of tradition and custom, to achieve its ends. The republic is architectonically fashioned to mimic the Forms insofar as these are directly grasped by the philosopher-king. In turn, Plato finds it necessary to regulate or banish the poets because their art might otherwise compete with the mimetic project of philosophy. When the object of imitation is a people rather than a block of stone or a poem, and its instrument a monarch's rule rather than a chisel or a tongue, then despotism (benevolent or otherwise) is to be expected.

Heidegger's disdain for the imitative nature of convention "left him

---

[41] Ibid., 53, 19; cf. 86, 88. For all its insight, Lacoue-Labarthe's *Heidegger, Art, and Politics* is marred by inconsistencies and confusions—for instance, when the author suggests despite earlier statements that he "at no point attributes to Heidegger [a national aestheticism], as critics have tried to make out" (102). Here I must side with the critics.

[42] Ibid., 66.

an unwitting prisoner," Lacoue-Labarthe writes, of a "Platonic mimetology: that mimetology which identifies *technē* with fiction."[43] Importantly, Heidegger historicizes Plato's political technē. The mimetic task
of the movement and the führer is to fashion a national people in accordance with its historic fate. Heidegger insists, in contrast to Plato, that
there exists no temporally transcendent Idea that might gain worldly
incarnation. Nevertheless, the historical self-realization of the collective
Dasein awaits instantiation, first in the movement, then in the nation as
a whole. Despite his rejection of Plato's ahistorical notion of political
art (cf. G 65:42–43), Heidegger effectively reinstates metaphysics in his
appeal to an immanent national destiny. The Platonic mimēsis of the
Idea itself becomes mimicked in Heidegger's understanding of the
führer's historically attuned sculpting of the Volk.[44] The colleague who
greeted Heidegger after his resignation with the sarcastic reference to
Syracuse hit the nail on the head. If we understand architectonic Platonism to be defined chiefly not by its ahistoricism but by its effort to
incarnate metaphysical ideals in the political world through a masterful,
representative artistry, then Heidegger's effort at Freiburg remains eminently Platonic. In his attempt to bridge the gap between philosophy
and the political exigencies of his day, Heidegger would seek the support of ancient metaphysical foundations.

Heidegger's fictioning of the political realm is not a making of something from nothing. The political realm is fashioned out of *Blut und
Boden* (blood and soil), out of physis. The "cryptophilia" of physis, its
love of hiding, demands technē to bring about its uncovering.[45] Technē
does not so much create as represent, in the sense of making present
what lies hidden. For the Nazis and Heidegger, what lay hidden was the
genius and historic destiny of the German people. To fiction the political, a people must be conceived as a unitary and organic whole with an
identifiable developmental potential. In other words, a belief in "political *organicity*" is necessary. The nation seeking self-realization is like
the caterpillar about to metamorphose or the flower about to bloom.
Hence the self-identification of a nation as it realizes its organic potential becomes "the political function of art."[46] Following Jean-Luc
Nancy, Lacoue-Labarthe calls this organicizing of the nation "immanentism." The nation attempts to produce itself out of itself, to actu-

----

[43] Ibid., 85.

[44] Heidegger's infatuation with Hitler's political artisanship perhaps lies behind the otherwise obscure response he gave to Karl Jasper's question of how anyone as uneducated as
Hitler could rule Germany: "It's not a question of education; just look at his marvelous
hands!" Quoted in Wolin, *Heidegger Controversy*, 145.

[45] Lacoue-Labarthe, *Heidegger, Art, and Politics*, 83.

[46] Ibid., 69.

alize its essence as a work of art, to achieve its historical potential in the present. With the Nazis, this task entailed a violent sculpting of the German nation. Impurities were to be systematically cut away. The detritus (the Jews) was to be ruthlessly disposed of. "This will to immediacy" that brought a people to seek its essence in immanence, Lacoue-Labarthe concludes, "was, ultimately, the crime—the boundless excess —of Nazism."[47]

Heidegger's belief in the führer's skillful capacity to instantiate the people's historical destiny did not last much beyond the rectorate. Unfortunately, the same cannot be said of his immanentism. Years after resigning the rectorate, Heidegger retained the hope that the Germans might still fulfill their unique historic mission as an organic people. It was a dangerous hope. The plurality of the human condition revealed in political life is severely threatened by any mythologizing of a people's destiny and unity out of its linguistic commonality. And this mythologizing, Lacoue-Labarthe rightly concludes, should have been spurned had Heidegger remained true to his own nonsubstantive understanding of Dasein and *Mitsein*. Being-with, or Mitsein, is an ontological phenomenon that has no ontic equivalent in the particular community, nation, or people. Dasein, in turn, is not a stable essence but an ontological relationship. Only its mythologizing allows its nationalizing. But, as Habermas remarks, beginning in 1933 the ontology of *Being and Time* suddenly is given "a collectivist turn. . . . now Dasein was the Dasein of the people, of the *Volk*."[48] Even after his resignation of the rectorate, Heidegger continued to write in terms of the "simple and essential decisions in the destiny of an historical people," and of a people's self-conception as "belonging to world history." History, Heidegger makes clear, is not conceived as "a sequence in time of events of whatever sort, however important. History is the transporting of a people into its appointed task as entrance into that people's endowment" (*PLT* 48, 74, 77). This "transportation" of a people into its ontological purity, Heidegger ominously insists, will not be without risk: "For the question 'Who is man?' is not as harmless as it may seem. . . . It can find its answer only in the exemplary and authoritative way in which particular nations, in competition with others, shape their history" (*ERS* 102). Immanentism will claim victims.

Heidegger would eventually distance himself from immanentism, just as he had formerly distanced himself from the cruder political technicism of the Nazis. Lacoue-Labarthe cites the year 1955, in which Heidegger wrote an important letter to Jünger (*The Question of Being*),

[47] Ibid., 70.
[48] Quoted in Wolin, *Heidegger Controversy*, 189.

as marking Heidegger's definitive denouncement of national aestheti-
cism as an inverted Platonism. We might note, however, that already by
1938, in his *Beiträge zur Philosophie,* Heidegger would admit that an
ontological focus on Dasein means that a "people can never be a goal
or program." He warns that a people must beware the danger of "becoming caught up in itself and idolizing what are only the conditions
[*Bedingungen*] of its existence as its *Absolute* [*Unbedingten*]" (G 65:
319, 398). Despite such veiled recantations, however, one suspects that
Heidegger could never bring himself to find the popular idol completely
hollow. In a letter to Karl Jaspers written in 1950, Heidegger insists of
his land and people that "despite death and tears, despite affliction and
horror, despite privation and suffering, despite dislocation and banish-
ment, what is happening in this state of *homelessness* is not nothing;
concealed therein is an Advent whose distant beckoning we may just be
able to divine in the faint stirring of the air."[49] Even after the war,
Heidegger continued to portray himself as a latter-day John the Baptist:
too often ignored, yet persistent in his prophecy to a chosen people of
the Second Coming of Being. At times Heidegger's chauvinism was
clearly German, at times European.[50] Regardless, the incarnation of a
transcendent destiny in an organic people can only be seen as the last
hurrah of metaphysical thought. Unfortunately, echoes of this cheer linger in Heidegger's work to the end.

　　Lacoue-Labarthe's and Bernstein's criticisms follow a line of thought
that has undeniable merit. Heidegger, well into the 1930s, identified
physis with Being itself. By making the further equation of physis with
the development of an organic nation, and by identifying the philosophic task as inherently linked to the achievement of national greatness
and destiny (*IM* 11), Heidegger lent his hand to the rise of the most
dangerous political immanentism and fictioning. Just as Plato employed
the Forms, so Heidegger employed the *Seinsgeschichte* (more specifically, the historical destiny of the German nation) to do his political
work for him. Heidegger propounded politics as a form of art that actualizes the latent essence of a people. In doing so, Heidegger forgot
about, or intentionally submerged, a political mode of revealing truth
distinct from artisanship that had already been given voice by Aristotle
in opposition to his idealist teacher.

　　This critique, for all its merits, neglects certain references in Heidegger's work that speak to modes of revealing truth beyond the poetic-

[49] Ott, *Martin Heidegger,* 24.

[50] Heidegger writes, for example, that "Descartes' thought, the metaphysics of Leibniz,
Hume's philosophy, are all European and therefore global. In the same way, Nietzsche's
metaphysics is at its core never a specifically German philosophy. It is European, global"
(*WPK* 251).

philosophic and the technological. Importantly, it ignores a crucial aspect of Heidegger's discussion of poiēsis during his Kehre. The parallels between Plato and Heidegger, in this regard, are only as important as their differences. If we understand Plato's philosopher-king to be a craftsperson who masters the mimetic production of objects at a politico-philosophic level, then Heidegger, shortly after the rectorate, developed a diametrically opposed view. Bernstein and Lacoue-Labarthe do not sufficiently engage the political ramifications of Heidegger's distinction between (poetic) art as a disclosive activity and technē conceived as a mimetic or utilitarian artisanship.[51] Their critiques fail to account for Heidegger's nonmetaphysical understanding of art, already developed in the mid-1930s, and Heidegger's intimation of a nonmetaphysical understanding of politics that bears discernible antifascistic tendencies.

The Disclosive Art of Politics

Having resigned the rectorate the year before, while much in doubt about the potential of the Nazi regime but perhaps still sanguine about the movement, Heidegger, in 1935–36, wrote and delivered his lecture called "The Origin of the Work of Art." Near the end of his life, Heidegger observed that his meditation on the origin of the work of art played a decisive role in his Kehre.[52] Indeed, this essay (along with the first Nietzsche lecture on *The Will to Power as Art* of the same period) is a crucial exposition not only of Heidegger's understanding of poiēsis and technē, but also, implicitly, of his understanding of politics. In proposing a conception of art distinct from that which orients modernity and much of antiquity, Heidegger also offers a rich, albeit veiled, conception of political life that shares with art and philosophy his highest accolades.

"Art is the origin of both artist and work," Heidegger declares enigmatically at the essay's outset (*PLT* 17). After some acknowledged thinking in circles, and a lengthy digression on the nature of things, Heidegger illuminates his earlier statement by bringing us to the crux of the essay: "*Art then is the becoming and happening of truth*" (*PLT* 71). The aesthetic or beautiful is that which shocks the soul into stillness so that it may receive, in wonder, the mystery of Being. Heidegger identifies art as this aesthetic ("composed, resolute") openness to beings (*WPA* 164). The work of art itself is only the concrete by-product of this disclosive event, its effective residue. Art must be seen as the origin

[51] Cf. Lacoue-Labarthe, *Heidegger, Art, and Politics*, 78, 113.

[52] See Jacques Taminiaux, "The Origin of 'The Origin of the Work of Art,'" in *Reading Heidegger*, ed. John Sallis (Bloomington: Indiana University Press, 1993).

of the art work, which constitutes simply the physical space in which truth becomes unconcealed. Truth, for Heidegger, is not a representation of reality but a happening. This happening of truth occurs in a particular way in the work of art (*PLT* 39). The work of art is not mimetic or reproductive. The work of art does not *portray* at all. Rather, it *conveys*. Specifically, the work of art conveys art, a particular (aesthetic) manner of revealing truth to which human being is privileged.

Art, we recall, is also the origin of the artist. The reasoning follows a similar course. The artist participates in a particular mode of revelation. Insisting that the artist finds her origin in art, and not the reverse, Heidegger rejects the traditional understanding of the artist as a sovereign entity aesthetically molding the world, regardless of whether this molding constitutes a mimicking of nature or a form of self-expression. The Heideggerian artist is neither the master craftsperson who willfully bends the world into preconceived form nor the self-expressive creator ex nihilo. Rather, the artist is someone who facilitates in a particular way the emergence of Being from beings. Artistic creation is less a giving form to what previously had none than an openness that allows ever-present yet hidden Being to come to presence in the world.[53]

Artistic creation is an aesthetic bringing forth that is aptly described as a "receiving" (*PLT* 62). The artist cultivates a receptive relation to the world and necessarily fails in this task if her activity is grounded in the pursuit of mastery, be it self-directed or mimetic of external form. "It is precisely in great art—and only such art is under consideration here," Heidegger maintains, "that the artist remains inconsequential as compared with the work, almost like a passageway that destroys itself in the creative process for the work to emerge" (*PLT* 40).[54] What is great in the artist, then, is her capacity to forgo possessive mastery in order to "let Being be" in the work of art. This is not to say that the artist is inconsequential in terms of how the work comes to be. Heidegger goes too far in dismissing the idiosyncratic importance of the individual. But his fundamental point is well taken. The artist's involvement with the work is participatory rather than sovereign.

This perspective follows from Heidegger's critique of metaphysics.

---

[53] Heidegger writes, "Creation is an emphasizing of major features, a seeing more simply and strongly" (*WPA* 117). In this regard, Zimmerman proposes an apt comparison: "Heidegger was in harmony with the expressionist painter Paul Klee, who said, 'Art does not reproduce what is visible, instead, it makes visible.'" Zimmerman, *Heidegger's Confrontation with Modernity,* 107).

[54] Elsewhere, Heidegger writes: "The master's presence in the work is the only true presence. The greater the master, the more completely his person vanishes behind his work" (*DT* 44).

"Modern subjectivism," Heidegger writes, "misinterprets creation, taking it as the self-sovereign subject's performance of genius." But creation is more appropriately described as a drawing forth, "as of water from a spring" (PLT 76). Importantly, it is the artist's eye for beauty that dissolves the distinction between subjectivity and objectivity, allowing a nonmetaphysical relation to the world. We find that "by having a feeling for beauty the subject has already come out of himself; he is no longer subjective, no longer a subject. In turn, beauty is not something at hand like an object of sheer representation. It is an attuning. Beauty breaks through the confinement of the 'object' placed at a distance, standing on its own, and brings it into essential and original correlation to the 'subject.' Beauty is no longer objective, no longer an object. The aesthetic state is neither subjective nor objective" (WPA 123). What is discovered in the work of art is not the genius's *production* of beauty out of mute matter, nor the genius's self-expressive *projection* of beauty out of the impenetrable darkness and depth of a sovereign soul. Rather, the work reveals the uncovering of beauty as a happening of truth, an attunement to Being.

The genius of the artist is in her ability to let Being be—aesthetically. As a passageway, the artist lets Being flow through her culturally, socially, and politically mediated being in order to take concrete form in the work of art. This is not to say that a striving for mastery does not frequently, and perhaps inevitably, evidence itself among artists, as among all creative people. Indeed, the tragic, because unfulfillable, desire for artistic mastery appears to be the cause of the "sadness of all created creators." "The creature," Heidegger states, never gains complete control over the ground. . . . Thence all creators, creative people, the poets, thinkers, and founders of the state, are 'melancholy spirits' according to Aristotle" (ST 164, 160). But the finitude of human being is both the cause of the artist's melancholy and her source of inspiration; the happening of truth in art can only emerge from the artist's historical worldliness, which provides the context of disclosure. What is "projected" in the work of art, Heidegger writes, "is only the withheld vocation of the historical being of man itself" (PLT 76). The work of art, in short, is the legacy of the artist as a historical Being-in-the-world-with-others. Like all legacies, it has an origin, but no master.

Art allows truth to happen. Better said, art allows truth to happen aesthetically. Truth also happens in other ways. Art is only one mode of disclosure. Heidegger explains: "But how does truth happen? We answer: it happens in a few essential ways. One of these ways in which truth happens is the work-being of the work. . . . *Beauty is one way in which truth occurs as unconcealedness.* . . . Another way in which truth occurs is the act that founds a political state. . . . Still another way in which truth becomes is the thinker's questioning, which, as the thinking of Being, names Being in its question-worthiness" (*PLT* 55, 56, 62). Truth, and hence freedom as participation in truth, may happen politically. This political mode of revelation occurs in the founding of a state. But when and how does this founding occur?

Heidegger, unfortunately, gives us little direction here. His own political biography might mislead one to assume that the political mode of revealing truth necessarily remains shrouded in the mythical (linguistic) beginnings of a Volk or nation. Yet Heidegger's philosophical insights prompt an investigation of how political founding might occur within the auspices of a democratic politics. Founding need not be a once-and-for-all affair, obscured in history and surfacing only during revolution. Democratic politics, by its very nature, constitutes a continuous founding, an ongoing reformulation and transformation of community, authority, and power by way of its evolving institutions, practices, and citizenry. This thesis, I believe, finds support within Heidegger's thought.

Heidegger summarizes his discussion of art as follows: "The nature of art is poetry. The nature of poetry, in turn, is the founding of truth. We understand founding here in a triple sense: founding as bestowing, founding as grounding, and founding as beginning" (*PLT* 75). Founding is indeed tied to origins. But origins do not always speak of the distant past. We may also refer to the *present* origins of things to come. Founding is about beginnings, to be sure, but included are those contemporary beginnings that lay uncertain foundations for the future. The argument may be extended to things political. Hannah Arendt provides some guidance.

Politics for Arendt is about beginnings. The primary political phenomenon is action and the essence of action is its inherent novelty. Action sets things on their way, introducing newness into the repetitious processes of life. Action, in short, is the stuff of origins. Political action is that starting of something new which assures that our time on earth is constituted by events in history rather than a chain of evolutionary development. But action begins—has the capacity for novelty—precisely because it does not copy transcendent forms, customs, or natural processes. Politics, most fundamentally, is neither a representational nor an instrumental endeavor. Arendt aestheticizes politics, as Heidegger eventually would, nonmimetically. Like dance or music, the virtue of politics lies in its performance.[55]

---

[55] Dana Villa cogently argues that Arendt is engaged in an aestheticization of politics that likens action to the playing of instruments or dancing—that is, to activities "whose value resides in the sheer performance of the activity itself" rather than in any instrumen-

But politics is not sheer initiation and novelty. It is also about safe-guarding and caretaking. Heidegger offers support for this position within his discussion of art. Upon declaring founding a bestowing, grounding, and beginning, Heidegger goes on to include all these categories under the rubric of that which founding most essentially is: a "preserving." Founding is actual only in preserving. "Thus," Heidegger concludes, "to each mode of founding there corresponds a mode of preserving" (PLT 75). Art, for Heidegger, is a founding in that it bestows, grounds, and sets in motion the revelation of truth. Simultaneously, art preserves this truth, for Being is taken into safekeeping, guarded in beings, through art, in the work of art. What, then, we might ask, is the political analogue of this aesthetic caretaking? How does a political founding that is a preserving occur?

Heidegger offers us a clue, but again one that we must extrude from the essay's central concern with things artistic. Art in general is a kind of poetry, a poiēsis, in the sense of a poetic creation that may assume, for instance, a linguistic, architectural, sculptural, or terpsichorean form. Among these diverse forms of art, however, linguistic art maintains preeminence. For Heidegger, "*All art,* as the letting happen of the advent of the truth of what is, is, as such, *essentially poetry.* . . . But poesy is only one mode of the lighting projection of truth, i.e., of poetic composition in this wider sense. Nevertheless, the linguistic work, the poem in the narrower sense, has a privileged position in the domain of the arts" (PLT 72, 73). Linguistic art is primary because all "art shapes its work within the realm of language" (EGT 19). Language begins human being on the path of disclosure. Language, Heidegger reiterates, is "not only and not primarily an audible or written expression of what is to be communicated," but rather that which "alone brings what is, as something that is, into the Open for the first time. Where there is no language, as in the being of stone, plant, and animal, there is also no openness of what is, and consequently no openness either of that which is not and of the empty" (PLT 73). We are artists originally because we are speakers, even though actual speech is silenced in various forms of art to allow the revelation of Being in other ways. But if language privileges poetry among the arts, we might question what other modes of disclosure also partake of its gift.

Philosophy and politics are the two other modes of revealing truth

---

tal purpose. The Heideggerian influence on Arendt in this regard is patent. But important differences persist. Heidegger ultimately grounds art and action ontologically, by way of its disclosive participation in Being. Arendt, as Villa's article suggests, offers no ground for politics: "sheer performance" is all. Dana Villa, "Beyond Good and Evil: Arendt, Nietzsche, and the Aestheticization of Political Action," *Political Theory* 20 (1992): 274–308.

that are essentially linguistic. Philosophic thinking is indeed a preserving and safeguarding of Being that is grounded in language. Politics bears a similar nature. Like philosophy, politics lets truth happen in speech. This happening occurs in three (overlapping) ways. First, our political deeds, like our philosophic ones, are done through language, even when they are carried out in silence. Whenever we act we act through language, even when words never leave our lips or come to mind. Second, the deeds of politics, much more than those of philosophy, entail actual communication. The vast majority of political actions are shared linguistic events: words that initiate, forbid, or institute. And third, speech is that which preserves the world and with-world of politics. All the beginnings that actions start on their way find their preservation, if they are to be preserved, in political speech. As Arendt claims, political speech assures us that the achievements of our deeds are not forever lost. Without the preservative function of speech, actions would vanish into oblivion as quickly as they arose in novelty. Speech preserves the political community as it secures its members, and their deeds, an abode in history.

Politics refers to the ongoing founding and preserving of a public place or site, a realm characterized by the initiating and preserving powers of action and speech. The polis signifies "the place, the there, wherein and as which historical Being-there is," Heidegger writes. "The *polis* is the historical place, the there *in* which, *out of* which, and *for* which history happens" (*IM* 152). In this sense the polis is really a *polos*—a pole (*Pol*) or vertebra (*Wirbel*) around which everything turns. According to Heidegger, the polis or city-state thus should be primarily understood neither as a city (*Stadt*) nor as a state (*Staat*), but first and foremost as a site or place (*Statt*). The polis is the "site of the historical dwelling of human beings in the midst of beings" (*G* 53:100–101). Despite Heidegger's own romantic susceptibilities, there need be no political immanentism here. To say that the polis is the place in, out of, and for which history happens is not to say that politics simply plays out the destiny of a particular people. History is precisely the arising of *novelty* through action, a newness so patent in its unpredictability that it solicits a preservative accounting in speech.

For a period, Heidegger succumbed to the Platonic temptation. He extended the notion of representational art's mastery to politics, and thus abetted a totalitarian regime not dissimilar in certain respects from the architectonically designed city in speech of the *Republic*. This aestheticization of politics proved catastrophic. With this in mind, critics of Heidegger have been understandably eager to dismiss any effort to link art and politics. But this position fails to account for Heidegger's rejection of the notion of mimetic or technicist art and his intimations of a new political aesthetics after his resignation of the rectorate. Differences do indeed exist between politics and art. But the key difference is not, as Bernstein insists, that of art's mastery through mimēsis versus politics' praxis through phronēsis. Both art and politics, properly understood, are resistant to mastery. Both ultimately rest on a mode of letting-be, a release that allows truth to happen. Both art and politics beget a happening of truth that is a founding, a beginning that is a preserving. The difference between art and politics, then, is in the manner in which these two modes of letting truth happen let it happen.

The chief vehicle of art is the individual. Art lets truth happen by way of the activity of individual artists, or through the choreographed, orchestrated, or directed activity of a group of artists performing together. Politics, on the other hand, lets truth happen through the interactions of many individuals. While political actions are generally coordinated, and while political engagement is frequently aimed at securing harmony or accord, politics nevertheless remains grounded in the differences among human beings. The essence of art is unity, with all parts (whether parts of an individual or of a group) subordinated to a singular, organic whole. The essence of politics is plurality, with all parts valorized in tandem with the whole. The citizen always enters, interacts, and remains within the political realm as one individual among many. Thus, unlike the member of an orchestra or troupe, the citizen's individuality is never completely dissolved in the whole through her actions.

In distinguishing physis from technē or poiēsis, Heidegger observes that "what presences by means of *physis* has the bursting open belonging to bringing-forth, e.g., the bursting of a blossom into bloom, in itself (*en heautōi*). In contrast, that which is brought forth by the artisan or the artist, e.g., the silver chalice, has the bursting open belonging to bringing forth not in itself, but in another (*en allōi*), in the craftsman or artist" (*QT* 10–11). To extrapolate: what presences by means of the polis is brought forth neither in itself, nor in a singular other, but by way of an irreducible plurality of citizens. With this in mind, we might view the distinction between art and politics as analogous to the distinction between the activity of an individual telling a tale and the activity of a group of individuals weaving a tale together.

We might imagine art (including, but not restricted to, actual spoken art) as the lone individual's storytelling. The solitary author retains a certain control over the story's course, development, and purpose. But the tale also becomes unintentionally and unavoidably filled with, and one might say structured by, the stuff of the artist's historical existence. The multivalence of words themselves saturates and informs the tale in uncontrollable ways. Meaning is discovered through the story's telling. Thus the artist, despite attempts to master her creation, may receive from it more than she (thinks she) gives. The story is hers, indubitably, and it is inconceivable apart from her idiosyncratic construction of it. But it is hers not as the property of a sovereign, but as the legacy of a being who in the midst of creative activity cannot help relying on the words, images, mythopoetic sources, historical contingencies, and relationships that constitute her world. In language, Humboldt once said, each individual feels most vividly that he is only the effluence of humankind. Likewise, the storyteller through her storytelling evidences herself as a thrown Being-in-the-world-with-others. The good storyteller is less a master of words than a perceptive participant in a cultural, historical, ontological, and linguistic reality that is given specific form in her tale. One can say nothing different of the painter or sculptor. The plastic arts, in this sense, represent a silent dialogue with the world, about the world, as it comes to be expressed through the work of an individual's hands. Ontologically speaking, the tale, like the sculpture, is a creative preservation of historical and worldly reality. The world of the artist takes particular form in the concrete work, with the historical self as a medium. I am not suggesting that a mystical external force named Being uses artists as tools to fashion works of art. Rather, as historical beings in the world, artists necessarily maintain a relation to Being (authentically or inauthentically), and cannot help instantiating difference, in some historically (socially, culturally, and politically) mediated fashion, whenever they create.

The collective—that is, cooperative and competitive—telling of a tale is something quite different. Such interactive storytelling is often engaged in by children. Someone typically begins, and sets the tone for the tale, with a preamble. Subsequently each participant adds a few sentences or phrases, contributing to the development of the story, sometimes sending it into strange (and, particularly with boys, often morbid) directions, and leaving his or her neighbor with something related, but also distinct from what came before. Many beginnings appear to go nowhere, fading away as a result of someone else's attempt to steer a different course. The story, having left one's care for a time, may come to serve a different, perhaps antagonistic, purpose, returning sometime later as a prodigal child. Regardless of how forcefully any one participant attempts to direct the story's course, inform its context, or structure its development, the tale is only a neighbor away from taking on new meanings and subverting every intention of mastery or prognosis. Typically, certain more imaginative, self-confident, and articulate speakers manage to steal the show. But while time, energy, and interest persist, no story line is secure and no contribution irretrievably lost. Occasionally, all efforts at coherence seem futile. Yet much is being preserved despite the apparent abundance of literary orphans and amid the seemingly endless and intrusive novelty. Language itself is preserved in the articulation and sharing of words, however they become stretched with use. The story's origins and its integrity are always partly preserved in the relationships of meanings that follow from neighbor to neighbor. Most importantly, the group engaged in the storytelling and the act of storytelling itself are preserved, and preserved precisely as a result of a sharing in speech.

The parallel to politics is clear. Political life unwinds as a story being told by many. As participants in a process, individuals may achieve hegemonic power, but never complete control. Aristotle rightly defined politics as ruling and being ruled in turn. In political life, power may be accumulated, but not monopolized. It is always shared. This sharing of power, as Aristotle observed, is seldom equal (or, in Aristotle's terminology, its equality may be "proportional" rather than "arithmetic"). But a sharing there must be. Tyranny and totalitarianism (as Arendt rightly concludes) are not politics but its limit.

In the political realm, one remains among many other speakers of words or doers of deeds. Attempts to direct the course of the community are plentiful. The achievement of hegemony by an individual (or oligarchy) is all too common, and typically the stuff of history books. But political life always evidences resistance to monologues, paths that take the community in novel, and one might say liberating, directions. And yet, for all the incessant introductions of speakers and doers and the inherent novelty of each contribution, preservation looms. Each beginning has a corresponding mode of preservation. As history reveals, a revolution that disdains all preservation will consume its own children. What is primarily preserved in the midst of the tumult of political activity is the public realm, the res publica, wherein citizens secure for themselves the opportunity to appear in the world and contribute to its maintenance—to tell their part of the story. Freedom in deed, political freedom, can thus never be owned or possessed by an individual: it is always shared.[56] In sharing political freedom, we create and safeguard a political space that guarantees other modes of revealing truth their own, often more private, domains. "Unconcealment occurs only when it is achieved by work," Heidegger writes, "the work of the word in poetry, the work of stone in temple and statue, the work of the word in thought, the work of the *polis* as the historical place in which all this is grounded and preserved" (*IM* 191). The political realm preserves both its own and other modes of disclosure by creating, securing, and maintaining the space wherein human thought, speech, and action may occur.

[56] As Holmes Rolston writes, "Liberty cuts both ways: those who only get and never give it cannot understand it; indeed, they do not yet fully have it themselves." Holmes Rolston III, *Environmental Ethics: Duties to and Values in the Natural World* (Philadelphia: Temple University Press, 1988), 289.

One final foray into Heidegger's understanding of art is required. Art is the happening of truth wherein the artist, through her work, lets Being be. Heidegger is explicit (in the addendum to "The Origin of the Work of Art") that this letting-be is the "opposite" of indifference or a fatalistic retreat from action. Far from being passive, it constitutes "a doing in the highest degree" (*PLT* 83). Letting beings be aesthetically is not a passive affair largely because art pushes us beyond familiar mediations of reality. "In contrast to all other modes of production," Heidegger writes, "the work [of art] is distinguished by being created so that its createdness is part of the created work. . . . it stands out from it, from the being thus brought forth, in an expressly particular way. . . . this thrust, this '*that* it is' of createdness, emerges into view most purely from the work. . . . But this 'that' does not become prominent in the equipment; it disappears in usefulness" (*PLT* 64–65). By making apparent its creativity, its instable and contingent glance at Being, art demonstrates our historical worldliness—that is, our own thrown Being-in-the-world. Art, in this sense, ceases to be art once it reinforces the familiar by becoming mere decoration, decorative equipment whose functionality obscures its creation out of our thrownness.

With this final characterization of art as a rudder, we may once again navigate those political waters Heidegger left largely uncharted. Politics is a mode of disclosure in which citizens let Being become manifest through their interactive words and deeds. Political disclosure, unlike its artistic counterpart, has numerous agents. It entails the recognition and letting-be of others, of other citizens, as coparticipants. Through political disclosure the with-world becomes manifest in its essential creativity. That which is brought forth politically, the public realm, unlike the equipment or utensil of the craftsperson, and like the work of the artist, does not hide its origins in utility. Rather, politics asserts its essential, nonmimetic creativity by explicitly manifesting our thrown Being-in-the-world-with-others. The analogue to art's becoming mere decoration, therefore, is politics' becoming sheer bureaucracy. In both cases, the creative, ungrounded, and self-consciously disclosive nature of the activity becomes lost in its functionality. Art and politics have their uses, let there be no mistake. But art and politics, unlike technical artisanship, do not have their meanings exhausted by utility. Once art or politics "disappears in usefulness," becoming decoration or bureaucracy, then it has ceased to be what it most essentially is. The point is not to diminish the utility of decoration or bureaucracy, for they are nothing if not useful. Inherent in politics, however, is its capacity to found, to begin something new, to initiate in a way that preserves, and in so doing, to disclose the world in novel ways through interaction and dialogue. This is possible for politics, no less than for art, because it is self-consciously grounded not in functionality but in disclosivity.

Politics, like art, is grounded in freedom. Heidegger focuses on three related but distinct modes of disclosure, and three corresponding types of freedom: philosophic, artistic, and political.[57] We might say that philosophic disclosure partakes primarily of freedom in thought, while artistic and political disclosure partake primarily of freedom in speech and freedom in deed. Yet each of these modes of disclosure remains importantly grounded in each of the types of freedom. Philosophy, Heidegger maintains, is an active thinking that is fundamentally a thoughtful saying; art is a creative doing that is a poetic thinking; and politics is that doing and saying which establishes and maintains the thoughtful interplay of self and other. Politics lets Being be in a particular manner, primarily as a Being-with. Political freedom manifests itself in the disclosure of the with-world.

The Question of Democracy

Is the political disclosure of the with-world likely to be democratic in nature? To put the question differently, does the political letting-be of others promote the disclosive (political) capacities of each and every individual? To respond, we must first recall that the acknowledgment of ontological difference is the foundation on which the acknowledgment of political difference—that of human otherness—ultimately rests. Denying ontological difference—the difference between beings and Being that exposes us to freedom and marks our contingency—results in existential resentment. Existential resentment is effectively a resentment of human finitude. Nietzsche focuses on the manifestation of this resentment in slave morality. But it is equally, if not more obviously, manifested in a master morality that leads to the domination or eradication those (or that) different from oneself. Both forms of resentment, at base, constitute refusals questioningly to affirm the indeterminate nature of human plurality and the unmanageable contingency of the human condition. To the extent that we come to be at home in the world, which includes coming to be at home with our inevitable anxiety at thrownness, we no longer need to strike out at others, as masters or slaves.

Reiner Schürmann questions the "principles" that historically have

---

[57] Heidegger also briefly mentions religious revealing ("the nearness of that which is not simply a being, but the being that is most of all"), as well as what I take to be an emotional revealing, corresponding to love (*agape*) that is capable of sacrifice ("another way in which truth grounds itself is the essential sacrifice") (*PLT* 62).

served as a bulwark against the storm of ontological uncertainty. He
alludes to the practical political benefits of a Heideggerian philosophy
that thrusts one into the storm of Being: "When one considers the suf-
ferings that men have inflicted and inflict on one another in the name of
the epochal principles, there can be no doubt that philosophy—or
'thinking'—is no futile enterprise: a phenomenology that deconstructs
the epochs 'changes the world' because it reveals the withering away of
these principles."⁵⁸ Heideggerian philosophy changes the world, Schürmann argues, by disallowing those metaphysical stabilizers that have
time and again been used to discriminate among the participants of the
with-world in preparation for their domination. Heideggerian philosophy, on this count, is inherently political and implicitly democratic.

In promoting this view, Schürmann maintains that Heidegger's anti-
humanism should not be saddled with biographical or historical ghosts:
"At Eichmann's trial in Jerusalem, it occurred to Hannah Arendt that
the evils of our century to which you allude resulted from thoughtlessness. And Heidegger's case against technology stands and falls with the
claim that it is dangerous because *gedankenlos,* thoughtless. This charge
is accompanied by a conviction: thinking changes the world. How can a
call for thoughtfulness be mistaken for a call for brutal force?"⁵⁹ On the
general point Schürmann is correct: Heidegger's philosophy does not
predispose one to fascist ideology, even though those with fascistic dispositions will always be able to find in Heidegger (as they do in
Nietzsche and Mother Goose) fuel for their fury.⁶⁰ Still, the drift of
Schürmann's position remains indefensible. The premise that thinking
would have prevented Eichmann from participating in the Third Reich's
barbarities leads one to expect that thinking should have prevented
Heidegger's involvement with Nazism. It did not. We must neither ignore nor obscure this fact. Philosophic thought, particularly given its
antipathy to common sense, provides no immunity from the pathologies
of politics.⁶¹

⁵⁸ Schürmann, *Heidegger on Being and Acting,* 11. Likewise, Hannah Arendt asserts
that the "purging component of thinking . . . which brings out the implications of unex-
amined opinions and thereby destroys them—values, doctrines, theories, and even convictions . . . is political by implication." Arendt, *Life of the Mind,* vol. 1, *Thinking* (New
York: Harcourt Brace Jovanovich, 1978), 192.

⁵⁹ Schürmann, *Heidegger on Being and Acting,* 59–60.

⁶⁰ Perhaps only the idiosyncratic nature of Heidegger's writing saves him from gaining a
spot on the reading list of the American neo-Nazis' National Vanguard Books catalogue.
Nietzsche figures prominently here. But then again, so do Homer, Aesop, Plato, Xeno-
phon, Polybius, G. B. Shaw—and Mother Goose. National Vanguard Books, catalogue
14, December 1992.

⁶¹ Arendt's own attempt to grapple with this fact is summarized by one of her commentators: "When she thought of Socrates, philosophical solitude seemed to provide a safe-

I say this despite my belief that Heidegger's vocal support of Nazism and (perhaps even more) his silence on the Holocaust constitute a blatant betrayal of the most fundamental imperative of his thought. With Jean-François Lyotard, I believe that the affirmation of human plurality that sits at the core of a democratic politics must be retrieved from Heidegger in spite of his withholdings. Lyotard writes, "Here lies the paradox and even the scandal: how could this thought (Heidegger's), a thought so devoted to remembering that a forgetting (of Being) takes place in all thought, in all art, in all 'representation' of the world, how could it possibly have ignored the thought of 'the jews,' which, in a certain sense, thinks, tries to think, nothing but that very fact?"[62] By "the jews," Lyotard means neither the nation nor the people, but most generally the other who gets excluded from consideration and subjected to domination. By forgetting the victims of fascism, Heidegger was implicitly forgetting the difference between being and Being that makes all worldly differences, including that of human otherness, possible.

Heidegger apparently hoped that his own work might "break through the narrowness of academic philosophy and reach much broader circles for the benefit of a large number of people."[63] Yet he chose, for the most part, to think apolitically. When he purposefully deviated from this vocation he was, for the most part, ill served by his judgment and disgraced by his arrogance. In some sense, then, I am in agreement with those who condemn Heidegger's philosophy as compromised by his politics. Yet I would argue that the problem to be confronted in tandem with Heidegger's political intrigues of the 1930s and 1940s is his former and subsequent apoliticism. All great thought and action must escape from the oppressive weight of tradition and convention no less than from the enticing but fickle winds of the zeitgeist. Yet the aspiration truly to stand above politics, above the polis, understood as the place of historical dwelling for human being, is dangerous and disturbed. Mugwumpery portends a haughtiness of character that easily leads to the type of authoritarianism Heidegger embraced. I believe, as

---

guard against moral and political errors, but when she thought of Heidegger Arendt's confidence evaporated. Her reflections on Kant suggest that if she had been able to finish *The Life of the Mind*, she would have concluded that philosophical thinking has two sides to it and is a mixed blessing from a political point of view, in that although solitary thinking can facilitate judging, which is politically beneficial, it is just as likely to deprive the thinker of all common sense in political affairs." Margaret Canovan, "Socrates or Heidegger? Hannah Arendt's Reflections on Philosophy and Politics," *Social Research* 57 (1990): 162.

[62] Jean-François Lyotard, *Heidegger and the Jews*, trans. Andreas Michel and Mark Roberts (Minneapolis: University of Minnesota Press, 1990), 4.

[63] Medard Boss, ed., *Zolikoner Seminare* (Frankfurt am Main: Klostermann, 1987), x; quoted in Dreyfus and Hall, *Heidegger*, 2.

well, that Heidegger's aspiration for a intellectually hermetic environment remains starkly at odds with the concerns that lie at the core of Heidegger's philosophy, for human freedom only emerges in the wake of our thrownness into a world with others.

No doubt Heidegger's political adventurism has tainted his philosophy for many. Jacques Derrida offers this wistful hypothesis: "Let us assume that Heidegger had not only said about 1933 'I have made a very stupid mistake' but also 'Auschwitz is the absolute horror; it is what I fundamentally condemn.' . . . What would have happened then? He would probably have immediately received an absolution. . . . And with one statement, which would have been aiming for an unproblematic consensus, Heidegger would have finished the affair; it would not be necessary for us to ask today what affinities, synchronisms of thinking, and common roots Heidegger's thinking could have with National Socialism, which is still an 'unthought' phenomenon."[64] Similarly, Gabriel Marcel regretfully muses that "the philosophical world's admiration for Heidegger would have doubled if after the war he had not maintained his stubborn silence and had said something about his behavior in 1933."[65] Such conjectures may be accurate. But I believe they convey the wrong lesson.

We should be grateful for Heidegger's Nazism. Of course, my point is not that Nazism, or Heidegger's support of it, was anything but abhorrent. Rather, Heidegger's Nazism and his intransigent silence may prove beneficial by inoculating us against a dangerous and historically tenacious fantasy. After examining the disgraceful political escapade of one of the world's greatest philosophers, we are forcefully reminded that the ambiguity and agonism of political life cannot be resolved through intellectual fiat or invention. Contemporary history, using Heidegger as its lesson, has most effectively chastised this inherently undemocratic hubris. Knowledge is not virtue, at least not always. Philosophic thought does not in itself prevent political vice. The temptation, in light of this truth, is "to liberate Heidegger from Heidegger, to . . . make Heidegger truly the name, not of a man, but of a matter to be thought."[66] But the matter to be thought, in this case, is that one can never achieve the complete liberation of the philosophical "matter to be thought" from the historical and political self doing the thinking—nor did Heidegger. When Heidegger sought such liberation, the resulting mugwumpery was almost as troubling as his politics.

The wedlock of philosophy and politics, as Heidegger demonstrates

[64] Derrida, "Heidegger's Silence," 147.

[65] Quoted in Graham Parkes, ed., *Heidegger and Asian Thought* (Honolulu: University of Hawaii Press, 1987), 95.

[66] Caputo, *Demythologizing Heidegger,* 117.

even better than Plato, proves disastrous. Politics and philosophy ought never to be married. But we should not go so far as to demand the dissolution of their relationship. Philosophy is not prescriptively empty from a political perspective. It is simply ambiguous. The task of wisdom is to discern the boundaries and balance that these enterprises might establish with each other. And this wisdom is to be gained in the only way it has ever been gained: through an open and careful involvement in the affairs of the world and those of the soul. Politics and philosophy ought never to marry, but they ought to have sustained affairs, full of procreative activity.

Philosophic and political maturity is evidenced to the extent that one explores and benefits from a work without persisting in the naive, often treacherous—and regarding Heidegger, already tedious—quest for a univocal precept as its moral or a unified figure as its author. This maturity is crucial to democratic life in the postmodern world. Contemporary democratic politics cannot escape ambiguity and the ongoing responsibility of judgment by lying at the feet of heroes, constructing monolithic demons to battle, or seeking to dissolve all ambivalences in a work or a life. The alternative, however, is neither perpetual vacillation nor enforced mediocrity. The point, as Galileo well understood, is not to cut off the heads of those who rise above the crowd, and here I am referring not only to outstanding individuals but to outstanding principles, and conventions. Many individuals, principles, and conventions deserve particular honor, respect, and support. To give anything less displays a resentful lack of magnanimity and a dangerous political naïveté.[67] But none is a half-god, a pure incarnation of virtue, or an unassailable ("epochal") truth. Conversely, few, if any, are unredeemably evil. Outside mythology and ideology, all are made from the same mix of crooked timber. And, outside mythology and ideology, the political edifice, however constructed, forever belies the trueness of its timber.

Heidegger's philosophy cannot be viewed as the seed of democratic thought and practice. But his philosophy can be tilled into a soil propitious for its growth. Heidegger explicitly reserved judgment about the virtues of democratic politics. "For me today it is a decisive question as to how any political system—and which one—can be adapted to an epoch of technicity," Heidegger acknowledges, and concludes: "I know of no answer to this question. I am not convinced that it is democracy"

---

[67] As C. S. Lewis remarked about the need to uphold principles in the face of a skeptical gaze: "If you see through everything, then everything is transparent. But a wholly transparent world is an invisible world. To 'see through' all things is the same as not to see." C. S. Lewis, *The Abolition of Man* (New York: Macmillan, 1947), 50. Perforce, to see through all things is the same as not to act. Moral and political principles should not be eschewed simply because they remain susceptible to having holes punched in them.

(*OGS* 55). Heidegger rightly fears that if technological, calculative thinking deprives us of our capacity for philosophic thought and worldly dwelling, then the particular political structures within which this horror occurs—and it could well occur under cover of what is presently called democracy—would be of little import. But Heidegger is wrong to assume that democratic politics has little potential for mitigating the probability that such a horror *will* occur.

Still, none of us should be "convinced" that democracy, understood as a set of political structures and procedures, is the "answer." No blueprint of a house can guarantee the trueness of its timber, and no blueprint of a public space can guarantee the virtuous dispositions of its dwellers. The problem with aristocracy is for the most part the aristocrats. The problem with tyranny is generally the tyrant. And, by and large, the problem with democracy is the people. No institutional arrangement can ensure the depth and integrity of the encounters between and among human individuals and groups. Only the cultivation of civic and other virtues can. Ultimately, these virtues must exist in tandem with what may only be described as a philosophic consciousness, broadly understood as a questioning relation to the transcendent and an openness to human contingency that fosters a receptivity to otherness.

The notion that communicative procedures, institutions, or conventions could obviate the need for this consciousness and its accompanying virtues is, in the end, simply another form of technological thinking.[68] Like Mahatma Gandhi, we should be wary of "systems so perfect that no one would need to be good." Certain structures and procedures do indeed facilitate the development of virtues among citizens better than others. But in the postmodern world, we would do well to greet with incredulity the technicist tale of how structures and procedures might become panaceas. Skepticism about the salvational power of political institutions, however, should not cause us to abandon what remains the greatest hope for worldly dwelling: the democratic experiment. If nothing else, the examples of totalitarian and tyrannical rule witnessed throughout history should dissuade us sufficiently from nondemocratic alternatives. To paraphrase Winston Churchill, democracy is the worst form of government to adopt in the present epoch of technicity—except for all the others.

To throw one's lot in with the democratic experiment is to hope that radical individualism and national tribalism—strange but frequent bed-

---

[68] While Habermas defends his communicative ethics as entailing more than procedural norms, he is insufficiently concerned with existential and ontological affairs to lend credence to his defense. Charles Taylor rightly criticizes Habermas on this point. "Habermas," Taylor observes, "elides the experiential problem under the public, as though the two could be solved for the price of one." Taylor, *Sources of the Self*, 510.

fellows—are unnecessary to ground social and political life. Minimally, it is to hope that the need for these ideologies and mythologies might be severely mitigated. This is the hope that a political and philosophic celebration of difference might be sustainable within community and might itself sustain community. Democracy, Plato admits, is the fairest regime because of the splendorous diversity of the citizenry. Plato also understands freedom to constitute the defining principle of democracy: it is *the* democratic good. But when freedom becomes licentiousness, Plato worries, difference becomes dangerous. Hence he sacrifices both freedom and difference for metaphysical certainties. Heidegger asks us to abandon metaphysics. He suggests that a solicitous acknowledgment of difference in the self, the questionable otherness of its Being, is the prerequisite and proper accompaniment for the solicitious acknowledgment of difference in the world. The political theorization of this philosophic position might be summarized by saying that democracy best begins at home. Freedom arises in the democratic negotiations of self and other.

This freedom is not to be possessed, only courted. Democracy is a journey toward freedom that remains ever under way. The journey is unending, as Vaclav Havel once observed, because the "horizon of freedom" is "eternally receding."[69] Yet the uncertainty of our quest serves to underline, not undermine, the need to embrace a politics that acknowledges contingency and celebrates difference. Disclosive freedom beckons to the democratic challenge.

The freedom to let Being be is the freedom to let Nothing be—to let the ungroundedness of Being be, to let indefiniteness and ambiguity be. Letting Being be marks a thoughtful and thankful dissolution of metaphysical certainties. I employ this phrase mindful of Claude Lefort's assertion "that democracy is instituted and sustained by the *dissolution of the markers of certainty*. It inaugurates a history in which people experience a fundamental indeterminacy as to the basis of power, law and knowledge, and as to the basis of relations between *self* and *other*, at every level of social life (at every level where division, and especially the division between those who held power and those who were subject to them, could once be articulated as a result of a belief in the nature of things or in a supernatural principle)."[70] Heidegger's philosophical dis-

---

[69] Spoken at a joint session of the U.S. Congress in 1990. Quoted in Al Gore, *Earth in the Balance: Ecology and the Human Spirit* (Boston: Houghton Mifflin, 1992), 172.

[70] Claude Lefort, *Democracy and Political Theory*, trans. David Macey (Minneapolis: University of Minnesota Press, 1988), 19. Lefort goes on to celebrate democracy as "distancing itself, as no previous regime had done, from the fantasy of an organic society" and "the fiction . . . of a collective individual" (55, 176). One is reminded of George Kateb's argument that democracy marks the victory of convention and indeterminacy and

solution of metaphysics has its political counterpart in a democracy infused with a disclosive freedom that celebrates relations of self and other in all their contingency. The political sensibility we may derive from Heidegger's philosophy, then, might be formulated as follows: Let not a resentment at our thrown Being-in-the-world-with-others become the impetus for the pursuit of possessive mastery. Strive for a home in difference and bear witness to its freedom.

Heidegger's most enduring philosophic legacy ensues from his understanding that the human condition is without an answer because it remains fundamentally grounded in questioning. That this legacy has political import without at the same time facilitating an unequivocal politics should neither surprise nor discourage us.

---

thus is symbiotically related to philosophic meditation on contingency. Kateb believes Heidegger's thought illuminates this understanding. See especially chaps. 4–6 of George Kateb, *The Inner Ocean: Individualism and Democratic Culture* (Ithaca: Cornell University Press, 1992). I have offered a critique of Kateb's effort in "Twilight of Modernity: Nietzsche, Heidegger, and Politics," *Political Theory* 22 (1994): 468–90.

Part Three _____

THE POLITICS OF DWELLING

Seven _____

Saving the Earth

THE PLIGHT OF HOMELESSNESS

> Philosophy is really homesickness,
> an urge to be at home everywhere.
> Where, then, are we going?
> Always to our home.
> (Novalis, *Fragments*)

HOMELESSNESS is politically provocative. "Bag people" walk the streets of our cities, redefining the nation's self-image. Refugees trenchantly place the question of homelessness in an international context. Conflicting claims by different nations, peoples, and ethnic groups to the same "homelands" transform the question into a global issue of war and peace. And the increasingly cosmopolitan and mobile nature of contemporary society challenges us to rethink the very meaning of having and maintaining a home. The significance of homelessness as a political category is increasingly apparent.

The sociopolitical context in which Heidegger thought and wrote was also saturated with the issue. When Heidegger began his university studies in the early 1900s, in stark contrast to the rootedness of previous generations, only half of Germany's sixty million inhabitants still lived at their place of birth.[1] Modernity and mobility apparently went hand in hand. Unlike the traditional societies of yesteryear, modern society seemed less concerned with establishing a home, and more bewildered by the meaning and consequences of its absence. In response, Heidegger participated in the National Socialist dream of a rediscovered and transformed homeland. But this dream soon turned to a nightmare, uprooting and denying haven to millions across Europe and around the world. By the late 1940s, Heidegger found himself in a land littered with heaps of rubble that were once the hearths of his fellow Germans.

Heidegger's word for home is *Heimat*, not *Heim*. The sense is that of a homeland rather than a household. Heidegger thus remains an easy target for those who, chiefly relying on political biography, depict his

---

[1] Noted in Zimmerman, *Heidegger's Confrontation with Modernity*, 7.

abiding concern for homelessness as xenophobic and protofascistic. It cannot be denied that Heidegger occasionally spoke of homelessness as if its remedy entailed a national retrenchment. But a national, racial, ethnic, or linguistic circumscription of home, which is indeed likely to produce a malignant chauvinism, is not intrinsic to Heidegger's thought. Heidegger's philosophic understanding of human being indicates that most fundamentally home is not found within the confines of national borders, though it is not, for that reason, a private domain. Home does not refer primarily to a spatial location. Rather, home is a relation of nearness to the world. In this light, Heidegger's lingering nationalism represents a nostalgic, and therefore misconstrued, effort that stands opposed to the thrust of his philosophy as a whole. Nostalgia refers to the often sweet but painful desire to return to or regain a home.[2] Yet the ontological task, and its corresponding ontic activity, is less a homecoming to a specific site (despite Heidegger's occasional use of the term) than a home-seeking, an enduring "urge to be at home everywhere," as Novalis formulated it.[3] The discovering of home and its caretaking are perpetual tasks. Such an understanding of home is appropriately embedded within an ecological framework that identifies the earth as the human habitat in need of caretaking. Though markedly distinct from naturalism, Heidegger's philosophy offers much support for this ecological disposition to dwelling.

Nostalgic Romanticism and Postmodern Nomadism

Heidegger's frequent ruminations on homelessness no doubt were stimulated by the political events, cultural developments, and demographics of his time. Nor was he the only one so concerned. Indeed, the company he kept in this regard makes us chary of the issue itself and suspicious of any solutions offered. The chauvinistic German obsession with *Blut und Boden* would, under Hitler's direction, be transformed into an all-out war for racial purity and lebensraum. Securing a home for Aryan Germans allowed the denial of home to neighboring Poles and Slavs as well as to "wandering" Jews and Gypsies. Nazism would create its own

---

[2] *Nostalgia* comes from the Greek *nostos*, the (desire to) return home, and *algia*, the feeling pain of loss.

[3] Jacques Derrida makes the same claim, asserting that in Heidegger "the solicitation of the Site and the Land is in no way, it must be emphasized, a passionate attachment to territory or locality, is in no way a provincialism or particularism. . . . The thinking of Being thus is not a pagan cult of the *Site*, because the Site is never a given proximity but a promised one." Jacques Derrida, *Writing and Difference* (Chicago: University of Chicago Press, 1978), 145.

refugee problem, and subsequently impose its own "solution," culminating in the massive destruction of the homes and lives of millions of Germans and of tens of millions of Germany's neighbors. This would not be the first time, nor the last, that the project of establishing and nurturing national roots for a people would lead to the violent denial of rights, home, and life to others. But the Nazi effort would surpass most if not all others in its viciousness and brutality. Heidegger's prewar invocations to an authentic German home anchored in blood and soil were alarmingly aligned with the yet-to-be-fully-revealed plans of the National Socialist Party. As a party member and ideological advocate, Heidegger participated, albeit naively, in Germany's intellectual preparation for the bloody attempt to expand the Germanic homeland while purging it of all threats to its imagined purity. Though Heidegger had no taste for the racist violence with which the restoration of the German Heimat was to be attempted, his nostalgic longing for the establishment of an organic national family rooted in tradition by blood, language, and soil allowed a dangerous accommodation.[4]

The defeat of the Nazis did not obviate the concrete problems of homelessness, or Heidegger's concern for authentic dwelling. After the war, Germany would experience a massive housing crisis as a result of its physical and economic destruction. The misery of those who weathered the storm of war but were left homeless in its aftermath was enormous. Heidegger's postwar preoccupation with homelessness is, then, perhaps understandable as the product of enduring national and cultural concerns. Unfortunately, his postwar addresses retain a dangerous nostalgia for what Germany had lost in its transition to modernity and had failed to regain through conquest. Heidegger's longing for a pastoral *communitas* remained not only out of touch with the realities of the postwar, increasingly global, and cosmopolitan civilization, but susceptible to fascistic formulations. More than fifteen years after an Allied victory had put an end to the threat of an expanded and purified German Heimat, while German reintegration into the family of nations was well under way, Heidegger would still wonder how he and his fellow Germans might set themselves up "as a bulwark against the on-rush of the alien." The answer offered is that they must "awaken unceasingly

---

[4] Heidegger's eulogy to Albert Leo Schlageter, shot for acts of sabotage by the occupying French in the Ruhr in 1923, provides a frightening prelude to the rabid nationalism that would later jell into a murderous war for lebensraum. In his role as rector, Heidegger romanticizes: "As he stood defenseless facing the rifles, the hero's inner gaze soared above the muzzles to the daylight and mountains of his home that he might die for the German people and its Reich with the Alemannic countryside before his eyes.... Student of Freiburg, let the strength of this hero's native mountains flow into your will." (Heidegger, "Political Texts," 97).

the bestowing and healing and conserving powers of Home . . . where Origin and the customs fostered from ancient times determine human existence."[5] One winces at the ease with which such romanticism might be integrated into a fascistic ideology targeting immigrants for persecution or expulsion. Heidegger stated a few years later that "according to our human experience and history, everything essential and of great magnitude has arisen only out of the fact that man had a home and was rooted in a tradition" (OGS 57); one only hopes that the Nazis' shriek of *Blut und Boden* was not lingering in Heidegger's mind.

We ought to deny ourselves the nostalgic romanticism to which Heidegger fell prey. And we are right to shun the national chauvinism of which this nostalgic romanticism often proves the cause or veneer. But we ought not ignore the social, cultural, political, psychological, and ontological significance of homelessness in the contemporary world. Particularly in his later writings, Heidegger would incisively flag the real dangers inherent in an increasingly cosmopolitan civilization. No longer securely rooted in traditions of land, language, ethnicity, and religion, humanity has found no substitutes for these stabilizing though treacherous possessions. If psyche no less than nature abhors a vacuum, then we must ask what will replace the tribal solidarities that have structured so much of human history. Heidegger believes that the will to power, in its guise as a will to knowledge, becomes the substitute by default. It feeds off the nomadic spirit of modernity, and drives humanity to ever intensified pursuits of possessive mastery. As we cease to share a world, but share only a desire for its control and conquest, the prospect of finding a common home evaporates. We cease to dwell and become uprooted, spiritually as well as physically. The question of home, then, should not be formulated as a concern for an exclusive national homeland. The question we confront today is whether humankind is losing its capacity to find its home on earth.

Marshall McLuhan insightfully describes the transition to contemporary times in terms of the evolution of human transience. He writes, "Man the food-gatherer reappears incongruously as information-gatherer. In this role electronic man is no less a nomad than his paleolithic ancestors."[6] Like McLuhan, Heidegger prompts us to question whether today we relate to each other less as inhabitants of a shared world than as deracinated participants of rationalized processes. Such uprootedness is particularly troubling because it cannot be remedied by technical linkages. And yet, as both Heidegger and McLuhan observe, such linkages

[5] Martin Heidegger, "Messkirch's Seventh Centennial," *Listening* 8 (1973): 45.

[6] Marshall McLuhan, *Understanding Media: The Extensions of Man* (New York: Mentor, 1964), 248.

are the only ones readily available in the contemporary world. Being nomadic gatherers of information, McLuhan continues, "we extend our central nervous system globally, instantly interrelating every human experience."[7] Here a shared sense of home and belonging is replaced with the sharing of information. This information, however, is not a stable possession; it is our own malleable and disposable creation. It arises not from a common world but from a common will to knowledge. In other words, the common world has been pulled from underneath us and atomized so that we might receive it back piecemeal, as a steady stream of data. Information may indeed interrelate every human experience today. But this feat can only be accomplished by the stamping of the vast diversity of human experience into a uniform, universal currency. The price of interrelation appears to be homogenization. And homogenization indicates not the capacity to share a home, but the incapacity to resist a process.

For Heidegger, the solution to modern homelessness consists in a humanity transformed by the opportunity to participate in worldliness. A discovery of our essential Being-in-the-world and our worldly shepherding of Being is required. This discovery is for Heidegger all too distant, and perhaps unlikely. Tribal gods, lands, and languages are gone. Disenchantment follows in the wake of an ubiquitous rationalization. Routinized and homogenized, Nietzsche foresaw, modern humanity is left without a nature and without a project. Heidegger describes the predicament with the lamentation that "we are too late for the gods, and too early for Being." He also indicates hope, however: "Being's poem, just begun, is man" (*PLT* 4). Hope rests on the possibility for a fundamental transformation. A humanity that is to serve as Being's poem cannot remain a humanity defined by its metaphysically grounded possession and mastery of the world. Yet today this seems to be the only game in town.

Homelessness, Humanism, and Anxiety

While rector, Heidegger spoke in numerous political addresses of the need for a revitalized German home. But in his philosophic works as a whole, the home in question is one for humanity at large. His primary concern is the meaning of human being, not the peculiarities of German being. At the same time, Heidegger's philosophic appeal to humanity should not be confused with humanism. The reason, spelled out most clearly in the 1947 "Letter on Humanism," is relatively straightfor-

---

[7] Ibid., 310–11.

ward. Humanism posits humankind as the center of a universe made available for exploration and exploitation. Being exists as a resource for the species and receives its value accordingly. The species, in turn, becomes defined in its essence by its jurisdiction over the universe of beings, their values, and their truths. For the humanist, the Being of being is always objective presence, that which relates as object to the species-subject. But this simply means that humanism is founded on and in turn reinforces metaphysical subjectivism. Heidegger asks us to abandon humanism because "every humanism is either grounded in a metaphysics or is itself made to be the ground of one" (*BW* 202). If Heidegger's goal is to promote our establishing a home in worldliness through a re-awakened, nonsubjectivist relation to Being, then humanism, traditionally conceived, remains an obstacle.

The question becomes one of tactics. Heidegger chooses to weather the admonitions of those for whom an abandonment of humanism amounts to an endorsement of barbarism or theism rather than to engage in the effort of forcing new meaning into a metaphysically saturated term. He asks: "Should we still keep the name 'humanism' for a 'humanism' that contradicts all previous humanism—although it in no way advocates the inhuman? And keep it just so that by sharing in the use of the name we might perhaps swim in the predominant currents, stifled in metaphysical subjectivism and submerged in oblivion of Being? Or should thinking, by means of open resistance to 'humanism,' risk a shock that could for the first time cause perplexity concerning the *humanitas* of *homo humanus* and its basis?" (*BW* 225). By rejecting humanism, Heidegger seeks to engage that thinking which questions human being anew. The hope is to discover in this questioning the essence of human being, to find that the mystery that situates this questioning constitutes an abode for human being, a place of dwelling.

The "shock" Heidegger elicits in rejecting metaphysical humanism is risked in the hope of awakening "a reflection . . . about the dimension in which the essence of man, determined by Being itself, is at home" (*BW* 225). The dimension in which the essence of humankind is at home is its Being-in-the-world. This "Being-in" does not primarily signify a concrete spatial relation. Rather, Being-in (*In-Sein*) refers to human being's capacity to "reside" alongside something "familiar." Being-in signifies a set of relationships to which one is "accustomed" and in which one is "absorbed." Importantly, however, these relationships remain susceptible to ontological questioning and an abode may be found in such questioning itself (*BT* 80). Being at home in the world has less to do with our ongoing relation to any particular plot of ground than it does with our relation to the ground of Being itself.

Being-in-the-world is in no sense an individual achievement. It is an intrinsic characteristic of the species. But being at home in the world is an achievement of sorts; for human being, as a creature capable of ontological reflection, necessarily understands itself as fundamentally not at home. That is what it means to exist as a thrown being. The worldly stage is neither of our making nor of our choosing, and we find ourselves cast in roles beyond our power fully to direct or control. The perception of our worldly being as an ungrounded thrownness produces anxiety. Anxiety is perhaps best described as the state of unease in which one's "there" is revealed to be not fully one's own. In anxiety one feels oneself displaced, alienated. The world becomes disclosed as foreign. In short, anxiety is the foreboding of homelessness.

Heidegger describes anxiety as *unheimlich*. Translators have generally rendered this as "uncanny," and the connotation of uneasy strangeness is also present in the German. Literally, however, unheimlich means unhomelike. Heidegger was appreciative of both senses of the word, and his explanation of its meaning summarizes the mood of anxiety, but with a surprising twist:

> In anxiety one feels "*uncanny*." . . . But here "uncanniness" also means "not-being-at-home." In our first indication of the phenomenal character of Dasein's basic state . . . Being-in was defined as "residing alongside . . . ," "Being-familiar with. . . ." This character of Being-in was then brought to view more concretely through the everyday publicness of the "they," which brings tranquilized self-assurance—"Being-at-home," with all its obviousness —into the average everydayness of Dasein. On the other hand, as Dasein falls, anxiety brings it back from its absorption in the "world". Everyday familiarity collapses. . . . Being-in enters into the existential "mode" of the "*not-at-home*." . . . When in falling we flee *into* the "at-home" of publicness, we flee *in the face of* the "not-at-home"; that is, we flee in the face of the uncanniness which lies in Dasein—in Dasein as thrown Being-in-the-World. . . . That kind of Being-in-the-world which is tranquilized and familiar is a mode of Dasein's uncanniness, not the reverse. *From an existential-ontological point of view, the "not-at-home" must be conceived as the more primordial phenomenon.* (BT 233–34)

Anxiety is the mood of homelessness that tears one away from the habitual dispositions that facilitate our coping with daily affairs. But anxiety is not a deprived state of being nor a deficient state of mind. On the contrary, anxiety is a basic disposition from which other moods may be seen to depart. Being at home in the world, in the sense of feeling comfortable within the weave of convention, is a fleeing into ontic familiarity in the face of ontological uncanniness. The problem, Heidegger maintains, is not that this flight occurs. We all necessarily live in the manner of everydayness as a condition of human being, shifting for ourselves or with others, and, in short, getting by. Life itself, one might fairly say, depends on this habitual management and ingenious coping. In turn, anxiety is not to be deprecated, because it brings to light a basic, if sometimes harsh, ontological reality: our thrown Being-in-the-world. The point is neither permanently to escape our anxious apprehension of contingency and the nothingness of Being nor self-destructively to languish in it. The problem is to live in the balance.

Anxiety is an awareness or foreboding of our homeless condition. If, following Heidegger, we refuse to flee from anxiety, then we must somehow learn to dwell with this uncanniest of moods. One must learn to become at home in homelessness. Heidegger proposes that we experience anxiety as our own, as belonging to us in the same sense that we belong to the world. He proposes that we make our abode in the world in a way that acknowledges rather than ignores or denies our sense of existential displacement. One never truly secures a home on this earth, Heidegger admits. Discovering a home is only a destiny we approach.[8] Still, we may learn to dwell in the ontological homelessness that anxiety brings to light. Indeed, the "unhomelike being at home of man on earth" (*unheimische Heimischsein des Menschen auf der Erde*) is precisely what is most worthy of poetry and thought, for "the becoming at home in not being home" (*das Heimischwerden im Unheimischsein*) is the meaning of humanity's worldly dwelling (G 53:150–51). The ongoing search for a home in our earthly homelessness defines human life. Engaging this search authentically in thought defines the philosophic life.

Being at home connotes a peaceful belonging, while anxiety indicates an uneasy displacement. How are the two reconcilable? The answer, Heidegger intimates, is that existential anxiety, although disruptive of everyday familiarity, is confluent with a deeper ontological serenity. He writes that "the anxiety felt by the courageous cannot be contrasted with the joy or even the comfortable enjoyment of a peaceable life. It stands—on the hither side of all such contrasts—in secret union with the serenity and gentleness of creative longing" (*EB* 343; translation emended). We may come to find a peaceful home in ontological questioning despite its attendant anxiety. Profound serenity prevails, however, only once one has learned truly to share the world with the intru-

---

[8] See G 13:156. The indebtedness of the deconstructivists to Heidegger is evident here. Richard Bernstein's description of Derrida's philosophy summarizes the point: "Derrida seeks to show us that we never quite are or can be at home in the world. We are always threatened by the uncanniness of what is canny; we are always in exile—even from ourselves. We may long and dream of being at home in our world, to find a 'proper' center, but we never achieve this form of presence or self-presence." (Bernstein, *New Constellation*, 179).

sive intimations of thrownness and contingency. One must experience oneself as belonging within, rather than threatened by, the limits marking the finitude of human being.

Belonging to the Fourfold

The world is the web of our social and cultural relations, our relations to artifacts, and our relations to nature. Relationships are defined as much by their boundaries as by their content. With this in mind, Heidegger defines the world as a "fourfold" (*Gevierte*) that encompasses and limits these relationships. "The unitary fourfold of sky and earth, mortals and divinities," Heidegger states, "we call—the world" (*PLT* 199). The sky serves as a limit to the earth, as the earth does to the sky. Mortals, in turn, are defined in their timely limitations in contrast to the (immortal) divinities. Being at home in the world, then, is not tantamount to gaining security for one's status or station. It does not mean securing our self-preservation, and certainly not the preservation of ourselves from eventual death. Quite the opposite: in discovering our place in the world we gain acceptance of a "good death." Not security but belonging is what characterizes being at home. The sense of belonging consists of a knowledge and acceptance of the boundaries of the place, or of the relationships, that one inhabits. The world as home is less a place of security than a relationship in need of securing, a set of boundaries in need of tending. It is a place of limits: limits to perception, limits to knowledge, and, most salient, limits to life itself. Being at home in the world is a self-reflective exploration of and living within limits.

The essence of human dwelling is the acknowledgment of that which human being is not, in the context of what is. The fourfold of earth and sky, mortals and divinities, defines the world of human beings in the same sense that the flowing water and impervious banks define the river. The river is neither the water without the banks, nor the banks without the water. The boundaries of each allow the identification of the whole. In being an issue for itself, human being makes the world its issue. With the world in focus, the question of boundaries arises, including those boundaries mortals never transgress.

Heidegger insists that human being discovers its home in the world primarily by means of poetic thinking, the thoughtful disclosure of Being through language. He writes that "poetry is what first brings man onto the earth, making him belong to it, and thus brings him into dwelling" (*PLT* 218). Heidegger frequently invokes and discusses this verse by Hölderlin: "Full of merit, yet poetically, man / Dwells on this earth." Human life is full of merit for its wondrous deeds and accomplishments, yet our capacity to dwell, to find a home in the world, is defined not by our productivity but by our poetry. To dwell is to discover and accept the world as a fourfold marking the human horizon. Such discovery and acceptance is a poetic act—that is, an act of thankful and thoughtful disclosure. To dwell in the fourfold is to shepherd Being poetically in the company of fellow humans, preserving its world and awaiting death. To say that humans dwell poetically on earth is not a question of geography, ethnicity, or technical mastery, but of ontological disclosure. Being homeless, in this sense, signifies the absence of a poetic—a thoughtfully disclosive—capacity. To be truly homeless, for Heidegger, is to lose one's ability to reveal the world as the place of human dwelling. To be truly at home is to exercise one's ontologically disclosive capacities. Being at home in the world and being free are the same. To be at home everywhere is to experience the freedom that allows our disclosure of the Being of our world.

Combating postmodern homelessness requires thinking through, and beyond, metaphysics. Preparing the way philosophically so that humanity might find the thinking of Being "more compelling" and hence come to dwell anew in the world is the Heideggerian task. In his last known address, given two weeks before his death in April 1976, Heidegger summarized this project: "To think properly the legacy which derives from the beginning of the history of Being and which remained necessarily unthought in and for that beginning—'Αλήθεια [aletheia] as such —and thereby to prepare the possibility of a transformed abode of man in the world."[9] Our worldly abode is transformed once it no longer is approached metaphysically, as an objective reality, but rather as a set of relationships in which we participate questioningly. Being at home in the world entails knowing that the question of dwelling is, as Heidegger insisted, "*the* question"—that is, that which remains "most worthy" of questioning. It follows that the difficulty of finding our home increases as the metaphysical orientation to human being gains sway and the question of dwelling increasingly declines in importance.

To the extent there persists a longing to dwell in the modern world, it typically manifests itself as a metaphysical drive to construct an abode. Herein homelessness becomes a problem to be resolved through social engineering and technological ingenuity. Heidegger is convinced that all such resolutions are ill fated, "for no technological equipment nor any of its achievements or aids, neither the powers of invention pushed to their limits nor endless activity have the power to give us homeland, i.e., that which sustains and determines and lets us grow in the core of our

[9] Heidegger, "Modern Natural Science and Technology," 4.

existence."[10] A proper abode for humanity can never be fabricated. It may only be discovered and rediscovered. True dwelling is not an imposition of the self on a foreign landscape, but, as Heidegger put it, a setting at peace, a preserving and a safeguarding of each thing in its nature. We read:

> To dwell, to be set at peace, means to remain at peace within the free, the preserve, the free sphere that safeguards each thing in its nature. *The fundamental character of dwelling is this sparing and preserving.* . . . human being consists in dwelling and, indeed, dwelling in the sense of the stay of mortals on the earth. But "on the earth" already means "under the sky." Both of these *also* mean "remaining before the divinities" and include a "belonging to men's being with one another." By a *primal* oneness the four— earth and sky, divinities and mortals—belong together in one. . . . The simple oneness of the four we call *the fourfold*. Mortals *are* in the fourfold by *dwelling*. . . . Mortals dwell in that they save the earth. . . . Mortals dwell in that they receive the sky as sky . . . they do not turn night into day nor day into a harassed unrest. Mortals dwell in that they await the divinities as divinities. . . . They do not make their gods for themselves and do not worship idols. . . . Mortals dwell in that they initiate their own nature—their being capable of death as death—into the use and practice of this capacity, so that there may be a good death. . . . To preserve the fourfold, to save the earth, to receive the sky, to await the divinities, to escort mortals—this fourfold preserving is the simple nature, the presencing, of dwelling. (*PLT* 149–51, 158–59)

The earth is fixed, concrete, sensuous, within our grasp—and for this very reason is in need of being saved. The sky lies beyond our reach, and therefore may only be received.[11] Gods, unlike the sky, not only escape our reach, but elude even our perceptual and conceptual grasp. They can only be awaited. Finally, mortals, as coinhabitants of the world, require caring accompaniment: they are to be escorted. The fourfold testifies to our awareness of what lies within our horizon and what lies beyond us. Dwelling is a preserving of these limits.

Are we to assume from this talk of gods and immortals that being at home in the world necessitates some sort of religious faith? Does Heidegger extol belief in immortal gods? Must we, before discovering

---

[10] Heidegger, "Messkirch's Seventh Centennial," 50–51 (translation emended).

[11] Today, however, as we blacken the sky with emissions, litter it with orbiting debris, and burn holes in it with chemicals, it too requires saving. Effectively, the sky, in the sense of the upper biosphere and stratosphere, has become part of the earth. Yet the sun and other stars still escape our reach in the way that the sky once did. They dwarf us with their distance and power, allowing us perspective on the frailty of human life and the need simply to receive what is.

our worldly home, rediscover a home in 'the beyond.' I shall postpone grappling with these questions until the next chapter, in order to focus on the meaning of "saving the earth." The issue here is whether this feature of dwelling corresponds to an ecological politics. The answer is a qualified yes. And the argument, once again, is grounded in Heidegger's understanding of the nature of human freedom.

Dwelling, Freedom, and Ecology

The god of Genesis and Jeremiah urged humankind to subdue the earth. Freedom in the Western tradition has been identified since the time of Adam with dominion. Neither positive nor negative liberty, nor its postmodern counterpart, mitigates this identification. Historically, positive libertarians have celebrated the domination of nature as indicative of the prerogatives of human rationality. Like the domination of the lower self (or of "inferior" peoples and classes), the domination of nature has served positive libertarians as a testimonial to human freedom. Negative libertarians, in turn, have fostered dominion over the earth because of their preoccupation with inalienable rights of property and person. Nature, incapable of bearing rights of its own, relinquishes all claim to protection, respect, or care to the extent that it is not accorded sanctuary under the aegis of private property. But private property, understood in a Lockean sense as the extension of the self (or the self's labor), is to be disposed of as its owner sees fit, unconstrained by anything save perhaps the obligation of efficient exploitation.[12] Postmodern liberty has been around for too short a time to have earned any historical indictment on ecological grounds. Yet my sense is that postmodern liberty, which valorizes the powers of artistic creation and the heroic struggle against subjectification, is as likely to depreciate as it is to celebrate qualities of guardianship. The postmodern worry with panoptic social administration, given its Nietzschean orientation to freedom, leaves postmodernists susceptible to a radically individualistic (even narcissistic) reaction. The all-out effort to escape the encroachments of "pas-

[12] Thus John Locke would justify the expropriation of native American lands without recompense because of the natives' insufficient exploitation of them. According to Locke, leaving lands unexploited was equivalent to wasting them; in wasting their lands, the "wretched inhabitants" of America forfeited all rights of ownership and defense. "Land that is left wholly to Nature," Locke writes in the *Second Treatise of Government* (sec. 42), "that hath no improvement of Pasturage, Tillage, or Planting, is called, as indeed it is, *wast[e]*; and we shall find the benefit of it amount to little more than nothing." John Locke, *Two Treatises of Government*, ed. Peter Laslett (New York: Mentor, 1960), 336–39; see also Wayne Glausser, "Three Approaches to Locke and the Slave Trade," *Journal of the History of Ideas* 51 (1990): 199–216.

toral power" places the ecological linkage of freedom to stewardship in disfavor.[13] In short, without an understanding of liberty divorced from the will to artistic mastery, the postmodernist is as unlikely as the negative or positive libertarian to foster an earthly caring.

The word ecology derives from the Greek *oikos,* meaning a house, home, or dwelling. Ecological practice, it follows, is about the caretaking of our earthly dwelling place. Heidegger's philosophy of freedom, which promotes the caretaking of home, corresponds to an ecological practice. Commenting on this linkage, Michael Zimmerman writes that "Heidegger's critique of anthropocentric humanism, his call for humanity to learn to 'let things be,' his notion that humanity is involved in a 'play' or 'dance' with earth, sky, and gods, his meditation of the possibility of an authentic mode of 'dwelling' on the earth, his complaint that industrial technology is laying waste to the earth, his emphasis on the importance of local place and 'homeland,' his claim that humanity should guard and preserve things, instead of dominating them—all these aspects of Heidegger's thought help to support the claim that he is a major deep ecological theorist."[14] There is much to what Zimmerman says here, and one might add to his list Heidegger's understanding of Dasein as care, and Heidegger's definition of human being as the "shepherd of Being." However, one must be wary of straightforward translations of Heideggerian philosophy into ecological theory.

Human being, Heidegger insists, is to be defined primarily not as the shepherd of beings, natural or otherwise, but as the shepherd of Being. This guardianship, Heidegger explicitly states, "is not fixated upon something existent" (*PLT* 184). One is indeed asked to experience truth (*Wahrheit*) as preservation, to understand dwelling in terms of guarding and sparing, and to acknowledge that "preservation belongs to the herdsman." Yet Heidegger is also quick to point out that this under-

---

[13] See Michel Foucault, "Governmentality," *Ideology and Consciousness* 6 (1979): 5–21 and his "Omnes et Singulatum: Towards a Critique of 'Political Reason,'" in *The Tanner Lectures on Human Values,* vol. 2, ed. Sterling McMurrin (Salt Lake City: University of Utah Press, 1981).

[14] Zimmerman, *Heidegger's Confrontation with Modernity,* 242–43. In a more recent article, Zimmerman reevaluates his position on Heidegger's affinity to deep ecology because of "the recent controversy about his support for National Socialism." Michael Zimmerman, "Rethinking the Heidegger–Deep Ecology Relationship," *Environmental Ethics* 15 (Fall 1993): 196. Heidegger's ecological credentials have become a frequent topic of discussion among philosophers and environmental ethicists. Charles Taylor, for example, writes that "Heidegger's understanding of language, its *telos,* and the human essence can be the basis of an ecological politics, founded on something deeper than an instrumental calculation of the conditions of our survival (though that itself ought to be enough to alarm us). It can be the basis of in one sense a 'deep' ecology." Charles Taylor, "Heidegger, Language, and Ecology," in Dreyfus and Hall, *Heidegger,* 266.

standing has "little to do with bucolic idylls and Nature mysticism."
The herdsman, he insists, "continues to hold the place of nothingness"
(*EGT* 36). Quite out of keeping with romanticized notions of a firmly
grounded pastoral life, the shepherding of Being throws one anxiously
into the abyss of groundlessness. Heidegger's is an ontological project,
rather than a naturalistic one. A questioning relation to Being may indeed erupt from a solicitous wonder at the vast diversity and beauty of
nature. But it may also ensue from gazing at stars, studying quantum
physics, or raising a child in the inner city.

The same tack must be taken regarding Heidegger's understanding of
care. Care is occasionally mistaken to mean altruistic love and caretaking, something that excludes "egoistic" or "greedy" dispositions.[15] Care
may indeed disclose itself as a love for humans and nature. But that is
not all care is. Because care permeates human being, modes of human
being that are neither loving, nor necessarily authentic, are also aspects
of care (*BT* 227; cf. *BT* 374). Care does not necessarily describe benign
relations humans establish with each other or with other forms of life.
Rather, care refers to the totality of human Being-in-the-world. Existence, falling, and facticity, all of which are constitutive of *das Man,*
also pertain to care (*BT* 293; cf. *BT* 84 and *BW* 210). Rather than
indicating a specific ethical or emotional relationship, care, like guardianship, signifies the ontological state of worldliness.

Despite such caveats, Heidegger's ecological credentials can be supported on a number of grounds. Our sense of self, always in part philosophically derived, impinges on our political, social, and cultural lives.
The way we act in the world depends on who we think we are—that is,
on how and what we think (of) ourselves. To define human being as
care, while not stipulating any particular ethical or environmental attitude or comportment, indicates that human being is not to be defined
by its possessive mastery of the world. "It is one thing just to use the
earth," Heidegger writes, "another to receive the blessing of the earth
and to become at home in the law of this reception in order to shepherd
the mystery of Being and watch over the inviolability of the possible"
(*EP* 109). Relations with others and nature would develop in a less
technologically exploitative and more preservative, ecological direction,
Heidegger suggests, once the understanding of human being as care displaces the subjectivism that grounds our metaphysical self-understandings. In writing that "man is not the lord of beings. Man is the shepherd

---

[15] Zimmerman writes: "What Heidegger means by care can perhaps best be understood
as love. . . . Only when we are freed from self-hatred, greed, and delusion can we really
love, for only then does egoism fade away." Michael Zimmerman, *Eclipse of the Self: The
Development of Heidegger's Concept of Authenticity* (Athens: Ohio University Press,
1981), 128.

of Being," Heidegger gestures at the changes to our concrete, worldly relationships that might ensue from changes in our ontological relationships (*BW* 221; cf. *N* 248). The ontology of dwelling engages the meaning of human being in a way that buttresses practical environmental concerns. Heidegger writes, "Mortals dwell in that they save the earth. . . . To save really means to set something free into its own presencing. To save the earth is more than to exploit it or even wear it out. Saving the earth does not master the earth and does not subjugate it, which is merely one step from spoliation" (*PLT* 150). The identification of human being as an ontologically care-full, worldly dweller facilitates an actual (ontic) earthly caretaking. Identifying oneself, and one's dignity, by the exercise of disclosive freedom precludes wholesale efforts at control and subjugation. To be free, we remember, is to set free, is to let be. The exercise of freedom coalesces our who and our how, our sense of self and our way of being in the world. To understand human freedom as a disclosure that preserves is to be well on the way to an ecological practice.

Heidegger, as Zimmerman notes, also supports a nonanthropocentric approach to the earth and the world. This is absolutely true, and has obvious ecological merit. But Heidegger does not suggest that we replace anthropocentrism with biocentrism. Biocentrism, intrinsic to most deep-ecological perspectives, relegates the human species to the same status as all other organisms.[16] Despite his fervent attack on subjectivism and humanism, Heidegger firmly maintains human exceptionalism. He maintains this exceptionalism because of human being's unique disclosive capacities; "it is man, open toward Being, who alone lets Being arrive as presence" (*ID* 31–32; see also *BT* 28, 35). Animals, Heidegger writes, cannot engage in the "work"—philosophical, artistic, or political—in which the disclosure of Being in thought, word, or deed occurs. And this incapacity of beasts arises for one simple reason: "they lack *freedom*" (*PT* 109). Our capacity for disclosive freedom makes our sojourn here on earth exceptional, however brief this sojourn is in cosmic or evolutionary terms. Heidegger writes that "the question of Being and its variations and possibilities is at heart the correctly understood question of man. Compared with the duration of cosmic galaxies, human

---

[16] Heidegger is frequently misinterpreted on this score. See, for example, Bill Devall and George Sessions, *Deep Ecology: Living as If Nature Mattered* (Salt Lake City: Gibb M. Smith, 1985), 99. An axiological biocentrism, if conceivable in practice, would certainly be undesirable. The AIDS virus and the useful bacteria of our digestive tracts are most interesting specimens of life. But that we should cease to exploit the latter or combat the former seems to me as silly as it is unnatural. Nature, as Nietzsche was fond of reminding us, is all about exploitation and battles to the death, and we should not be arguing for a world in which viruses and grapes have the same "rights" to life and growth as children.

existence and its history is certainly quite fleeting, only a 'moment.' But this transiency is nevertheless the highest mode of Being when it becomes an existing out of and towards freedom" (*MFL* 18). There is, in short, a special place reserved for human being in Heidegger's universe because in that place freedom appears.

Zimmerman hedges his praise of Heidegger's ecological credentials at this point, citing the above passage as indication that Heidegger "over-estimated our importance" compared to that of the rest of nature.[17] But Zimmerman overlooks Heidegger's earlier statement that humankind's fundamental questioning is "far removed from any noisy self-importance concerning the life of one's own soul or that of others" (*MFL* 16–17). Moreover, Heidegger was clear that giving ontological priority to human being in no way suggests that the natural world, or the material world at large, exists (solely) for our benefit.[18] Indeed, disclosive freedom appears only in the absence of the possessive mastery that underlies such an assumption. Human being is the highest being (as opposed to the most powerful being) only to the extent that human being gains release from all self-aggrandizing subjectivism. If there is any claim to greatness in our being, it arises not from the human capacity to dominate and exploit but from the unique human capacity to dwell and disclose in a way that preserves.

Heidegger's unwillingness to exchange anthropocentrism for biocentrism, however, does not weaken his contribution to an ecological politics. Arguably, it makes his contribution more significant. Celebrating the unique capacities of human being to disclose in a way that preserves best ensures humanity's caretaking of the earth and the world. The fostering of human freedom, understood as a disclosive letting-be rather than a sovereign control, is precisely the measure that will best safeguard the earth's ecological diversity and health. One of Heidegger's favorite Heraclitean fragments is "Nature loves to hide." Nature loves to hide, one might say, because it resists becoming an open book. However we disclose the natural world, something else remains hidden yet beckoning: relationships of interdependence, evolutionary legacies, biological and aesthetic properties. The vast diversity of nature solicits the manifold modes of disclosure to which humans are heir because of their capacity for freedom. Hence our disclosive guardianship of nature marks, at the same time, the preservation of the greatness and uniqueness of human being.

[17] Michael Zimmerman, "Toward a Heideggerian *Ethos* for Radical Environmentalism," *Environmental Ethics* 5 (Summer 1983): 121.

[18] We read, for example, "That all functional relations are grounded ontologically in a for-the-sake-of in no way decides whether, ontically, all beings are as beings for the sake of the human Dasein" (*BP* 295).

In advocating a disclosive, caretaking orientation toward nature, Heidegger supports what in ecological circles is called bioregionalism. Bioregionalism is an orientation toward environmental care that advocates human guardianship of nature organized around relatively small communities sustainably integrated into local ecosystems. Likewise, Heidegger stresses that intimate ties to soil and locality are the antidote for the destructive exploitation of the earth and the technological manipulation and extortion of nature. Heidegger envisions living and working with, rather than against, natural processes. In contrast to high-tech agribusiness, for example, Heidegger affirms that "the work of the peasant does not challenge the soil of the field. In the sowing of the grain [the peasant] places the seed in the keeping of the forces of growth and watches over its increase" (QT 15). The remedy for our earthly homelessness, Heidegger maintains, "remains most readily possible and most enduringly effective there where the powers of encompassing nature and the echo of historical tradition abide together side by side. . . . Only the rural regions and the small country towns are today still adequate to this decisive task."[19]

We ought to maintain our critical edge here, however, for ecological and political reasons. In romanticizing the peasantry, Heidegger fails to acknowledge that small-scale farming may be every bit as unacquainted with the preservation of the land and as intent on its unsustainable exploitation as large-scale agribusiness. If the peasant proves less destructive, it may only be because of the relatively small size of the enterprise. Indeed, to the extent that poverty forces peasants more intensively to cultivate smaller and smaller plots of land, ecological devastation looms. In any case, peasants, like businesspeople, are neither born nor necessarily encultured with specifically technological or nontechnological dispositions. Care for the land, and for people, must be fostered culturally. I believe Heidegger is right in thinking that this care is fostered much better within small farming communities than through large-scale agribusiness. Still, we had best eschew the bucolic romanticism that Heidegger often found irresistible, for the rootedness in soil that Heidegger longed for has a seamy political side. In its thrall, Heidegger himself succumbed to a dangerous infatuation with the power of blood and soil that neatly aligned him with Nazism.

Agrarian provincialism has other political and ecological drawbacks. Many of the most pressing environmental concerns today remain impervious to anything but a globally regulated redress. To the extent that localism stymies rather than fosters such efforts, it may actually work against ecological health. In any case, the global management of certain

[19] Heidegger, "Messkirch's Seventh Centennial," 45.

ecological problems does not necessarily disrupt our rootedness to community or bioregion. Indeed, the environmental slogan "Think Globally, Act Locally!" is based on the compatibility—even synergy—of global concerns and local care. In any case, there are no eternal demarcations of one's place of dwelling. Rootedness for some will pertain mostly to a valley or watershed, for some to a city or nation, and for some to the earth itself. Moreover, the boundaries of these places of dwelling need not be defined by static geography or sovereignty. They may frequently overlap and remain ambiguously in flux, becoming redrawn in light of changing concerns and memberships. In other words, Heidegger's own predilection for Swabian peasant culture need not constrict our own sense of habitat. Heidegger's Arcadian nostalgia and lingering tribalism notwithstanding, I submit that fully dwelling within the fourfold today requires our willingness to live beyond—though not necessarily without—local, ethnic, and national enclosures. A discovery of our earthly home is warranted.[20]

The chief threat to this discovery is the technological temperament that transforms contemporary human being into a nomad in pursuit of physical and cognitive mastery. Within this nomadic worldview, all problems and mysteries, including those most fundamental to the human condition, are proposed as resolvable. They are expected to dissolve in the fast-moving stream of technological progress. There is a class of problems, however, that have no technical solutions. Only a change in consciousness will provide for their resolution. The problem of the overuse and abuse of public lands, Garrett Hardin submits in his famous article "The Tragedy of the Commons," is a case in point. Individuals who gain personally from the exploitation of the commons by grazing their stock on it will seek to maximize these gains by grazing ever more stock. This lack of self-restraint at a collective level eventually, and often quite rapidly, yields a commons overgrazed and eroded beyond further use, to everyone's detriment. Hardin's concern is not only the overuse of land but the overuse and abuse of water and air. Most pressingly, his concern is with the overpopulation of the earth itself. If individuals produce more progeny than the earthly commons can sustain, they will ensure a tremendous collective loss despite any (perceived) personal gain. The tragedy of the commons is the ecological

---

[20] William Connolly rightly observes that "the nostalgia in political theory (and the culture at large) for a 'politics of place' in which territoriality, sovereignty, electoral accountability, and belonging all correspond to each other in one 'political place' has the double effect today of depoliticizing global issues and weakening the ability to challenge state chauvinism." William E. Connolly, *The Terms of Political Discourse*, 3d ed. (Princeton: Princeton University Press, 1993), xvi.

tragedy of a common earth in an age of burgeoning populations and massive consumption.

Hardin's conclusion follows: "Ruin is the destination toward which all men rush, each pursuing his own best interest in a society that believes in the freedom of the commons. Freedom in a commons brings ruin to all."[21] Hardin admits that restrictions on breeding and ecologically destructive ways of living will precipitate vociferous denouncements of unjustified curtailments to "freedom." "But what does 'freedom' mean?" he asks. On the horns of our ecological dilemma, Hardin answers, following Hegel, that freedom can only mean "the recognition of necessity."[22] Heidegger would agree with Hardin that many problems, including that of the caretaking of our earthly home, are without technical solutions. Only a change in the way we think and feel—in the way we "are"—will allow their redress. Heidegger would also support Hardin's critical challenge to the traditional understanding of freedom. Nevertheless, Heidegger would disagree with Hardin, and Hegel, about the meaning of freedom.

Freedom is not the recognition of necessity. Indeed, it would be better to say that freedom is the necessity of recognition; freedom bespeaks not the acceptance of fate, but the active re-cognition of contingency and difference. We are not free because we mentally or physically master our fate by either submitting to or exploiting its decrees. Rather, we are free when we release ourselves from the will to master the world, and thus open ourselves fully to its mystery. Averting the tragedy of the commons, for Hardin, entails submitting everyone to coercive force. Effectively, we must do away with the commons altogether. Heidegger, on the other hand, asks us to expand the commons. He prompts us to discover the commonality of our worldly being and to make it our home. The point is not that laws (regulations and taxes) discouraging or prohibiting ecologically unsustainable practices (including the practices of overconsumption associated chiefly with Western nations) are unnecessary; they most certainly are. The point is that these laws (regulations and taxes) are unlikely ever to be sufficiently promulgated and observed if they are held to strike at the very freedom that secures human dignity and uniqueness.

Given a choice between liberty or collective death, the pursuit of the former is unlikely to be sufficiently checked by fear of the latter. In other words, freedom in a commons does bring ruin to all, but only if

---

[21] Garrett Hardin, "The Tragedy of the Commons," in *Managing the Commons*, ed. Garrett Hardin and John Baden (San Francisco: W. H. Freeman, 1977), 20.
[22] Ibid., 29.

freedom is understood to entail the possession and mastery of things, the ability to act arbitrarily or wantonly in the world. By Heidegger's reckoning, however, freedom is something quite different. Disclosive freedom is what allows a commons to be perceived as a commons in the first place—that is, a place defined not by ownership or dominion, but by guardianship. Disclosive freedom is precisely that which preserves the common world from ruin by preserving the meaning of a common world.

In exploring the nature of problems that have no technical solutions, Hardin points to the difficulty of winning a game of tic-tac-toe. Hardin explains that no procedures, regardless of their sophistication, will allow victory in such a game against a competent opponent. One can win only by radically redefining what the word "winning" means, or radically redefining the game itself.[23] The reader might suspect that this is precisely the nature of Heidegger's nontechnical, philosophically inspired resolution to the problem of saving the earth. "Freedom," like "winning," has simply been redefined so as to resolve by linguistic fiat the dilemma of preserving liberty without destroying the commons. Surely such verbal gymnastics cannot adequately address a concrete problem embedded in real worldly practices. Heidegger, however, is not proposing a solution by linguistic fiat. A change in the meaning of freedom follows, and follows only, from changes in the actual experience of freedom. If the tragedy of the commons is to be averted without sacrificing human dignity, then the *experience* of disclosive freedom must become manifest in our thoughts, words, and deeds.

Our relation to the earthly commons, despite all efforts to "tread lightly," will always include elements of exploitation. Indeed, all organisms engage in the exploitation of their environment to a greater or lesser degree. Only human beings, however, assume that nature as a whole is to be made an object of possession and mastery. The reason, one might speculate, is that everything that remains beyond our possession and mastery is perceived as a threat to our freedom and an affront to our dignity.[24] What threatens the earth's ecological health, in other words, is not so much the variety of our technological capacities as the uniformity of our technological drive. This drive has its limits defined, or rather has its limits left undefined, because of our identification of possessive mastery with freedom.

---

[23] Ibid., 17.

[24] As William Connolly notes, "in a world driven by the drive for mastery, any absence of control is experienced as unfreedom and imposition." William E. Connolly, *Political Theory and Modernity* (Ithaca: Cornell University Press, 1993), 2.

Ecological concerns have erupted in postmodern times largely as a result of the increasingly apparent limits to human growth. The more these limits are ignored—or worse, viewed as obstacles to be overcome—the graver the crisis becomes. Heidegger develops a philosophy of limits. More to the point, Heidegger describes our freedom as dependent on rather than curtailed by our worldly boundaries. Once the boundaries of human being are experienced neither as a threat to human freedom nor as an affront to human dignity, the tragic attempt to conquer the earth might be abated and the opportunity for its caretaking approached.

Eight

Receiving the Sky and Awaiting Divinities

THE CHALLENGE OF TECHNOLOGY

> All technology has the Midas touch. When a
> community develops some extension of itself,
> it tends to allow all other functions to be
> altered to accommodate that form.
> (Marshall McLuhan, *Understanding Media*)

WE LIVE in a world of furious technological growth. Human beings modify as never before the world in which they live. Increasingly, they attempt to create this world anew. Yet the question remains whether this world, frantically produced under the law of exponential growth, provides a home. Despite our power to fashion our habitat—indeed, largely because of this increasing power—we are left without an abiding sense of place. This alienation is evident whenever the earth is treated less as a place of dwelling than as a quarry from which resources are to be extracted and refuse deposited. Having accumulated the power to pitch the planet into an irreversible ecological "coma," as a recent news report indicated in an extreme illustration of the point, we are already fantasizing about our escape to its celestial neighbors, which would be prepared for human habitation through massive "terraforming" techniques. As Heidegger foresaw, "The partly conceded, partly denied homelessness of man with regard to his *essence* is replaced by the organized global conquest of the earth, and the thrust into outer space" (*N* 248). Our profound sense of homelessness, more than a description of the cosmopolitan, transient, and accelerated pace of contemporary life, also marks our status as nomads in the realm of thought and spirit. As our nomadic conquests wax, our capacity to dwell on earth wanes. In the last address given before his death, Heidegger would ask his hometown friends at Messkirch to "reflect whether and how in the age of the technologized, uniform world civilization home can still exist" (*G* 13:243).

Complacency in homelessness threatens to become the postmodern condition. The defining feature of this complacency, however, is not lassitude. To the contrary: it fosters an acceleration of technological growth. In the wake of this growth, the remedy for our homelessness, if we may speak in such terms, remains elusive. But a solution will not arise from the willful attempt to fabricate an abode for ourselves. Technological attempts to create a world are ill fated, for our technological capacity to build a home remains improperly channeled so long as our capacity to find a home in this world remains dormant. Heidegger warns:

> *Only if we are capable of dwelling, only then can we build..* . . The *real plight of dwelling* does not lie merely in a lack of houses. The real plight of dwelling is indeed older than the world wars and their destruction, older also than the increase of the earth's population and the condition of the industrial workers. The real dwelling plight lies in this, that mortals ever search anew for the nature of dwelling, that they *must ever learn to dwell.* What if man's homelessness consisted in this, that man still does not even think of the *real* plight of dwelling as *the* plight? Yet as soon as man *gives thought* to his homelessness, it is a misery no longer. Rightly considered and kept well in mind, it is the sole summons that *calls* mortals into their dwelling. But how else can mortals answer this summons than by trying on *their* part, on their own, to bring dwelling to the fullness of its nature? This they accomplish when they build out of dwelling, and think for the sake of dwelling. (*PLT* 160–61)

Building, Heidegger indicates, must arise out of the spirit of dwelling, not as its substitute. To dwell (*Aufenthalten*) is to find one's place. The assumption is that this place presents one with the *ongoing* task of its discovery and preservation. To find one's place is not to forge it through the power of technological will. It is to receive and care for an abode. Our capacity to maintain this caring reception in the face of inevitable technological growth will determine our future as worldy dwellers.

Metaphysics and Technology

Technology is one of Heidegger's enduring and foremost concerns. Though Heidegger only explicitly formalized this concern in his later work, he expressed his worry about the systematic rationalization of the world early on. In 1919, Heidegger clearly described in a personal letter what over two decades later would become a preoccupation of his published work. He writes: "The unbridled, basically Enlightenment directive to nail life and everything living onto a board, like things, orderly and flat, so that everything becomes overseeable, controllable, definable, connectable, and explicable, where only many pure and unrestrained (*sit venia verbo*)—'ables' exist—this directive underlies all the many quasi-memories of life, which are being attempted today in every sphere of experience."[1] For Heidegger, the "Enlightenment directive" to control and standardize life ensues from the metaphysical drive to objectify the world. Modern technology and metaphysics, it follows, are largely equivalent terms (*EP* 93). Both arise from and evidence a refusal to think Being in their systematic (conceptual and practical) effort to possess and master being. Modern technology and metaphysics stand entwined. As such, neither allows a proper perspective from which to evaluate or overcome the other (*OGS* 59). Technology entices us into a productive process that precludes questioning thought, yet only such questioning could adequately reveal the nature of metaphysics. In turn, metaphysical humankind, engaged as a subject in the reductive objectification of being, is left little alternative but a technological apprehension and manipulation of the world.

Heidegger denies that insight into the nature of technology lies implicit in our ability to build and maintain machines. Technical knowledge—know-how about machines and techniques—does not constitute an understanding of the essence of technology. Essentially, technology is not even about machines, complex techniques, or the fabrication of artifacts. These are indeed the products of a technologically oriented world, but they are not the foundation of that world. As Heidegger neatly formulates the issue: "Our age is not a technological age because it is the age of the machine; it is an age of the machine because it is the technological age" (*WCT* 24). He pursues this point, saying that "the essence of technology is by no means anything technological" (*QT* 4). Unwrapping this perplexing statement will bring us to an understanding of the threat, and promise, of technology.

Heidegger acknowledges a fundamental relationship between machines and technology. But the modern (over)production of machines is to be viewed simply as a ramification of a particular way of thinking, or a particular way of being. Machine technology is only "the most visible outgrowth" of modern technology (*QT* 116). But if the essence of technology is not machinery, what is it? Machines might be viewed as extensions of tools. Unlike tools, however, machines do not conform to the human anatomy and rhythm, but, in most cases, actually induce human conformity to their own movements and timing. Nevertheless, machines, like tools, remain in an important sense mere means. As means they do not strictly entail goals but can be made to serve sundry purposes. Machines, as is often said, are "neutral" with regard to the

---

[1] Martin Heidegger, "Heidegger's Letter to the Boss' Daughter," *Telos* 77 (Fall 1988): 126.

ends to which they may be put.[2] With technology, however, this is not the case. "Technology is . . . no mere means," Heidegger writes. "Technology is a way of revealing" (*QT* 12). From an ontological perspective, technology is neither neutral nor merely instrumental. It is neither an artifact nor merely a means of producing artifacts. Rather, technology signifies a particular mode of disclosure. What technology reveals in a particular manner is the Being of beings.

Reflecting on the ancient Greeks, Heidegger notes that the root of the word "technology" is technē, which signifies not so much the making of something as its production in an etymologically strict sense: its leading or drawing forth. For the Greeks, technē signified a revelation of something, its uncovering or bringing to light. According to Heidegger, then, the word *technē* denotes "a mode of knowing. . . . *Techne*, as knowledge experienced in the Greek manner, is a bringing forth of beings in that it *brings forth* present beings as such beings *out of* concealedness and specifically *into* the unconcealedness of their appearance; *techne* never signifies the action of making" (*PLT* 59). Modern technology is also a revelation or bringing forth, but its manner of doing so, Heidegger maintains, is distinct from that of the ancients. The Greek experience of technē was a revelation of what lay in potential, as the form of the sculpture might be thought to lie concealed in the unchiseled stone. Hence technē was a form of "care," a way of enticing from beings their potential shapes, forms, and functions. This enticement, Heidegger believes, evidences a "resolute openness to beings" in the attempt "to ground beings on their own terms" (*WPA* 164, 165). Openness to beings, of which technē constitutes one particular mode, thus describes human being's assumption of a solicitous relationship to the world. This solicitation, Heidegger indicates, is the burden of freedom.[3] Ironically, human freedom (at least in the Western world) has typically been identified not with the solicitation of what lies in potential, but with the power to master and possess what is actual. Modern technology receives its defining characteristics therefrom.

Modern technology reveals the world not in the manner of a leading or bringing forth (*her-vor-bringen*) but as a challenging forth (*Herausfordern*). This challenging forth undeniably draws out what lies in

---

[2] Many would disagree with this statement, insisting that the complexity, size, and cost of machines, or the expertise required for their production and use, may make them antidemocratic forces and hence far from neutral in a political sense. See, for example, David Dickson, *The Politics of Alternative Technology* (New York: Universe Books, 1974). There is something to this point. However, the increasing sophistication of technology often allows it to serve democratic ends. Low-cost personal computers, "user-friendly" software, and desktop publishing techniques come to mind.

[3] Heidegger, *Essence of Reasons*, 101, 103.

potential. But it does so in a way that confronts this potential not as a phenomenologically discoverable essence in need of safeguarding. Rather, it extracts it in order to use it. Heidegger explains that "this setting-upon that challenges forth the energies of nature is an expediting [*Fördern*], and in two ways. It expedites in that it unlocks and exposes. Yet that expediting is always itself directed from the beginning toward furthering something else, i.e., toward driving on to the maximum yield at the minimum expense" (*QT* 15). To the extent that we may speak of a goal for technology as a whole, it is the endless pursuit of efficiency in the exploitation of resources.

In the technological drive for efficiency, the earth, its creatures, and our fellow human beings are reduced to the status of raw material—Heidegger's word is "standing-reserve" (*Bestand*). Technologically conceived, the world as a whole becomes standing-reserve. It exists in the mode of awaiting our use, of its being put to most efficient use. In a technological world, Heidegger writes, "everywhere everything is ordered to stand by, to be immediately at hand, indeed to stand there just so that it may be on call for a further ordering" (*QT* 17).[4] Heidegger suggests the term "enframing" (*Gestell*) for the mode of disclosure that displays everything as standing-reserve. Enframing, then, is the essence of modern technology, being that ordering which challenges everything forth as standing-reserve. Technology, in this sense, is totalizing. The development of any particular machine, artifact, or set of procedures is not the point. Heidegger's concern is that such developments are merely the symptoms of an expansive technological drive that recognizes no boundaries and makes no (ontological) distinctions in its effort to enframe the entire experiential field of human being.

Machines, techniques, and elaborate artifacts—what we generally understand as technology—remain of secondary concern to Heidegger. Foremost in his mind is the totalizing reach of enframing as a particular mode of human being. It follows that enframing, as the "way of revealing which holds sway in the essence of modern technology . . . is itself nothing technological" (*QT* 19–20). Machines are only the most patent examples of that which awaits use as standing-reserve and integrates the world as standing-reserve. The essence of modern technology is itself nothing technological because technology is grounded not in the production of machines (its most apparent effect), but in the ontological disclosure of the Being of being as standing-reserve. Technology is no mere means but a way of revealing, Heidegger says, because from a

---

[4] A Sierra Club newsletter describes the modern attitude toward forests as a standing reserve: "The truth is, we've been managing our national forests as though they were outdoor warehouses of living trees, held in inventory until the lumber companies are ready to take delivery."

technological viewpoint all disclosure is reduced to a mere means. In other words, technology cannot be neutrally applied within manifold modes of disclosure because technology imposes a single mode of disclosure: everything, everywhere, uniformly, is revealed as standing-reserve.

The Devastation of the Midas Touch

Technology has the Midas touch, and a particularly contagious one at that. Everything with which it comes in contact becomes uniformly subsumed into a framework of efficiently exploited resources. Indeed, technology reconfigures human society itself to accommodate the exigencies of its furthest extensions and intrusions. What is essential to modern technology is its refusal of limits, its rejection of boundaries and difference. In the end, humanity itself becomes part and parcel, indeed a most crucial element, of technological ordering. This is true in a number of respects. First, humankind is, by and large, the only producer of technology. Second, the efficient and endless production of technological artifacts requires their equally efficient and endless consumption. Once again, humankind is, by and large, technology's only consumer. But the circle is only fully completed when humanity becomes not simply the primary producer and consumer of technology, but that which technology primarily produces and consumes. The novelty of the postmodern world, in this light, is not that we live in a consumer society, but that society itself has become the consumed. Heidegger lays out in detail the ramifications of this total ordering:

> The "world wars" and their character of "totality" are already a consequence of the abandonment of Being. They press toward a guarantee of the stability of a constant form of using things up. Man, who no longer conceals his character of being the most important raw material, is also drawn into this process. Man is the "most important raw material" because he remains the subject of all consumption. He does this in such a way that he lets his will be unconditionally equated with this process, and thus at the same time become the "object" of the abandonment of Being. The world wars are the antecedent form of the removal of the difference between war and peace. . . . War has become a distortion of the consumption of beings which is continued in peace. Contending with a long war is only the already outdated form in which what is new about the age of consumption is acknowledged. . . . Since man is the most important raw material, one can reckon with the fact that some day factories will be built for the artificial breeding of human material based on present-day chemical research. (*EP* 103–6)

Written after Hitler's rise to power and before the war had revealed its final devastations, Heidegger indicates in the above passage, though only backhandedly and without assuming personal responsibility, that he has glimpsed the terrible error in his support for Nazism. Once in power, the Nazis quickly displayed their technological demon.

No more horrific and ruthless example of the total ordering of humanity as standing-reserve has ever been constructed than that of the Nazi concentration camps. Here technology's limitless scope and capacity for summoning horror was made evident in the unbridled exploitation of and experimentation with human raw material, the literal using-up of human bodies and minds. In the Nazis' "final solution," technology, understood not as a neutral tool or technique but as an overpowering ontological condition, came most dangerously to the fore. Yet present-day genetic research, which bears out Heidegger's prediction of the artificial breeding of human material, is ultimately no less dangerous for all its humanistic appeal. And present-day politics generously pays its dues to the technological demon. The success of contemporary political candidates largely rests on their ability to promote themselves as efficient managers of the growth of the forces of production and consumption. Wars are won and lost because of this same proficiency, and in large part with the singular purpose of deciding which state is to control what share of the global market. Yet amidst intense and occasionally bloody competition, the significance of national boundaries actually diminishes as states become equally subject to the same technological forces. Heidegger concludes that the distinction between national and international is becoming increasingly untenable (*EP* 107).

Technology is the chief historical ramification of the subjectivism introduced by Western metaphysical thought. Metaphysical subjectivism posits human being in relation to its world as a subject standing before an object of perception and (mental) representation. As Heidegger notes, a view of the world as an object (*Gegenstand*—literally, that which stands against) is the prerequisite for its instrumental use and domination. Subjectification is the precondition for objectification. Heidegger explains that "a being can be experienced as object only where man has become the subject, the one who experiences his basic relation to beings as the objectification—understood as mastery—of what encounters him."[5] With Nietzsche, subjectivism evolved into a radical individualism. For the most part, the subjectivism underlying modern technology has taken a different though analogous route. It has been translated into a radical humanism. That is, subjectivism in the modern

---

[5] Heidegger, Φύσις in Aristotle's Physics B, 1," 227.

age becomes a species-level orientation, effectively an objectifying an-thropocentrism. By means of this objectification, the technological mas-tery of the world by humanity at large is encouraged. The world is reduced to an object of manipulation for the species-subject. Here again, technological activity—the production of artifacts, the develop-ment of techniques, and the use of machines—is but a ramification and contributing condition, not the origin or cause, of subjectivism.

Heidegger illuminates the nature of species subjectivism in his discus-sion of the emerging world picture. "World picture" refers to the meta-physical reduction of the world to a human representation. It is a con-ceptual enframing. The significance of this reduction, Heidegger maintains, cannot be exaggerated. Indeed, the transformation of "the world . . . into picture and man into *subiectum*" constitutes the "funda-mental event of the modern age" (*QT* 133–34). The world conceived as picture takes us beyond the primitive subjectivism of the early modern age. No longer is the world objectified piecemeal by the representation and instrumental use of its components. Rather, the inclusive represen-tation of world as world-object becomes the most basic human experi-ence. The world picture is not, in this sense, a mere representation of an external, higher-order reality. Rather, the world picture becomes hu-manity's chief measure of reality. Effectively, it becomes reality itself. Today, for instance, customers may buy time in audio-video-tactile ma-chines that transport them into "virtual reality." Here one experiences and directs the course of sights, sounds, and sensations made available through highly sophisticated computer simulations. This epitomizes postmodern technological culture. Fact melds with fiction, history with drama, the discovered with the fabricated. The result is a cultural pas-tiche that bespeaks our unlimited extension into the world, or rather the unlimited fabrication of our world. By world picture, Heidegger is not simply referring to a visual image of the earth made possible by photo-graphs taken from orbiting spaceships or satellites.[6] Rather, he is indi-

---

[6] The ambition to control this imagery is, however, perhaps the impulse behind much satellite photography. One might reflect on the following environmentalist's concern: "For the first time in human history, our image of the Earth is not told to us by friends, elders, or family, nor is it gleaned through the direct experience of our own senses. The NASA image of the Earth is brought to us from the depths of cold space by immensely sophisticated machines to which only a few have access. . . . The photographic act can be a form of violence . . . when it transforms the external world into a spectacle, a commod-ity, a manipulable package. . . . With its single encompassing and privileged viewpoint, this contemporary image visually epitomizes the modern quest for a unified totalizing framework. . . . the local knowledge that was informed by many senses evaporates in the face of this uniform global picture. The same monotheistic impulse that replaced the pantheon with a single god and the plurality of psychic personages with a single heroic ego, has now given us a single Earth image." Yaakov Jerome Garb, "Perspective or Es-

cating that we have effectively reduced the world to our representation of it: "What is, in its entirety, is now taken in such a way that it first is in being and only is in being to the extent that it is set up by man, who represents and sets forth" (*QT* 129–30). Through the creation of a world picture, the human subject begins to produce its own reality.

We are confronted with what amounts to technological solipsism. Wherever we look, we encounter a reflection of ourselves. At this point, in an ironic twist, the objectivity of the world itself vanishes. All that exists now comes to exist, from a technological perspective, because it is represented or produced by us. As Heidegger notes, "whatever stands by in the sense of standing-reserve no longer stands over against us as object" (*QT* 17). We are, therefore, no longer speaking solely of an anthropocentrism that objectifies its world in order to exploit it. We are speaking of an "unconditioned *anthropormorphism*" that creates a world in its own image (*WPK* 174). The modifier "unconditioned" must not be overlooked, for it speaks to the scope of the technological drive that Heidegger finds definitive of contemporary life. Enframing engages humanity and world, being and time, as standing-reserve. This standing-reserve is revealed not as an object that stands against, apart and opposed to a subject, but as the extension of that subject. The real meaning and most devastating effect of the Midas touch is revealed. Whatever technological humankind comes in contact with becomes an extension of itself. This, for Heidegger, is the foreboding danger of technology:

> As soon as what is unconcealed no longer concerns man even as object, but does so, rather, exclusively as standing-reserve, and man in the midst of objectlessness is nothing but the orderer of the standing-reserve, then he comes to the very brink of a precipitous fall; that is, he comes to the point where he himself will have to be taken as standing-reserve. . . . the impression comes to prevail that everything man encounters exists only insofar as it is his construct. This illusion gives rise in turn to one final delusion: It seems as though man everywhere and always encounters only himself. . . . Thus the challenging Enframing not only conceals a former way of revealing, bringing-forth, but it conceals revealing itself and with it That wherein unconcealment, i.e., truth, comes to pass. (*QT* 26–27)

The Midas touch of technology is ontologically devastating. Its defining characteristic is not simply that it reveals the world in a particular way, but that it usurps all other modes of revelation. In the most fundamental event of the contemporary age, the world becomes totally enframed

---

cape? Ecofeminist Musings on Contemporary Earth Imagery," in *Reweaving the World: The Emergence of Ecofeminism*, ed. Irene Diamond and Gloria Feman Orenstein (San Francisco: Sierra Club Books, 1990), 267–69.

as a picture. Worldly life becomes the analogue of film production, a celluloid reality whose boundaries depend only on our own imaginations and technological skills.

With everything standing in reserve for our use, "distance" disappears. Heidegger is speaking here not of distance as a literal extension in space, but as an existential sense of our proximity to horizons: chiefly those between earth and sky, mortals and immortals. Indeed, as our relation to the world becomes technologized, we gradually cease to differentiate distance and nearness. With everything awaiting production or made ready for consumption, we find ourselves without the means to discriminate between what sits within our court and what remains beyond our ken. This blurring and transgression of borders is the chief indicator of an unconditioned anthropomorphism. Heidegger writes: "In the absence of distance, everything becomes equal and indifferent in consequence of the one will intent upon the uniformly calculated availability of the whole earth. This is why the battle for the dominion of the earth has now entered its decisive phase. The all-out challenge to secure dominion over the earth can be met only by occupying an ultimate position beyond the earth from which to establish control over the earth. The battle for this position, however, is the thoroughgoing calculative conversion of all connections among all things into the calculable absence of distance. This is making a desert of the encounter of the world's fourfold—it is the refusal of nearness" (*WL* 105–6). In other words, enframing brings the world completely within our grasp. Like a closely held picture, Heidegger foresaw early on, everything becomes "overseeable, controllable, definable, connectable, and explicable." The refusal of nearness marks a lost sense of relatedness to the world as a place of boundaries.

Technology yields the (physical) nearness of distant things in its overcoming of time and space. But in so doing, technology makes us truly distant from the world as a fourfold home in need of preservation. Technology invades the sky. No longer is the sky revealed as that which stands beyond us, worthy of contemplation for its otherness. The sky has ceased to be other. It has become integrated as standing-reserve. Hence the sky is no longer received. Rather, it is used. It becomes a sponge to soak up our gaseous wastes. It becomes a port for thousands of satellites that allow the transmission of data. It becomes an object of increasing militarization (and with this, demilitarization; arms control today would be impossible without "open skies" for reconnaissance and verification). It becomes a vessel for clouds that may be "seeded" to extort precipitation. For millennia, the sky was beyond human reach. Today, this distance has disappeared.

By "sky" Heidegger signifies, most broadly speaking, the cosmic forces. These manifest themselves not only above us, in the sun and stars of the sky, but below and within us, in the molecular and atomic structure of earthly matter. The reach of technology extends not solely into space but deep within the earth. Above, below, and within us, these cosmic forces solicit reception. But earthly matter, like the sky, is endlessly harassed into standing-reserve. Nature loves to hide. But there is nowhere to hide from Midas's touch. Nature has become indelibly smudged by the human fingerprint. In his meditation on the "end of nature," Bill McKibben offers a lament in accord with Heidegger's concern. McKibben suggests that nature has indeed been irreversibly integrated into humankind's utilitarian calculus, permanently brought out of hiding and within reach. How, McKibben asks, "can there be a mystique of the rain now that every [acidic] drop—even the drops that fall as snow on the Arctic—bears the permanent stamp of man? Having lost its separateness, it loses its special power. Instead of being a category like God—something beyond our control—it is now a category like the defense budget or the minimum wage, a problem we must work out. . . . What will it mean to come across a rabbit in the woods once genetically engineered 'rabbits' are widespread? Why would we have any more reverence or affection for such a rabbit than we would for a Coke bottle?" McKibben wistfully concludes: "Someday, man may figure out a method of conquering the stars, but at least for now when we look into the night sky, it is as Burroughs said: 'We do not see ourselves reflected there—we are swept away from ourselves, and impressed with our own insignificance. . . .' The ancients, surrounded by wild and even hostile nature, took comfort in seeing the familiar above them—spoons and swords and nets. But we will need to train ourselves not to see those patterns. The comfort we need is inhuman."[7] Heidegger would heartily agree. Yet corporations are currently exploring the possibility of placing gigantic Mylar billboards in the stratosphere along with gigantic reflectors to allow nighttime industry. We are, as Heidegger said, turning night into day and day into a harassed unrest. In turn, the genetic manipulation of plants and animals accelerates without pause. With each passing day the likelihood increases that as we look high into the heavens, or deep within nature, the only impressions we receive will be those made by our own hands.

The limitlessness of our technological penetration, however, is only an "illusion" that, in turn, gives rise to the "delusion" of our omnipresence. However close to species solipsism the rule of enframing brings man, as Dasein he necessarily inhabits a "there," exists outside himself in the world, and therefore "*can never* encounter only himself" (*QT*

[7] Bill McKibben, *The End of Nature* (New York: Random House, 1989), 210–17.

27). Are we to be reassured? To agree with Heidegger that human being is a thinking Being-in-the-world, that is, a situated and limited being rather than a disembodied mind that might grasp hold of the universe from an Archimedean point, is to understand that the ultimate victory of technological humankind is indeed delusory. But its reign would not, for that reason, be any less catastrophic, for delusion may become accepted as reality. Then the human capacity to experience its worldliness would become dormant. According to Heidegger, the stakes in the technological game remain the highest. Human nature and human freedom lie in the balance.

The age of planetary mastery, technological dominance, and the end of metaphysics, Heidegger speculates, will likely endure for a long time (*EP* 95). Indeed, there is no certainty that, from humanity's point of view, a succession to some other mode of revealing truth is ordained. The technological quest may reach its climax, as it were, without us. In the absence of an ontological reorientation, humanity would then be "left to the giddy whirl of its products so that it may tear itself to pieces and annihilate itself in empty nothingness" (*EP* 87). Estimating the likelihood of this apocalyptic conclusion is not Heidegger's concern. In any case, it is fair to say that the physical annihilation of humanity is not Heidegger's most proximate worry. Foremost in his mind is the ontological meaning of this potential self-annihilation.

If, as Heidegger put it, "the will to action, which here means the will to make and be effective, has overrun and crushed thought," then our chances of escaping the catastrophic whirlwind of enframing are slim indeed (*WCT* 25). The danger is that intensive technological production may simply overpower human being's capacity for manifold modes of disclosure, displacing the freedom inherent in philosophic thought, artistic creativity, and political action. Undeniably technology fosters thinking, creating, and acting of sorts. Calculation, cognition, innovation, and engineering are highly valued within technological society, though even here it is not clear that computers and robots might not eventually displace more of these capacities than their production demands. The real menace, however, is that social engineering would obviate political action, endlessly innovative production would leave artistic creativity to atrophy, and utilitarian cognition would fully displace philosophic questioning.[8]

Because the human capacity for thought is the foundation for artistic

---

[8] In George Grant's opinion, postmodernity is such an event. It is characterized by a "pure will to technology" that marks the "closing down of willing to all content except the desire to make the future by mastery, and the closing down of all thinking which transcends calculation." George Grant, *Technology and Empire* (Toronto: House of Anansi, 1969), 40.

creativity and political action, Heidegger indicates that its loss is his most pressing concern. He writes, "In this dawning atomic age a far greater danger threatens—precisely when the danger of a third world war has been removed. . . . the approaching tide of technological revolution in the atomic age could so captivate, bewitch, dazzle, and beguile man that calculative thinking may someday come to be accepted and practiced *as the only* way of thinking" (*DT* 56). In the wake of this revolution we find ourselves desperately in need of "an education in thinking" (*TB* 72). Such an education would, at a minimum, allow us to discern why calculative thought could never adequately substitute for philosophic thought. In the absence of such learning, and in the continued thrall of enframing, our capacity for philosophic thought may wither beyond resuscitation. Most disturbing and dangerous, however, this situation need not disturb or appear dangerous at all. Technological calculation and innovation may satisfy both our intensified material needs and our diminished spiritual demands. As Heidegger warns: "The devastation of the earth can easily go hand in hand with a guaranteed supreme living standard for man, and just as easily with the organized establishment of a uniform state of happiness for all men" (*WCT* 30). Devastation need not mean discontent. Indeed, technological devastation may consist in humanity's creation of a brave and exciting new world. Utopia and oblivion, as Buckminster Fuller prophesied, may well coincide.

Devastation, Heidegger states, "is the high-velocity expulsion of Mnemosyne" (*WCT* 30). Mnemosyne, or remembrance, designates not simply a recollection of what was, but also a "steadfast intimate concentration" on and a "devotion" toward worldly things and affairs. Remembrance is the "constant concentrated abiding with something—not just with something that has passed, but in the same way with what is present and with what may come. What is past, present, and to come appears in the oneness of its own *present* being" (*WCT* 140). The expulsion of memory, therefore, is the loss of the capacity to abide by, rather than challenge forth, the world. Once the fourfold is reduced to an extension of our cerebral computations and technical orderings our capacity to dwell within its horizons vanishes. We sit complacent in homelessness. The devastation is complete.

What Is to Be Done?

In light of this devastation, Heidegger's enduring and primary concern is that the essence of technology come to light "in its undisguised form" (*MHC* 44). The chains that bind us to technology are strongest, Heidegger maintains, when we mistake (its outgrowth of) technical devices for (its essence of) enframing, naively coming to believe in the neutrality of technology (*QT* 4). What is dangerous is not complex machinery and techniques per se, but the philosophic somnolence that may overtake us if, in our excited involvement with machines and techniques, and more generally in our subjectivist framework, we fail to think what enframing means. Heidegger writes, "There is no demonry of technology, but rather there is the mystery of its essence. . . . The rule of Enframing threatens man with the possibility that it could be denied to him to enter into a more original revealing and hence to experience the call of a more primal truth. . . . '*But where danger is, grows / the saving power also.*' Let us think carefully about these words of Hölderlin" (*QT* 28). Hölderlin's words, from his hymn "Patmos," suggest that the menace of enframing harbors its own opportunities for redress. Indeed, the danger posed to human being by technology reveals a saving power in the very thinking of its profound threat.

"Homeless is man," Heidegger wrote, "though there is scarcely a place on earth to be found anymore where mankind does not establish itself and meddle about" (*G* 13:156). Enframing does not coincidentally occur in the age of homelessness. Enframing is the root from which this condition grows. Thus the depth of humankind's homelessness corresponds precisely to the extent of its meddling about—to humankind's turning the world, as picture, into its property. Our opportunity to re-member this homelessness in the face of our consuming penetration of the earth is the saving power. That is, the threat of losing our ability to find a home on earth and an abode in thought stirs us to recollection. We are given to recall loss in the face of abundance.[9] In short, the philosophical and historical task before us today is the challenge of technology, for technology threatens the human capacity for disclosive freedom. Hence the question of Being, "properly understood," comes down to the question of technology.[10] However, Heidegger insists that "*before considering the question that is seemingly always the most immediate one and the only urgent one, What shall we do? we ponder this: How*

[9] Heidegger's poem entitled "Hints," in *Philosophy Today* 20 (Winter 1976): 287, is, in this sense, autobiographical.

The more insistent the calculators,
the more measure-less the society.
The fewer the thinkers,
the lonelier the poets.
The needier the divining ones,
divining the distance
of the saving hints.

[10] Heidegger, "Letter from Martin Heidegger," 18.

must we think?" Only in this way, he states, may we prepare ourselves for "the surmounting of Enframing" (*QT* 40–41).

An aspect of Heidegger's thought that is much misunderstood might be fruitfully discussed here. In his well-known *Spiegel* interview entitled "Only a God Can Save Us" (conducted in 1966 but only released after his death a decade later), Heidegger addressed the question "What is to be done?" He elaborated on the notion that waiting, not willing, was the proper response to the nihilistic, technological frenzy of our age. Asked if not even philosophy was an appropriate remedy, he answered: "Philosophy will be unable to effect any immediate change in the current state of the world. This is true not only of philosophy but of all purely human reflection and endeavor. Only a god can save us. The only possibility available to us is that by thinking and poetizing we prepare a readiness for the appearance of a god, or for the absence of a god in [our] decline, insofar as in view of the absent god we are in a state of decline. . . . We cannot bring him forth by our thinking. At best we can awaken a readiness to wait" (*OGS* 57). A mistaken notion has arisen that Heidegger suggests that we fatalistically abandon reflective thought and action in order to abide in religious faith. Nothing could be further from the truth. Awaiting some (anthropomorphic) god is precisely the "waiting for," effectively a willful action, that Heidegger deprecates. Moreover, the waiting he proposes cannot be equated with fatalism because, most simply put, God is not the (awaited) answer to our problems but simply an element of our questioning. There is no deus ex machina here, not even one that might save us from the machine. No all-powerful entity will redeem our finitude or fallenness. God may save us only as that which reappears as most questionable—that is, as most worthy of questioning. Waiting for a god, then, is an attendance upon the reawakening of our capacity for fundamental questioning, nothing more or less. This waiting moves one beyond metaphysical and theological representations toward a thankful thinking of the enigmatic Being of being. Such a thinking necessarily awaits Being's disclosure without knowing what that disclosure will entail. We may then "look out toward the divine," as Heidegger suggests, because we have come to understand the relation of human being to Being as *the* question (*QT* 47).

Let there be no mistake: the moral, redemptive God is every bit as dead for Heidegger as for Nietzsche. There is no expectation or hope of a resurrection. Indeed, for Heidegger, as for Nietzsche, philosophy is something of a jealous god. It permits no religious deities before it. We read that "philosophical research is and remains atheism, which is why philosophy can allow itself 'the arrogance of thinking.' Not only will it allow itself as much; this arrogance is the inner necessity of philosophy and its true strength. Precisely in this atheism, philosophy becomes what a great man once called the 'joyful science'" (*HCT* 80). Philosophy and religious faith are not only distinct; they are mutually exclusive. "Faith is so absolutely the mortal enemy that philosophy does not even begin to want in any way to do battle with it," Heidegger writes. "Accordingly, there is no such thing as a Christian philosophy [or, one might conclude, any religious philosophy]; that is an absolute 'square circle'" (*PT* 20–21). The problem with religious belief is not that it moves one to contemplate the divine—indeed, that is its virtue. The problem is that in naming the divine, religious belief defines what can only remain beyond definition and hence subject to questioning.

If Heidegger encourages atheism, it is not to promote a disbelief in God—and even less to promote a belief in the nonexistence of God—but as a means of remaining oriented in awe to that which is unknown, escapes comprehension, and marks our horizon. Hence he finds it "preferable to put up with the cheap accusation of atheism, which, if it is intended ontically, is in fact completely correct," because "the presumably ontic faith in God [might] be at bottom godlessness" (*MFL* 165). Not unlike Nietzsche, Heidegger finds pretensions to a familiar relationship with the deity to be blasphemous. Such pretensions are, at base, impiety masquerading as its opposite. Herein piety becomes, as Socrates claims in the *Euthyphro*, "a certain art of commerce for gods and human beings." Such a market theology, Heidegger agrees, signals true impiety. Here the sacred becomes the profane, a much valued prize, and salvation gets measured with scales specifically developed for human crafts. Heidegger might well have echoed Alexander Pope's words from *An Essay on Man:*

> Know then thyself, presume
> not God to scan.
> The proper study of
> mankind is man.

Pope's verse, though rightly dissuading religious presumption, conceals something crucial. Proper study necessarily entails attention to the divine, for the divine is that which human being necessarily questions. Observe the following exchange from Heidegger's *Discourse on Thinking:*

> *Scientist:* Toward the last you stated that the question concerning man's nature is not a question about man.
> *Teacher:* I said only that the question concerning man's nature makes a consideration whether this is the case unavoidable. (*DT* 58)

What the teacher implies is that humankind makes its own being an issue by questioning that which lies beyond its horizon. Being human makes unavoidable the querying of whether our being is not (only) about us but about that which transcends us.

The questioning of divinity sets humanity apart, marking its unique status and nature. In making its own being an issue, human being makes immortal divinity, as its horizon, an issue. It recognizes its horizon as a horizon. But to acknowledge a horizon is not to see beyond it. Indeed, the attempt to do so, conceptually or practically, is the mark of impiety. Accordingly, Heidegger emphasizes the "onto-theological character of metaphysics" and the metaphysical character of theology (*ID* 55). He finds that a "god-less thinking" which abandons God insofar as God comes to be metaphysically constructed "is thus perhaps closer to the divine God" (*ID* 72). Only such god-less thinking keeps God from becoming "known," the object that we, as subjects, evaluate and subsequently elevate. "The heaviest blow against God," we read, "is not that God is held to be unknowable, not that God's existence is demonstrated to be unprovable, but rather that the god held to be real is elevated to the highest value" (*QT* 105). Heidegger rejects all religious belief for its complicity in this project.

Traditional sacrilege involves worshiping idols, the fabrications of human hands. Heidegger cautions against the form of sacrilege that involves worshiping the fabrications of human minds. Heidegger might be held to ascribe to a negative theology, with the understanding that Being, as *theos,* is higher than human logic and conceptualization. It alone forces us to think beyond the doctrine of the excluded middle, to understand how *A* and *not-A* do not exhaust Being, which *is* nothingness. Heidegger's orientation to the transcendent, to God, stands piously in opposition to the pursuit of certainty and proof. Heidegger's atheism thus comes closer to certain forms of religious faith than a simple suspension of belief or a skeptical "addiction" to doubt. Effectively, Heidegger rejects theism *and* atheism; both doctrines provide answers where questions rightfully reign alone.

Despite his religiosity, Eric Voegelin describes "the life of the soul in openness toward God" in a way that Heidegger would have approved. For Voegelin, this life is defined by a "waiting" that proves "too heavy a burden for men who lust for massively possessive experience."[11] When this lust comes to rule, as it does with the shallow atheism manifested in technological behavior, the human relationship to the suprasensory is threatened. Formerly mediated through a belief in anthropomorphic gods, this relationship has now lost its bearing. With god's demise, transcendent aspirations become deflected; "the suprasensory world is without effective power" (*QT* 61). But the death of God does not mean that we are condemned to remain insensible to transcendence. Hei-

---

[11] Eric Voegelin, *The New Science of Politics* (Chicago: University of Chicago Press, 1952), 122.

degger hopes that our wonder at the transcendent might somehow survive this event to unfold as the question of Being. Until then, however, we may only wait to discover "whether Being will once again become capable of a god, as to whether the essence of the truth of Being will lay claim more primally to the essence of man" (QT 153). By waiting without faith, we acknowledge that any god that might save us would not be subject to conceptualization or valuation as the redeemer of earthly life. A god that is susceptible to representation or evaluation is no god.

Nonetheless, divinity may endure, we are told, in philosophic questioning. "Thus God is not dead," Heidegger writes. "For his divinity lives. It is even nearer to the thinker than the believer" (G 13:154). To think God as a question is not to make God the answer. Any such making available of a god for our own (salvational or epistemological) purposes belies the same willfulness that led to God's original disappearance. It evidences the same unwillingness or incapacity to think (in a way that is not a "thinking for") that one finds in the nihilistic refusal of openness to transcendence. Those who would interpret Heidegger's words about waiting for a god politically rather than religiously, as a veiled metaphor for a charismatic leader or revolutionary event that might put the human condition right, are also mistaken.[12] Heidegger's point in speaking of gods is not to suggest the possibility of salvational figures, but to orient us disclosively to worldly life in a way that marks the limits of human power and ingenuity.

To wait for gods is to acknowledge that the disclosure of the transcendent is not solely under human command. The transcendent would not really be transcendent if it remained within our power to procure at will. Heidegger concludes that the loss of the question of the transcendent within the technological world, the "overshadowing of Being by beings," is not completely within the purview of human being to redress (WPK 157). However, the obverse of this statement also holds. If only a god can save us from technological nihilism, then this nihilism itself, its coming to be, must also exceed the ambit of human directives. Heidegger writes: "The essence of nihilism is not at all the affair of man, but a matter of Being itself, and thereby of course also a matter of the *essence* of man, and only in *that* sequence at the same time a human concern" (N 221). The point is not that nihilism is not our concern. Nihilism ought to be our foremost concern, but not solely as our doing. Nihilism

---

[12] Hubert Dreyfus, for example, worries that Heidegger is referring to "a charismatic figure or some other culturally renewing event . . . [that] exposes us to the risk of committing ourselves to some demonic event or movement." Hubert L. Dreyfus, "Heidegger on the Connection between Nihilism, Art, Technology, and Politics," in Guignon, *Cambridge Companion to Heidegger*, 314.

concerns us because it fosters the concealment of the transcendent, while the questioning of the transcendent bespeaks the essence of human being. To assume that nihilism is of our making, and consequently completely within our capacities to exorcize, is itself a nihilistic position characteristic of a technological frame of mind. From this technological perspective, nihilism becomes part of a world picture that we might erase or paint over at will. Yet as Heidegger observes, "those who fancy themselves free of nihilism perhaps push forward its development most fundamentally" (*QT* 63). The belief that we might subdue technological nihilism at will is part of the disease, not the cure.

Heidegger employs our questioning relation to divinity in a way that underlines the difference between receiving the sky and the natural earth and invading it technologically. We read that "man first receives the measure for the breadth of his being . . . [in] the godhead against which man measures himself. . . . the god who remains unknown, must by showing *himself* as the one he is, appear as the one who remains unknown. . . . the unknown god appears as the unknown by way of the sky's manifestness. This appearance is the measure against which man measures himself. . . . only this measure gauges the very nature of man. For man dwells by spanning the 'on the earth' and the 'beneath the sky'" (*PLT* 222–23). Awaiting divinities is not an action grounded in the hope of salvational demonic forces, but a way of Being-in-the-world, a way of living in the fourfold. It signifies nothing more nor less than an openness to (not a belief or faith in) that which transcends human being. There is no proof that this openness will save us, nor could there be. Answers may be provable; questions never are. And the orientation of human being to the disclosure of Being remains, fundamentally, interrogative.

Nietzsche evaluated the "rank" of individuals by investigating both the sorts of questions they posed and their need for answers. In this regard, Heidegger understood what Nietzsche glimpsed but tragically lost hold of: that the ungrounded nature of human being, though unsatisfying for representational or metaphysical thought, bears the seed of a freedom beyond willfulness. Most threatening to this freedom is the absence of openness manifest in enframing:

> What has long since been threatening man with death, and indeed with the death of his own nature, is the unconditional character of mere willing in the sense of purposeful self-assertion in everything. What threatens man in his very nature is the willed view that man, by the peaceful release, transformation, storage, and channeling of the energies of physical nature, could render the human condition, man's being, tolerable for everybody and happy in all respects. But the peace of this peacefulness is merely the undisturbed continuing relentlessness of the fury of self-assertion which is

resolutely self-reliant. . . . What threatens man in his very nature is the view that technological production puts the world in order, while in fact this ordering is precisely what levels every *ordo*, every rank, down to the uniformity of production, and thus from the outset destroys the realm from which any rank and recognition could possibly arise. (*PLT* 116–17)

The problem with the creation of the world picture, in other words, is that everything gets reduced to two dimensions. Whatever is disclosed is disclosed uniformly as a product of human ingenuity, as a (man-made) object or value. As such it becomes measurable, calculable, and exchangeable in a free market of resources. Technology mints a universal currency. Though values certainly vary within the technological marketplace, all ordering is conducted on a single scale; everything is assessed in terms of its rank within the standing-reserve. Art becomes serviceable, myth and religion useful, families functional, nature adaptable, and the fourfold of earth and sky, mortals and divinities all part of a panoply of resources awaiting efficient use. As the world becomes increasingly anthropomorphized, humanity comes to trade only in its own coin.

Heidegger summarizes the problem and intimates its resolution: "The coming to presence of technology threatens revealing, threatens it with the possibility that all revealing will be consumed in ordering and that everything will present itself only in the unconcealedness of standing-reserve. Human activity can never directly counter this danger. Human achievement alone can never banish it. But human reflection can ponder the fact that all saving power must be of a higher essence than what is endangered, though at the same time kindred to it" (*QT* 33–34). Here Heidegger observes that we cannot simply ransom our escape from enframing with a hefty tribute of coins bearing our own image. Enframing cannot be brought under control through willfulness. Certainly machines and techniques, their production and use, can and should be harnessed. But the essence of technology, unlike technical devices, is not susceptible to willful mastery. Like the attempt to reduce one's level of intolerance by liquidating those individuals found overly objectionable, the attempt to master enframing is self-defeating. The problem of technology is one of willfulness itself. In other words, technology is symptomatic of a subjectivist and anthropomorphic enframing of the world. Retouching the picture is not an adequate response.

E. F. Schumacher insightfully compared "people of the forward stampede" with the "home-comers." The former believe that technological fixes exist for each and every problem. Theirs is a world wherein the solution to the problems that human mastery confronts or creates is always more mastery. The latter, in contrast, seek to care for an earthly habitat and its boundaries without recourse to technological panaceas. Theirs is a world of waiting that is active and watchful but not willful. Despite Heidegger's characterization of this activity as a waiting for gods, religion does not come into the picture. It is therefore mistaken, I believe, to characterize homecoming, as Schumacher does, in religious terms—as a product of "deep convictions" and a "return to certain basic truths about man and his world" that may be unearthed from gospel.[13] Homecoming, as Heidegger understands it, is most fundamentally a returning not to basic truths but to basic questions, not to religious faith but to ontological interrogation.

Neither heroic action nor religious faith can overcome enframing and deliver us from our technological addictions. Only a nonwillful doing grounded in reflective thinking will avail. Thought, however, is not in the business of overcoming. It only summons. Although the technological world is full of quandaries and challenges, thought can provide no answers. But it does keep questioning alive. And once the nature of modern technology is brought into question, its hold is loosened.

Dwelling with Technology

Heidegger offers a hint about the nature of the thinking that might loosen the grip of technology. He writes that "the coming to presence of technology will be surmounted [verwunden] in a way that restores it into its yet concealed truth. This restoring surmounting is similar to what happens when, in the human realm, one gets over grief or pain" (QT 39). Importantly, one gets over grief not through a willful overcoming. Such self-mastery only displaces grief, with the likelihood of its resurgence at some other time, in an invidious form. Like moods in general, grief is overcome not by mastery, intellect, or will, but only by another mood (WPA 99). And moods, Heidegger insists, cannot be created, only summoned (ST 105). The mood that allows our overcoming of grief might best be described as one of rediscovered sanctuary. One gets over grief by once again coming to feel one's belonging in a world that, because of to its cruel deprivations, had for a time become alien. Hannah Arendt often called to mind Isak Dinesen's saying that "all sorrows can be borne if you put them into a story or tell a story about them." Dinesen's point is that we get over grief by reflecting on our grief-stricken selves and becoming interpretively reintegrated in the world. Looking back on our grieved selves allows us to surmount grief not by denying our misfortune but by finding meaning in the story of

[13] Schumacher, *Small Is Beautiful*, 155–56.

our sorrow. To look back on ourselves in time is to gain distance, and, at the same time, a nearness to the ongoing and often tragic saga of worldly habitation. Homelessness is the mood of the technological age. Rediscovering our worldly home (as threatened) signals the "restoring surmounting" of technology. This rediscovered sense of (threatened) sanctuary is chiefly summoned, Heidegger indicates, by memory or recollective thought.

Recollecting our worldly habitat not only fosters resistance to enframing, but also provides guidance in negotiating relations with the products of technology, namely machines and techniques. Heidegger acknowledges that we should neither reject nor do without technological artifacts or skills as a whole. He neither advocates nor accepts a retreat to a pretechnological state of being. Nor, despite much misinterpretation by his commentators, does he suggest that we fatalistically resign ourselves to the victory of enframing. Its victory, he emphatically states, is not inevitable (*OGS* 61). "We cannot, of course, reject today's technological world as devil's work, nor may we destroy it—assuming it does not destroy itself," Heidegger maintains. "Still less may we cling to the view that the world of technology is such that it will absolutely prevent a spring out of it" (*ID* 40–41). To confuse our destined relation to Being as if it were a fate, particularly one that leads to the inevitable decline of our civilization because of technological rule, is itself a historically determinist, and therefore metaphysical and technological, understanding. According to Heidegger, "All attempts to reckon existing reality morphologically, psychologically, in terms of decline and loss, in terms of fate, catastrophe, and destruction, are merely technological behavior" (*QT* 48).[14] Fatalism is no answer because fatalism reflects the same absence of thought that is evidenced in a naive complacency with technological "progress." Heidegger's admonition to think the nature of technology, though far from a resigned musing, is not the devising of a counteroffensive. We are asked to respond first to the question "What shall we think?" rather than the question "What is to be done?" But the point is not simply that we must think before we act. The needed thinking of what we are doing and how we are being is not solely a strategic

[14] Many of Heidegger's readers fail to observe this point. They misinterpret Heidegger's talk of the "destining of Being" to mean that human actions are "heteronomously 'fated,'" and understand Heidegger's description of the technological stamping of the age to indicate a technological determinism. See, for example, Wolin, *Politics of Being*, 155, and Jerry Weinberger, "Politics and the Problem of Technology: An Essay on Heidegger and the Tradition of Political Philosophy," *American Political Science Review* 86 (March 1992): 112–27. Even generally sympathetic readers, such as Michael Zimmerman, mistakenly conclude that Heidegger believed Western history to be "the story of humanity's degeneration." Zimmerman, "Rethinking the Heidegger–Deep Ecology Relationship," 219).

preparation for more informed and effective behavior. Thought must first save us from our typical *modes* of behaving, namely those oriented to possessive mastery.

Heidegger warns that "so long as we represent technology as an instrument, we remain held fast in the will to master it" (*QT* 32). The more we fail to experience the essence of technology as enframing, persevering in the mistaken notion that complex machinery is the danger, the more we will believe that salvation lies in our mastering technology before it masters us. With this in mind, Heidegger explicitly states that he is "*not against* technology," nor does he suggest any "resistance against, or condemnation of, technology" (*MHC* 43–44). Indeed, the development of complex machines and techniques—technology as it is commonly understood—has enormous benefits that must not be depreciated. It would be shortsighted to condemn such technology out of hand. Apart from our obvious dependence on technical devices, their development also often "challenges us to ever greater advances" (*DT* 53). From political, social, cultural, and environmental standpoints, technology demonstrates many virtues. Indeed, given the unrelenting extension of human power and population, technological developments that buffer the earth from our predaceousness seem both urgent and indispensable. A good bit of the destruction humanity presently visits on the earth and itself makes sophisticated technological remedies necessary. Having machines efficiently serve our needs is neither evil nor regrettable. But this service must be grounded on our discovery of what needs we truly have. More importantly, it must be grounded on our discovery of what transcends human need.[15] These, decidedly, are not technological questions, and our capacity to answer them largely rests on our recovery of the capacity to think beyond the criterion of instrumental service.

Heidegger, I believe, would be an advocate of what is called "alternative," "soft," or "appropriate" technology. What makes a technological artifact appropriate is its capacity to secure us within the fourfold. An artifact's contribution to ecological sustainability would then become the criterion of selection in respect to the dictum of saving the earth. To be commensurate with receiving the sky and awaiting the gods, an artifact must not be developed in the indiscriminate and hubristic effort to master nature. Rather than institute human being as the intrusive arbi-

---

[15] Heidegger writes: "One settles for beings and forgoes Being so decidedly, that one does not acknowledge this abnegation as an abnegation, but presents it as a gain, as the advantage of never more becoming disturbed by 'the abstract' while meddling with beings. From where does this strange parsimoniousness originate? Perhaps this self-sufficiency in his experiencing and ordering of beings comes from this, that man in the midst of beings only thinks of what he needs" (*G* 51:40).

ter of life, it should serve the guardianship of nearness and distance. In turn an artifact would have to facilitate, or at least not impede, the escorting of fellow men and women as codwellers in social and natural habitats. Such technology would be closely adapted to natural cycles and processes, would be primarily based on renewable sources of matter and energy, and would be largely decentralized with respect to location and control. In confronting the appropriateness of any particular technological development, then, the right question to ask is whether that development encourages or hinders the philosophically, artistically, or politically mediated disclosure that delivers us into the fourfold. Laborsaving devices may allow the leisure that facilitates such disclosure, just as technological developments that supply adequate levels of food, shelter, medical care, education, and recreation are frequently its prerequisites. But like "mind-expanding" drugs, technological instruments and innovations may become addictive. At this point, they facilitate an escape from, rather than an interrogative embrace of, our worldly finitude. The problem with inappropriate technology is neither its origin in human skills and needs, nor the sophistication of its development per se, but its denial of boundaries. This denial expels us from the fourfold.

The expulsion is not inevitable, according to Heidegger. We may learn to abide within human limits, in technical endeavors no less than in philosophical ones. Heidegger writes: "Building and thinking are, each in its own way, inescapable for dwelling. The two, however, are also insufficient for dwelling so long as each busies itself with its own affairs in separation instead of listening to one another. They are able to listen if both—building and thinking—belong to dwelling, if they remain within their limits and realize that the one as much as the other comes from the workshop of long experience and incessant practice" (*PLT* 160–61). Humans are inherently builders. Although it is crucial to perceive the danger of our technological constructions lest they come to dominate us, it is unnecessary and futile to forswear them completely. But the alternative to becoming the slaves of our own machines, clearly the most deplorable state, is not simply to become their masters. The goal is to integrate technology within a bounded worldly dwelling no longer structured by possessive mastery.

The task before us is cultural and political no less than philosophic in nature, even though Heidegger tended to emphasize the latter and ignore the former aspects of it. Despite this shortcoming, Heidegger aptly describes the comportment needed to disengage ourselves from possessive mastery and achieve an appropriate relation to technology. He writes:

We can use technical devices as they ought to be used, and also let them alone as something which does not affect our inner and real core. We can affirm the unavoidable use of technical devices, and also deny them the right to dominate us, and so to warp, confuse, and lay waste our nature. But will not saying both yes and no this way to technical devices make our relation to technology ambivalent and insecure? On the contrary! Our relation to technology will become wonderfully simple and relaxed. We let technical devices enter our daily life, and at the same time leave them outside, that is, let them alone, as things which are nothing absolute but remain dependent upon something higher. I would call this comportment toward technology which expresses "yes" and at the same time "no," by an old word, *releasement toward things.* (*DT* 54)

Heidegger's description of the "wonderfully simple and relaxed" way we may come to abide with technology recalls, and reverses, Max Weber's gloomy assessment. We may, pace Weber, learn to wear technology "like a light cloak, which can be thrown aside at any moment." Learning this comportment allows us to escape fate's decree that "the cloak should become an iron cage."[16] Many theorists of technology, such as Jacques Ellul, follow Weber's lead in yielding to pessimism and cynicism. This attitude follows necessarily from their philosophic assumptions. Not unlike Heidegger, Ellul defines technology (or rather technique) as the pursuit of *"absolute efficiency."* Ellul also proposes that the only hope of escape from the clutches of technology comes from "an increasing number of people" who are determined to "assert their freedom."[17] However, for Ellul, as for Weber, freedom remains a metaphysical concept tied to subjectivity and control. Hence the hopelessness of Ellul's and Weber's prognosis. Neither the pessimism or cynicism of the naysayers nor the heroic self-assertion or complacency of the yeasayers is called for. We may say both "yes" and "no" to technology.

Awaiting gods is an openness to the mystery. Receiving the sky is a releasement toward things. Together they allow our liberation from enframing without at the same time forswearing our technological achievements and skills. Awaiting and receiving, openness and release-

[16] Weber writes: "[The modern economic] order is now bound to the technical and economic conditions of machine production which to-day determine the lives of all the individuals who are born into this mechanism, not only those directly concerned with economic acquisition, with irresistible force. Perhaps it will so determine them until the last ton of fossilized coal is burnt. In Baxter's view the care for external goods should only lie on the shoulders of the 'saint like a light cloak, which can be thrown aside at any moment'. But fate decreed that the cloak should become an iron cage." Max Weber, *The Protestant Ethic and the Spirit of Capitalism* (New York: Charles Scribner's Sons, 1958), 181.

[17] Jacques Ellul, *The Technological Society*, trans. John Wilkinson (New York: Vintage, 1964), xxv, xxx. See also Jacques Ellul, *Le système technicien* (Paris: Calmann-Levy, 1977), 34.

ment, are summoned by recollective thinking. Only thus is the mood of homelessness attendant on technological ordering displaced. "Releasement toward things and openness to the mystery belong together," Heidegger writes. "They grant us the possibility of dwelling in the world in a totally different way" (DT 55). But Heidegger misspeaks here somewhat. The worldly dwelling to which we may aspire is not merely different from that experienced in the midst of willful technological endeavors. There is no true dwelling in an enframed world, only the visitation of a boundless ordering upon it. To dwell is already to have found an abode in the mystery of Being and to have gained release from the possessive mastery of things. Until this occurs, our attempts to control the products of technology will only perpetuate our subordination to its imperative. The greatest irony is that the freedom that has been systematically nurtured and cherished for two and a half millennia in the West has fostered this technological servitude.

Nine

Escorting Mortals

BEING WITH OTHERS IN TIME

> Man is the only creature who refuses to be
> what he is.
>   (Albert Camus, *The Rebel*)

THE TIMELINESS of human being is manifest in the historical nature of our disclosure of Being. The timeliness of human being is also manifest in another, equally foundational, sense: we are mortal. Hence human beings are defined by what Heidegger calls finitude, which speaks both to their historical contingencies and their inevitable mortality. A political sensibility arises from the philosophic comprehension of the twofold nature of our timely being. To live without resentment of time, or rather to celebrate one's time as the opportunity for disclosive freedom, is, politically speaking, to understand oneself as an escort of one's fellow mortals. To escort, as Heidegger puts it, is to recognize our "belonging to men's being with one another" (*PLT* 149). To escort is respectfully to abide by another. It is to subsume neither the other in the self nor the self in the other. Nor is it to isolate the self from the other. Rather, to escort is to accompany. It signifies less a destination sought than a journey shared. Means are not sacrificed to the end. Escorting mortals requires opening oneself fully to otherness in its finite everydayness. Escorting mortals is the exercise of disclosive freedom in common affairs.

The everyday exercise of disclosive freedom demands a search for the philosophical in the mundane and the extraordinary in the ordinary.[1] It demands an extension beyond habitude and prescription. With this in mind, I engage Eastern thought as a supplement and corrective to Heidegger's characteristically Western orientation. What follows is not a thorough comparative study.[2] Rather, I loosely weave strands of Eastern

---

[1] For a philosophical and literary examination of the extraordinariness of the ordinary, primarily with reference to the American transcendentalists but also to Heidegger, see Stanley Cavell, *In Quest of the Ordinary: Lines of Skepticism and Romanticism* (Chicago: University of Chicago Press, 1988).

[2] Certain comparative efforts have been made, though they, too, remain largely exploratory. See, for example, Parkes, *Heidegger and Asian Thought*; Steven Heine, *Existential*

religion and philosophy into the fabric of Heideggerian ontology, resuscitating and expanding on Heidegger's own limited excursions beyond his tradition. The strands of Eastern thought chosen to enhance and strengthen Heidegger's work are not proposed as exhaustively representative. I should not want to make the mistake of assigning a near-monolithic structure to the East after explicitly criticizing Heidegger for imposing one on the West. Nor is there any claim here of sufficiency regarding these Eastern excursions: they are and remain forays, perhaps pilgrimages, meant to supplement—and occasionally sublimate—Heidegger's work.

It has been suggested that the affinity between Heidegger's philosophy and Eastern thought underlines the apolitical nature of his work. Eastern religious and philosophical traditions are generally viewed as less political in substance and tendency than those of the West. Be that as it may, my intent in investigating the relationship of Heidegger to the East is a political one. I wish to argue for an increasing opening to otherness on both a personal and a global scale. In this sense, the argument might be cast as metaphor, as a device that carries one over to another part of the world and self. I might also have attempted to navigate from north to south, or more extensively from male to female. I choose the East not to exclude that which primarily identifies itself with neither East nor West, but to signal the need for a more inclusive philosophical and political panorama and, ultimately, to flag the dangers of thinking and acting within the strictures of such dichotomies in the first place. The effort, to borrow a phrase from one of Heidegger's more distinguished former students, Hans-Georg Gadamer, is to "fuse horizons." It is a gesture of respectful if tentative opening to otherness, an opening intrinsic to Heideggerian philosophy but too seldom actualized by Heidegger.

Ontological Refusal and the Revenge of Time

Albert Camus identified human beings by their inherent refusal to be what they are. This refusal occurs in two fundamental ways. Heidegger affirms what might most appropriately be called its *interrogative* form. Human being, he maintains, displays its essential nature when it profoundly questions its horizons. Human being, most fundamentally, is a "why asker." Through questioning, authentic human being finds a home in the mystery of worldly life, ironically learning to dwell within

---

and Ontological Dimensions of Time in Heidegger and Dōgen. (Albany: State University of New York Press, 1985); and vol. 20, no. 3m of *Philosophy East and West*.

the anxiety of homelessness. As questioners, we are indeed the only creatures who refuse to be what we are: not simply because questioning undermines authority and enables transgression, but because questioning is itself a reaching beyond. To question is to challenge, as any parent beleaguered by a child's incessant "whys" well knows. Yet Dasein's interrogative refusal is not a rebellious challenge in Camus's sense. It is to reach but not to grasp. Its reaching beyond is a reaching out. To question is to remain attendant upon a response. In philosophic questioning, this attendance constitutes a disposition to wait, and this disposition is, in the end, an affirmation, a thinking that is a thanking.

Heidegger developed a philosophy not of rebellion against the human condition, but of understanding and appreciation of its limits. He investigates that which situates us inevitably within boundaries: of earth and sky, gods and mortals, within a world and in a with-world. He uncovers those specific and relatively determinate dimensions of human being that make it an abode for Being.

The second form of refusal is a product of resentment. Resentful refusal signifies a refusal of the contingency of our Being-in-the-world. It fosters the will to be more, or less, than a questioner of and worldly participant in Being's disclosure. This refusal typically manifests itself today in the pursuit of technological control and conquest. In this way, it extorts compensation or seeks revenge for human limitations. Unsatisfied with or incapable of a disclosive freedom, resentful refusal manifests itself in the possessive mastery of being. At its height, this refusal is identifiable by its antagonism to the most fundamental medium and horizon of human being: time itself.

The chorus from *Antigone* states that human beings are the strangest of earth's creatures. What makes humans so strange, Heidegger observes, is their violent surpassing of limits. Heidegger translates the word 'strange' (*deinon*) in the passage from Sophocles as "the uncanny" (*das Unheimliche*), which, he notes, "casts us out of the 'homely' [*das Heimische*]—that is, the customary, familiar, secure. The unhomely prevents us from making ourselves at home" (*IM* 151). The wonder of human being is its refusal to find itself completely at home in its world. But this refusal of stagnant security can bring humanity to good or ill. It might prompt us resentfully to wear away the earth and ruthlessly to dominate its inhabitants. Alternatively, it might prompt us questioningly, and anxiously, to dwell with care. Sadly, it is the former activity that humanity has too frequently chosen with mistaken pride as its distinguishing characteristic. Heidegger describes this refusal, which has visited much destruction upon the earth, as the historical ramification of a metaphysical drive that finds its apogee in the technological will to power. His philosophy of limits offers critical reflections on this chief expression of contemporary ontological refusal. Heidegger writes: "The unnoticeable law of the earth preserves the earth in the sufficiency of the emerging and perishing of all things in the allotted sphere of the possible which everything follows, and yet nothing knows. The birch tree never oversteps its possibility. The colony of bees dwells in its possibility. It is first the will which arranges itself everywhere in technology that devours the earth in the exhaustion and consumption and change of what is artificial. Technology drives the earth beyond the developed sphere of its possibility into such things which are no longer a possibility and are thus the impossible" (*EP* 109). The technological, and highly successful, human pursuit of the impossible is the ontological refusal Heidegger attempts to exorcise. It thrives within the homelessness of postmodernity.

Like Heidegger, Nietzsche addresses the fundamental refusal and rebellion of human being. His thought, like Heidegger's, wrestles with the question of homelessness. Those who accept the limitations of belief and social convention, habit and morality, Nietzsche calls the Last Men. They sit complacently ensconced within herd life. Centuries of resentment have encased them in a cocoon that shields them from the tragedy of human life. Here they incubate ideals out of their frustration with earthly contingencies. In the past, religious projections of heavenly realms were their chief solace. Now, in the age of nihilism, these projections have lost their allure. No longer are the strains of a limited being with limitless aspirations experienced with awe and anxiety. A comfortable happiness suffices. Confronted with this complacent resignation, Nietzsche attempts to resuscitate the spirit of the ancient Greeks. When faced with Silenus's wisdom (that the best thing is not to be born, or quickly to return whence one came), the Greeks opted nonetheless for a fiery burst of life. Nietzsche also makes a tragic and heroic choice. He refuses to accept all-too-human limitations. He attempts to break free of social, moral, and historical encasements. He observes desperately the wasteland of mummified specimens about him and refuses company with any but higher types. These higher types are the meteors that streak across the firmament. They light up the sky with a fire that consumes them to avoid the task of sharing a home on earth.

Nowhere are the stakes and meaning of this tragic and heroic game made clearer than in Nietzsche's discussion of time. Human limitation is most harshly endured in our powerlessness to master time. Human freedom, the highest value, is most fundamentally threatened by time itself. The escape from time, or the mastery of it, thus constitutes the ecstatic victory of the Overman. Failure in this regard, a failure that Nietzsche finds characteristic of humanity at large, is a recipe for the revenge and resentment of slave morality. Zarathustra proclaims:

To redeem the past and to transform every "It was" into an "I wanted it thus!"—that alone do I call redemption! . . .

The will cannot will backwards; that it cannot break time and time's desire—that is the will's most lonely affliction. . . .

It is sullenly wrathful that time does not run back; "That which was"— that is what the stone which it cannot roll away is called.

And so, out of wrath and ill-temper, the will rolls stones about and takes revenge upon him who does not, like it, feel wrath and ill-temper. . . .

This, yes, this alone is *revenge* itself: the will's antipathy towards time and time's "It was".

Truly a great foolishness dwells in our will; and that this foolishness acquired spirit has become a curse to all human kind.

The spirit of revenge: my friends, that, up to now, has been mankind's chief concern; and where there was suffering, there was always supposed to be punishment.

"Punishment" is what revenge calls itself: it feigns a good conscience for itself with a lie.

And because there is suffering in the willer himself, since he cannot will backwards—therefore willing itself and all life was supposed to be—punishment.[3]

In light of this predicament, Nietzsche attempts the impossible: to will backward. One must approach one's past anew. Thus he proposes the "Eternal Recurrence of the Same." To will the eternal recurrence, Nietzsche claims, is to master time. This willing is not simply the resentful resignation to time's "It was" of slave morality. Rather, one wills the past to be again, as that which will return, endlessly and the same. Consequently, to will the eternal recurrence is to strive to make each thought, word, and deed of each moment of each day endlessly worth repeating. Willing the eternal recurrence, thinking the most difficult thought, is Nietzsche's heroic redemption from human limitation and its vengefulness. It is freedom from time itself.

So conceived, the thought of the eternal recurrence appears as the greatest vindication of the here and now. The intent, Nietzsche stipulates, is for the present never to be depreciated as a mere means to the future: each moment is to be self-fulfilling. Were it not an end in itself but only a means to some other end, each moment would not merit eternal repetition. Instrumentality must disappear altogether in the brilliance of performance. Nietzsche's vision is enticing. But Heidegger gives us pause to reflect on the meaning of Nietzsche's thought experiment. Truly to live in the here and now is resolutely to will that what is,

[3] Nietzsche, *Thus Spoke Zarathustra,* 161–62.

is. To live in the here and now is to let being be. Letting being be, however, entails letting time be, for being is only in time. Full participation in the timely disclosure of what is, then, is the greatest celebration of life and being. Nietzsche's effort to *will* the eternal return, in other words, signifies not the living of one's being in time but the attempt to administer its unfolding. Yet as thrown, human being neither sets this unfolding in motion nor overcomes its contingency. Psychologically and philosophically (no less than socially and politically) to flee the horizons of one's historical finitude is to give up the task of dwelling in time.

Nietzsche's effort to will life's endless repetition does not fully translate into an affirmation of life, for it implicitly denies and deprecates that aspect of human life which it seeks to overcome: its timely and bounded nature. The freedom won is not the freedom to disclose what is, but the freedom to control and conquer the (psychological or spiritual) effects of historical and worldly dwelling. Freedom becomes a possessive mastery of time. But herein the slave's basic antipathy toward time is not really overcome. It is simply redirected. Time is now forced to swallow its tail. Effectively, Nietzsche exchanges the resentment of the slave for that of the master. He fails to discern the spirit of revenge inherent in the drive to overcome temporal horizons. The attempt to conquer time by willing the eternal return, to undo time's "It was" by way of a voluntaristic imposition of ultimate value on the endless repetition of its component parts, is perhaps the most sublime resentment yet achieved. But it is resentment nonetheless.

Heidegger offers an alternative. Human being, he agrees with Nietzsche, is not the naysayer who resentfully projects life as a punishment. But neither is human being the yea-sayer whose willful affirmation is "a highly spiritualized spirit of revenge" (*ERS* 228). Human being is the "why asker." The questioner is neither slave nor master of time. The questioner seeks neither to escape this world for the next, nor to dominate this world in lieu of any next. Rather, the questioner lives *in* time, in anxious and awe-full interrogation of the very medium of her worldliness. The questioner thinks Being *as* time, as an unfolding disclosure in which she is privileged to participate but will never fully control. To practice this questioning is to gain wisdom, as an acceptance of limits. And it is wisdom, Heidegger writes, that teaches us how to dwell in the here and now of the "permanent everywhere."[4] Among the many types of refusal that humankind has ingeniously invented, only interrogative refusal does not reduce itself to resentment. Only in profound questioning, which is neither complacent nor rebellious, is chagrin at existence

---

[4] Heidegger, "Plato's Doctrine of Truth," 268.

altogether eschewed. Only for the questioner are mundane and historical limits encountered not as constraints on an insatiable will, but as the
very conditions for a freedom manifest in their disclosure.

The Work of Memory in the Historical Present

The tradition of Western philosophy produced something quite different from the interrogative guardian. By Heidegger's reckoning, the
world has largely been delivered over to the technician. And in our frenzied quest for technical power we have forgotten the meaning of dwelling in time. Metaphysics began with Plato's separation of Being, the
unchanging Forms or Ideas, from becoming, the changeable and timely.
Metaphysics ended with Nietzsche, who wills the eternal recurrence in
an attempt to displace all Being into an endless becoming. In short,
metaphysics is characterized by an unwillingness to accommodate Being
and time, to understand Being *as* time.[5] Modern technology brings this
unwillingness to a head. Technology is the pursuit of efficiency, defined
as the achievement of given ends, such as knowledge, wealth, power, or
pleasure, with a minimum expenditure of resources. Key among these
resources is time itself. Yet the underlying impetus of technology is not
so much the saving of time as its mastery. Time is that antagonistic
cosmological force that technology most seeks to harness. But one cannot truly dwell in time if one orients oneself to it as a hostile and fleeing
force to be mastered. Time is not simply a necessary medium for our
activities. Time is that which makes Being-in-the-world what it is. Temporality, Heidegger proposes, is "the meaning of the Being of that entity
which we call 'Dasein'" (*BT* 38; see also *HCT* 197). In other words,
human beings can only find its home in time; for the world only truly
becomes a home through the careful disclosure of the Being of being as
time (*HCT* 213–14, 319–20; see also *WBG* 215–16).

The remedy that Heidegger proposes for our untimely and homeless
state is memory. Edgar Guest once famously observed that "it takes a
heap o' livin' in a house t' make it a home." Making the world a home
takes no less recollective living. Memory (Mnemosyne), as the mother
of the Muses, fosters poetic work. Such work constitutes a building that

[5] In his later work, Heidegger suggests that the ontological unity of timely becoming
and Being requires a name that might dissuade further metaphysical bifurcations. He
hesitatingly chooses appropriation (*Ereignis*). However, Heidegger is quick to forewarn
that "appropriation is not the encompassing general concept under which Being and time
could be subsumed." Were appropriation to assume this role it would represent "a contin-
uation of metaphysics" and constitute yet another "obstacle" to the thinking of Being (*TB*
21, 24).

is a preserving (*EGT* 36). As artists, we remember whenever we preserve Being in beings, illuminating difference in the work of art. As citizens, we remember whenever we found and maintain a political space for interactive words and deeds, illuminating difference in the caretaking of a public world of self and other. As philosophers, we remember whenever we resolutely question the hiddenness of Being in thoughts and words that arise out of our temporal and worldly sedimentation. Memory, in short, is a recalling, or calling forth, of how we are in the world. Mnemosyne is a Titan daughter of Ouranos and Gaia. Memory is the offspring of Heaven and Earth. In reaching back to memory we recollect our dwelling "on the earth" and "beneath the sky."

Human being, Dasein, is "the being which *is itself its 'there'*" (*HCT* 253). The "there" of human being is not only a worldly place, however, but a historical time as well. Memory is a calling forth of our temporal way of being in the world. To remember is to re-collect oneself historically, to live one's historical "there" authentically. As Heidegger put the point: "The question of how it stands with Being proves to be the question of how it stands with our Being-there in history, the question of whether we *stand* in history or merely stagger" (*IM* 202). The degree of our openness to temporal Being-in-the-world determines whether we are truly living historically—that is, living our historicity with resoluteness.

Philosophy is an effort *"at once recollective and focused on the present"* (*MFL* 9). A philosopher stands in history, Heidegger maintains, "precisely by being, most intrinsically, the word of his time" (*HPS* 32). Thought, far from establishing its abode in the clouds, as the Western tradition has portrayed it since Aristophanes, remains firmly grounded in the world and the historical present (*WCT* 8, 15). As Heidegger admonished his students: "You do not get to philosophy by reading many and multifarious philosophical books, nor by torturing yourself with solving the riddles of the universe, but solely and surely by not evading what is essential in what you encounter in your current Dasein devoted to academic studies. Nonevasion is crucial, since philosophy remains latent in every human existence and need not be first added to it from somewhere else" (*MFL* 18). Philosophy in general, and Heidegger's philosophy in particular, is a timely meditation. If through one's philosophical work one is separated out from the crowd, its traditions and fashions, then it is precisely because one remains timely in an untimely age. Thinking (like resolute speaking and acting) "lets itself be given, by whatever shows itself however it shows itself, what it has to say of that which appears" (*PT* 27). In other words, the historical context of the thinker (speaker and actor) is a precondition of, rather than a hindrance to, her task of disclosing Being.

A common charge is that Heidegger's philosophy, because of its radical ontology, remains untimely and apolitical. Karsten Harries, for example, argues that "Heidegger's thinking, as he himself interprets it for us, has pushed beyond his own time in such a way that given all that the age considers important it must seem beside the point. The work of the later Heidegger is an extended untimely meditation. This untimeliness helps to explain the apolitical character of this work."[6] Heidegger admitted that because of the hegemonic subjectivism of modern society, "a philosophy which has overcome the stand-point of subjectivity is not even permitted to participate in the discussion" (*MHC* 39). But this does not mean that Heidegger's work has pushed beyond the needs of contemporary society to the point of becoming inconsequential. Rather, Heidegger's philosophy pushes contemporary society to question that which it considers important. In so doing, his philosophy does indeed meet with resistance, often to the point of having deaf ears turned toward it. But precisely for this reason we must consider it timely rather than untimely. A message is timely if, by offering new information or a new point of view, it allows one to avert danger. In a world of simmering social injustices and looming ecological threats, any message worthy of being called timely must challenge our perspectives and habituations, counseling us to alter the present course.

Heidegger is timely in a revolutionary sense. But "the greater a revolution is to be," he observes, "the more profoundly must it plunge into its history" (*WPA* 203). Heidegger asks us to plunge into the history of metaphysics and uncover the subjectivist roots that continue to feed our technological drive. In this historical descent, Heidegger suggests (with Nietzsche) that we strike bottom with the Greeks. The imperative of their retrieval is declared: "We not only wish to but must understand the Greeks better than they understood themselves. Only thus shall we actually be in possession of our heritage. Ancient ontology . . . represents the first necessary step that any philosophy at all has to take, so that this step must always be repeated by every actual philosophy. Only a self-complacent modernity lapsed into barbarism can wish to make us believe that Plato, as it is tastefully expressed, is done for" (*BP* 111– 12). Philosophy, understood as metaphysics, is fundamentally Greek in origin, in nature, and in historical development (*WP* 31). In his more expansive moments, Heidegger did not restrict the meaning of "Greek" to designate the ancient inhabitants of the Aegean (*EGT* 25). By Greek Heidegger means all those roots of Western philosophy that we must dig up and expose if we are to understand and grapple with its current effects.

[6] Harries, "Heidegger as a Political Thinker," 304.

Unfortunately, Heidegger's persistent confrontation with Western philosophy largely remains deaf to the call of other philosophic traditions. Heidegger is not completely remiss on this score. Despite his own envelopment in the study of Western thought, he was quite informed about Eastern traditions. As early as the 1920s, Heidegger had established personal relationships with Japanese scholars.[7] He read translations of Eastern scripture and remained interested in and enthusiastic about Eastern philosophy throughout the latter half of his life. He enthusiastically investigated Zen Buddhism, noting its similarities to his own thought. Indeed, it is reported that upon reading one of Daisetz Suzuki's books on Zen Buddhism, Heidegger remarked: "If I understand this man correctly, this is what I have been trying to say in all my writings."[8] In turn, Heidegger was much interested in Taoism. He would quote Lao Tzu in his writings (e.g., *PT* 56), and for a time after the war was even engaged with a Chinese scholar in the translation into German of the *Tao Te Ching*. He also observed the Taoist parallels to his own concerns and the foundational affinity of Taoism to Greek thought (*ID* 36). One cannot say with certainty to what extent Heidegger was influenced by these Eastern teachings. But he certainly held them in great esteem.

Occasionally Heidegger would gesture at the potential confluence of his (Western) thinking with its Eastern counterpart. He writes, for example, "Perhaps the mystery of mysteries of thoughtful Saying conceals itself in the word 'way,' *Tao*, if only we will let these names return to what they leave unspoken. . . . All is way" (*WL* 92). Such references are relatively sparse and undeveloped. Any similarities and parallels we may discern, moreover, compete with numerous disparities. Both Zen and Taoist thought, for instance, generally depreciate the power of words. Speech is considered, as often as not, a hindrance to the goal of enlightenment.[9] For Heidegger, on the other hand, speech is the preeminent

---

[7] See Heinrich Wiegand Petzet, *Encounters and Dialogues with Martin Heidegger, 1929–1976*, trans. Parvis Emad and Kenneth Maly (Chicago: University of Chicago Press, 1993), 166.

[8] D. T. Suzuki, *Zen Buddhism: Selected Writings of D. T. Suzuki*, ed. William Barrett (Garden City, N.Y.: Doubleday Anchor, 1956), xi. The relationship between Heidegger and Zen Buddhism, it turns out, was in certain respects mutual. The Kyoto school of philosophy was much influenced by Heidegger's work, and boasts numerous translations of *Being and Time*. In turn, Zen scholars have found common roots with Heidegger in certain Western figures. Daisetz Suzuki, perhaps Zen's foremost modern expositor, borrows much from Meister Eckardt, as did Heidegger. Daisetz T. Suzuki, *Zen and Japanese Culture* (Princeton: Princeton University Press, 1959), 289–312.

[9] Zen Buddhism spread to Japan from China after Mahayana thought underwent a fusion with Taoism to form the *Ch'an* school. *Zen* is a transliteration of the Chinese *ch'an*, which comes from the Sanskrit *dhyana*—literally, concentrated absorption or meditation. Zen, like Taoism, is centered in silent meditation.

structure of human being and language remains the venerable house of Being. Likewise, while the Zen and Taoist traditions find history a distraction to the search for the eternal now, for Heidegger the historicity of Being and human being remains crucial. Indeed, in conversation with a Buddhist monk, Heidegger emphasized that the Eastern nonrecognition (of the importance) of history is what mostly separated their philosophies.[10] These two important differences between Heidegger's philosophy and Zen or Taoist thought are noted not for lack of others but because they illustrate the obstacles that kept Heidegger from further exploring the East.

The West shares a particular history. It looks back on a common heritage of cognate languages. Being, Heidegger seems to say, speaks to the West over some three millennia in ways powerful and unique. Because of the centrality of history and language to his thought, Heidegger largely resists extending his philosophic purview beyond the Western tradition. He insists that "only in the same place where the modern technical world took its origin can we also prepare a conversion (*Umkehr*) of it. In other words, this cannot happen by taking over Zen-Buddhism or other Eastern experiences of the world. For this conversion of thought we need the help of the European tradition and a new appropriation of it" (*OGS* 62). Given that Zen Buddhism has rendered Japan no less technocratic than the non-Buddhist world, and that Eastern philosophy and religion in general have not prevented massive ecological destruction or ensured social harmony in the countries of the East, Heidegger's suspicion of exotic panaceas might be taken to heart.[11] At the same time, Heidegger implicitly acknowledges that all his digging into the Western tradition is only the prerequisite for an eventual opening to the East. He maintains that "every reflection upon that which now is can take its rise and thrive only if, through a dialogue with the Greek thinkers and their language, it strikes root into the ground of our historical existence. That dialogue . . . remains for us the precondition of the inevitable dialogue with the East Asian world" (*QT* 157–58). Though Heidegger cautioned against philosophical trips abroad for fear that they might forestall a deeper excavation of domestic soil, the voyage was considered inevitable.[12]

[10] Petzet, *Encounters and Dialogues with Martin Heidegger,* 176. See also Caputo, *Mystical Element in Heidegger's Thought,* 216–17.

[11] See Philip Novak, "Tao How? Asian Religions and the Problem of Environmental Degradation," *ReVision* 9, no. 2 (1987): 33–40.

[12] There is a practical, or perhaps personal, side to Heidegger's position. When Hans--Georg Gadamer was asked why Heidegger rarely mentioned Taoist thought if, as is generally known, he was enthusiastic about it, Gadamer replied: "You have to understand that a scholar of the generation to which Heidegger belongs would be very reluctant to say anything in print about a philosophy if he were himself unable to read and understand the relevant texts in the original language." Quoted in Parkes, *Heidegger and Asian Thought,* 7.

The confrontation of the West Heidegger inspired and engaged in remains incomplete. Its completion, however, rests on the sort of extension Heidegger was averse to making. We must be cautious about sacrificing historical depth to cultural breadth in our philosophic investigations. But our capacity to reach new layers in our Western excavations now largely depends on increasing the breadth of our understanding of non-Western (or non-Northern or non-patriarchal) thought. Heidegger writes that "the recollection from historicity is necessary not because we have already a long history of philosophy behind us, nor because piety demands that we also heed the ancients. Even if there were no explicit history of philosophy, it would still be necessary to go back and take up the tradition in which every human Dasein stands, whether it has a developed historical consciousness or not, and whether or not what it has to recollect is expressly called 'philosophy'" (*MFL* 9). Today the "tradition" we must recollect is not one but many, not unilinear but a product of multiple social and historical vectors. "The West" is no longer monolithic. Indeed, it never truly was. But we "stand" today, more than ever, in an integrated world of hybridized cultures. The philosophical clarification Heidegger sought, if it is truly to bring the historical present into focus, requires an expanded aperture.

In this matter, and ironically so, we might still take our guidance from the ancient Greeks. As Heidegger acknowledges (following Nietzsche), "the Greeks did not become what they were by means of cocooning themselves in their own 'space.' Only by virtue of the sharpest yet creative confrontation with that which was to them most foreign and difficult—the Asian—did this people rise up to their short-lived historical uniqueness and greatness" (*G* 13:21). Heidegger persistently calls upon us to think Being. This means we are to ponder Being without regard to metaphysics. Overcoming metaphysics means leaving it alone. It is time for us to take this recommedation to heart. Leaving metaphysics alone need not, indeed should not, entail our ignoring it. Nor need it, or should it, entail our devotion to its Western history if that devotion prevents our confronting other traditions of thought that testify to the global historical present.

Being-in-the-World: East and West

Buddhists and Taoists devote relatively little attention to the characteristics of historical development. Yet Eastern thinkers have also asserted that wisdom constitutes an authentication of one's worldly "there." We may better understand Heidegger's work, including his confrontation with the Western tradition, through their efforts. Daisetz Suzuki illustrates the difference between Eastern and Western under-

standings in this regard by comparing Rodin's sculpture *The Thinker* to
Sekkaku's *Zen Master in Meditation*.[13] Rodin's figure sits atop a pedestal. He is removed from the earth, and gains through this distance the
objectivity necessary for abstract reflection. Sekkaku's monk, on the
other hand, is portrayed as seated on the ground. He remains firmly
rooted in worldly life and his musings derive therefrom. Students of Zen
are taught to think in ways that do not veer into abstract conceptualization. Zen thinking always circulates around concrete there-being in its
temporality. In large part, this worldliness of the Eastern tradition stems
from its unwillingness to embrace the strict dichotomies of spirit/body,
heaven/earth, and subject/object that Neo-platonism, Christianity, and
Cartesian thought potently fostered in the West.

The Western tradition emphasizes the need to escape the bodily and
worldly—the prisons of the spirit, as Plato calls them—to attain a
higher plane of existence. The Eastern traditions, on the other hand,
seek to transcend such dichotomous thinking. The goal in the East is
attunement: the establishment of a harmonious abode in the world that
dissolves the antipodes of spirit and body, heaven and earth, subject
and object. As one Eastern commentator remarks, this distinction between East and West is evident in their respective religious figures: "Returning home, returning to the motherly earth is the ideal of the Orient.
The form of death must be painless. Sakyamuni Buddha returns in
peace into Nature after he has lived for eighty years. In the East the
man whose death is not natural is not qualified to be a saint. In this
regard the spiritual tradition of the West differs from that of the East.
Here a question arises as to why a man who was murdered can be the
most ideal man in the West."[14] The point, no doubt, is overstated. The
East has also known the persecution and martyrdom of a number of its
philosophically or religiously venerated figures. Nevertheless, a significant distinction remains: the wise person of the East is no less honored
for having escaped persecution and established a harmonious life. Attunement with the world serves as testimony to spiritual greatness.

Both the Taoist and the Zen practitioner do not so much seek to
escape the constraints of earthly life as to transform them. To be sure,
most Eastern religious traditions speak of our earthly domicile as a temporary abode, although one typically revisited numerous times in rein-
carnated forms. Moreover, release from the cycle of earthly birth and
death, from samsara, is assiduously sought. But the practitioner's goal is
not escape to an abode in the heavens. (Though the Buddhist scriptures

---

[13] Suzuki, *Zen and Japanese Culture*, 105.
[14] Takeshi Umehara, "Heidegger and Buddhism," *Philosophy East and West* 20, no. 3
(1970): 275.

speak of a heavenly paradise, it too is considered only a temporary resting place.) Ultimately, the goal is nirvana, the nonplace marking the cessation of desire and willfulness. The aim is to achieve that nirvanic wisdom which does not desire escape at all, either to a heavenly or an earthly rebirth. In the East, Being-in-the-world, though a temporary condition, is to be greeted with grace rather than rebellion or resentment. Freedom is evidenced neither by escaping nor by dominating the temporal world. Rather, freedom, including the ultimate liberation of nirvana, is approached through harmonious integration.

Metaphysically speaking, freedom is manifest in a sovereign doing, while (passive) being denotes its absence. Attunement and belonging are generally understood as a way of being rather than as a form of doing. Hence the Western tradition, in identifying freedom with possessive mastery rather than integration, effectively celebrates doing and depreciates being. Heidegger, in accord with Eastern thought, rejects the bifurcation between doing and being as well as the metaphysical concept of freedom on which it is grounded. Doing and being are synchronized in the human capacity for dwelling. Authentic Dasein "is not a thing" but "only a way to be" (*HCT* 247). Human being is a how rather than a what, a relation of disclosure rather than a subject or object. Human being is a doing, and human doing is a way of being. That is the meaning of authentically Being-in-the-world. Ontology, in this sense, structures ethics. The experience of the pervasive harmony of the way, the Tao, or of the Buddha-nature, like the Heideggerian disclosure of Being, is a transformative act. It fundamentally affects the way we are in the world.[15]

Just as we may stagger or stand in history, so Heidegger holds that we may be authentic or inauthentic in our doing. To stand in history is to remain open to the question of one's worldly being in time. To be authentic in one's doing is to accept thrownness as foundational and yet not abdicate active being for resentful resignation. Pindar's invocation to become what you are, much admired by Nietzsche, is based on this ontology. One always already *is* one's there, contingently thrown in the world, whatever one *does*. For Heidegger, "only because the Being of

[15] Like Heidegger, Taoists subsume ethics under what might be called ontology. The Tao is considered broader, deeper, and older than any morality. Chuang Tzu, in words that remind us of Heidegger's early belief in the primordial Greek relation to Being, records that only as the Tao came increasingly to be forgotten did morality arise: "Still the deterioration and decay continued. . . . They left the Tāo, and substituted the Good for it, and pursued the course of Haphazard Virtue." Chuang Tzu, "The Writings of Chuang Tzu," in *The Texts of Taoism*, trans. James Legge (New York: Dover, 1962), 1:370. Zen Buddhism has a similar orientation. Ethical comportment is subordinated to what is best described as ontological attunement.

the 'there' . . . *is* what it becomes (or alternatively, does not become), can it say to itself 'Become what you are', and say this with understanding" (*BT* 186). The difficulty we may experience in coming to grips with this thought might be alleviated by means of a long-standing debate within Zen circles.

Saijojo Zen is considered by the Soto sect to be the highest stage of Buddhist practice. Here "means and end coalesce" as one sits in meditation (zazen), convinced that one's true Buddha-nature is at every moment already realized. One does not self-consciously strive for enlightenment, known as satori or *kensho* (literally, seeing into one's own nature), lest willfulness obstruct one's further development. Acknowledging the ubiquity of the Buddha-nature, and understanding the self as its instantiation, allows a waitful but nonwillful discipline oriented to the actualization of what (already) lies in potential. All doing is thus governed by being, for one cannot discover what is not there. Awaiting the incipient realization of one's (Buddha) nature is all there is to do. And it is a great effort indeed. In this (*shikan-taza*) mode of Zen meditation "you sit with the conviction that your essential nature is no different from the Buddha's, so there is no *purposeful* striving for kensho. Still, you must believe that your sitting will one day eventuate in awakening."[16] In other words, one sits with simultaneous questioning and conviction. The questioning is that refusal to remain unawakened that sustains spiritual work. The conviction is that acknowledgment that one's lack of wakefulness is less an obstacle to be overcome than a reality to be embraced as an intrinsic feature of one's development. Becoming what one is is only assured once one resolutely accepts its profound necessity.

In the Eastern traditions, spiritual work and discipline are designed to make the harmony pervading life a self-conscious reality. Everything we do, say, or think, at all times, to all things, is held to manifest (one's) Buddha-nature or rest in accordance with the Tao. Heidegger, in contrast, is generally interpreted as presenting us with two distinct modes of human being: authentic and inauthentic existence. To the extent that we view the notion of authenticity as analogous to enlightenment, Heidegger seems to be saying that everyday life, the bulk of our experience, necessarily remains unenlightened. Illumination is only a sporadic phenomenon, evident in flashes of philosophic thought, artistic creation, and political founding, that stands in sharp contrast to the preponderance of inauthentic experience. If we transpose the early Heidegger to the later and characterize authenticity by releasement and openness,

---

[16] Philip Kapleau, *The Three Pillars of Zen* (New York: Doubleday, 1989), 133; see also 49, 64.

then Heidegger may be interpreted to propose an inevitably double life. Moments of authentic existence distinguished by an openness to Being and releasement to things stand in stark contrast to extended periods of inauthentic existence characterized by absorbed coping with everyday concerns or by technological obsessions. No doubt certain aspects of Heidegger's writings validate this interpretation. But I believe it to be an unnecessary constriction of his thought. With the help of certain Eastern reflections, one may reformulate the Heideggerian understanding of human being in a manner less bifurcated and more receptive to the exercise of freedom in the everyday.

Authenticity and Enlightenment

Authenticity does not signify the eradication of inauthenticity. With the onset of authenticity, inauthenticity is simply suspended. In *Being and Time* we read that "*authentic* existence is not something which floats above falling everydayness; existentially, it is only a modified way in which such everydayness is seized upon" (*BT* 224). Everydayness remains an indispensable foundation for the authentic. It may be superseded, but never extinguished. Heidegger maintains that "inauthenticity belongs to the essential nature of factical Dasein. Authenticity is only a modification but not a total obliteration of inauthenticity" (*BP* 171). Authenticity and inauthenticity simultaneously exist together in every individual.[17] Moreover, as a distinct and inevitable mode of human being, inauthenticity is neither undesirable nor regrettable. Heidegger makes clear that "the inauthenticity of Dasein does not signify any 'less' Being or any 'lower' degree of Being. Rather it is the case that even in its fullest concretion Dasein can be characterized by inauthenticity— when busy, when excited, when interested, when ready for enjoyment. . . . And here too Dasein's Being is an issue for it in a definite way; and Dasein comports itself towards it in the mode of average everydayness, even if this is only the mode of fleeing *in the face of it* and forgetfulness *thereof*" (*BT* 68, 69). Heidegger identifies idle talk as conversation not grounded back to the issue of one's Being. Inauthentic behavior is similarly ontologically dispossessed through its mundane absorption and forgetfulness. But it is not, for that reason, to be denied or deprecated.

To be busy, excited, lost in interest or occupied with opinions, to

---

[17] Richard Wolin completely misses the interdependence of authenticity and inauthenticity when he writes of Heidegger's "*de facto* separation of human natures into authentic and inauthentic," which "suggests that human beings are divided by nature into leaders and followers." Wolin, *Politics of Being*; 56.

await enjoyment or to fear the oncoming: all this is part of human being and may be genuinely experienced. Tying one's shoes in the morning, discussing schedules during the day, or washing dishes in the evening are generally inauthentic acts, but quite unavoidable and unregrettable ones. We are inauthentic, in other words, whenever we presume "to grasp the 'real' at a single glance," even though such presumption is frequently necessary and "fully adequate for everyday life."[18] The point is that the ontological and the ontic, the authentic and the inauthentic, simply cannot be evaluated by the same standards (WCT 192). Hence Heidegger insists that the term *idle talk* (and one might add the term *inauthentic action*) "carries no disparaging connotation whatsoever" (HCT 269). Authentic speech and action are not "higher" or "better" than everyday talk and activity. They are, at once, less forgetful of Being and less adequate to our everyday transactions with beings.

It is unfortunate that Heidegger chose the Judeo-Christian term "falling" to describe the phenomenon of inauthenticity. But as Heidegger emphasizes, falling is not meant to indicate a descent from a state of grace to one of sinfulness, certainly not a state of grace that might, at one point and hence forever, be regained. He insists that we must not understand fallenness as "a 'fall' from a purer and higher 'primal status.'. . . We would also misunderstand the ontologico-existential structure of falling if we were to ascribe to it the sense of a bad and deplorable ontical property of which, perhaps, more advanced stages of human culture might be able to rid themselves" (BT 220). Falling is the inevitable movement of human being away from resolution. It is not a descent into turpitude that might be avoided.[19] One must detach

[18] Martin Heidegger, "The Problem of Reality in Modern Philosophy," *Journal of the British Society for Phenomenology* 4 (January 1973): 64. There is a common perception that for Heidegger the everyday is necessarily technological. Regarding "the everyday life . . . within which our most important moral or ethical concepts play their roles," Stephen K. White states that "Heidegger could never see anything here other than more or less disguised iterations of a technologizing attitude." Stephen K. White, "Heidegger and the Difficulties of a Postmodern Ethics and Politics," *Political Theory* 18 (1990): 96. White confuses the issue. Heidegger does not claim that everydayness or inauthenticity is inherently technological. One may operate in an everyday manner without in the least being technologically oriented. Enframing is a relatively recent development, yet the Greeks, like people before them, had their life of the everyday. Inauthenticity today is often caught up within enframing, but it need not be.

[19] Heidegger explicitly writes: "The term 'falling' designates a *movement of the Being of the happening of Dasein* and once again should not be taken as a value judgment, as if it indicated a base property of Dasein which crops up from time to time, which is to be deplored and perhaps eliminated in advanced stages of human culture. Like discoveredness, Being-with and Being-in, falling refers to a constitutive structure of the Being of Dasein. . . . It should be noted here that the explication of these structures of Dasein has nothing to do with any doctrine of the corruption of human nature or any theory of original sin" (HCT 274, 283).

Heidegger from any (Judeo-Christian) religious affiliation that deprecates mundane aspects of life and seeks their eradication. Inauthenticity
is decidedly neither a sinful nor an inadequate state.

Inauthenticity consumes the lion's share of our lives. We accept most
things at face value. We operate in the world with skills that do
not demand—indeed, could not properly function in the midst of—profound ontological questioning. This worldly coping, according to Heidegger, is a fundamental and inescapable aspect of the human condition. Indeed, the attempt to deny or escape the inauthentic facet of
human being is reprehensible. The "inauthentic self-understanding of
the Dasein by no means signifies an ungenuine self-understanding. On
the contrary, this everyday having of self within our factical, existent,
passionate merging into things can surely be genuine, whereas all ex-
travagant grubbing about in one's soul can be in the highest degree
counterfeit or even pathologically eccentric" (BP 160).[20] Though neither
higher nor lower than authentic being, inauthentic being necessarily ignores the Being of human being and its fundamental finitude. But precisely for this reason, inauthenticity cannot be escaped, nor should it be
deprecated. The finitude of human being, acknowledged by the authentic self, is made manifest by the inauthentic self. As Heidegger writes,
"*recollection* is possible only on the basis of and because of the original
forgottenness that belongs to the Dasein and not conversely" (BP 290).
Authenticity constitutes an affirmative questioning of the limits of human being: it is decidedly not a denial or impugning of these limits, and
therefore not a denial or impugning of inauthentic life.

To be authentic is to be resolute. But being resolute is far from being
stubbornly set on some "higher" purpose or procedure while remaining
deaf to anything or anyone that shares one's world and time. On the
contrary, "resoluteness is freedom to *give up* some definite resolution,
and to give it up in accordance with the demands of some possible
Situation or other" (BT 443). Quite the opposite of a heroic ordering of
the future, resoluteness is a disclosive openness to the historical present.
The resolute individual is defined by his or her receptivity to the (nov-
elties of the) here and now. Heidegger writes: "When resolute, Dasein
has brought itself back from falling, and has done so precisely in order
to be more authentically 'there' in the 'moment of *vision*' as regards the
Situation which has been disclosed" (BT 376). Resoluteness detaches

[20] Zimmerman makes the mistake of interpreting inauthenticity as a perverse form of
everydayness. Zimmerman, *Eclipse of the Self,* 44. He claims that Heidegger is inconsi-
stent on this point because Heidegger often equates the everyday and the inauthentic.
Indeed, this is Heidegger's thesis. Zimmerman, it seems, is too anxious to suggest affinities
between Heidegger's thought and the existentialism of Pascal and Kierkegaard (and perhaps Sartre). Therefore he portrays inauthenticity as a type of bad faith.

one from convention and habit not to deliver one into a realm of abstract principles or future projects, but precisely to bring one authentically into the populated present.

Heidegger prompts us to remain open to the "moment of *vision*" which "discloses the authentic 'there'" of human being (*BT* 398). Heidegger makes clear that this temporal and worldly dwelling in the here and now is the essence of authenticity and resoluteness: "Resoluteness, as *authentic Being-one's-Self*, does not detach Dasein from its world, nor does it isolate it so that it becomes a free-floating 'I'. And how should it, when resoluteness as authentic disclosedness, is *authentically* nothing else than *Being-in-the-world?* Resoluteness brings the self right into its current concernful Being-alongside what is ready-to-hand, and pushes it into solicitous Being with Others" (*BT* 344). To be authentic is to hand oneself over to the inexhaustible richness of Being as it is manifest in a world shared with others. In the face of the finitude of human being, authenticity allows one respectfully to accompany one's temporal cohabitants of the with-world. Authentic existence pertains to the task of escorting mortals.

Heidegger cannot rightfully be accused of deprecating our mundane, social existence in the name of authenticity. However, Heidegger fails adequately to discourage an understanding of authenticity that places it in categorical distinction to inauthenticity. Many readers are misled to believe that everyday inauthenticity is always and everywhere a seamless web of human being, with authentic human being an equally pure phenomenon marking its complete, albeit temporary, interruption or suspension. There is to be found in Heidegger's work no argument or discussion grounding such a position. We have no reason to suspect that moments of vision are always uniformly authentic or that daily, mundane activities are homogeneously inauthentic. What Heidegger often alludes to as a category, is, I propose, a continuum. Authentic vision is typically adulterated with inauthentic distraction. Inauthenticity, our absorption in the everyday, is not only interrupted by authenticity, but laced with it. While there is no need to deny the possibility of completely authentic and inauthentic moments, they are best portrayed as poles of a continuum whose interstices constitute the basic stuff of human existence.

This amendment to, or clarification of, Heidegger's thought has significant ramifications. Freedom, in thought, speech, and deed, must now be conceived as a somewhat elusive goal, typically achieved in manifold yet abridged forms in the midst of daily affairs. Disclosive freedom is a composite process and practice, not a final, enduring, or unadulterated achievement. Hence we may justifiably speak of *everyday freedom*. To be sure, freedom in thought, speech, and deed may be most clearly and purely evidenced in the flights of philosophic meditation, the creation of great art, or the founding resolutions of political bodies. Yet freedom may also be experienced, albeit in diluted and dispersed form, throughout everyday life. Every thought, word, and deed testifies, obscurely or otherwise, to the Being of what is. Each day of every human being contains the seeds of freedom in some state of germination. Freedom is not prescribed to certain places or persons or moments. In practice, however, the luminosity of its purest manifestations may cast all kin into the shadows of workaday life.

There is an undeniable realism in this position. Moreover, viewing authenticity and inauthenticity on a continuum allows us to eschew a dualism lingering in Heidegger's thought. Again, a momentary turn to the East proves helpful. Zen and Taoist literature is rife with stories of the search for and achievement of enlightenment during banal activity. Indeed, the stories of greatest inspiration typically expound an individual's realization—in the midst of mundane affairs—that the distinction between the ordinary and the extraordinary is illusory. Precisely the commonplace awaits one's opening to its luminosity, to what simply yet profoundly is. Zen monks are instructed to engage every practice and duty, whether rigorous meditation or the serving of tea, with a resoluteness and concentration that befits the opportunities for enlightenment lurking in quotidian affairs. Absorbed in sweeping, cooking, archery practice, or flower arranging, practitioners are to attune themselves to the Buddha-nature within everyday life. Eschewing the planning, judging, and ordering—aspects of possessive mastery—that preempt one's full experience of the here and now, Zen practitioners discipline themselves to discover the extraordinary within the ordinary. In Taoist traditions, the practice is similar. As Chuang Tzu ably states, "The Tao does not exhaust itself in what is greatest, nor is it ever absent from what is least; and therefore it is to be found complete and diffused in all things."[21] The point is not, as Bentham famously said, that it all comes down to what gives us the most pleasure, and that prejudices apart push-pin is as good as poetry. Push-pin is as good as poetry only if poetry is reduced to a solely recreational diversion rather than an interrogative saying of Being, or if push-pin becomes the sort of exercise in attunement that sweeping floors or drinking tea does for the zen master.

Heidegger defines the everyday as the realm of the inauthentic. But that is not to say that he remains blind or deaf to the greatness and mystery of that which is unadorned with ceremony or fame. Quite the opposite is true. He maintains that Being may shine forth most clearly when attention is not diverted by the grandiosity of events and things.

---

[21] Chuang Tzu, "Writings of Chuang Tzu," 1:342.

Heidegger underlines this position by focusing on what he calls "the simple." The simplest things and events beget the profound question of why they are at all. Those inured to the mystery of Being, however, perceive in the simple only an arid uniformity: "To the disoriented, the simple seems monotonous. The monotonous brings weariness, and the weary and bored find only what is uniform. The simple has fled. Its quiet power is exhausted."[22] Boredom with the simple often leads not to inaction but to technological action without bounds. In contrast, for those who remain attentive, the "ever-same astonishes and liberates."[23] The mundane is pregnant with Being. This pregnancy, to borrow a Socratic image, calls us to midwifery. What lies hidden in the everyday solicits ontological rediscovery. Without appreciation of this potential, boredom usurps the experience of freedom.

To disclose the Being of ordinary beings is to experience what Heidegger calls the "nearness of things." Because of our frenzied manipulation of the world, we often remain impervious to this nearness (*Nähe*). In our technological relations, "despite all conquest of distances the nearness of things remains absent" (*PLT* 166). The resulting alienation forbids experience of the mystery of Being within the most ordinary of beings. To overcome this alienation we must "dwell as those at home in nearness" (*QT* 49). The everyday is never irretrievably lost to authentic being. Rather, we must learn to experience the everyday and the simple anew in their uncanny nearness. Being underlies all that is, and therefore anything and everything may allow for its disclosure. To remain astonished at the simple is to witness the ever-same of Being amidst the diverse flux of beings.

Being is not to be experienced as an overpowering, uniform presence that blinds us to difference. It is a presencing of difference. "Being has identity as its essence," Heidegger maintains. But he quickly adds, "Identity is unity as the belonging together of what is different" (*ST* 105). Heidegger's discussions of the belonging together of identity and difference resonate with Eastern thought. The Buddha-nature, we are told, is everywhere as one in multiple forms. As Daisetz Suzuki observes, a "central perception of the truth of Zen is 'the One in the Many and the Many in the One,' or better, 'the One remaining as one in the Many individually and collectively.'"[24] In the East, the search for wisdom typically takes the form of a search to discover the One in the

[22] Martin Heidegger, "The Pathway," in Sheehan, *Heidegger,* 70.

[23] Ibid., 71. Heidegger's treatment of "boredom" (*Langeweile*) has been largely ignored. I address its importance in "Changing Moods: Heidegger on Boredom in a Technological Age" (paper presented at the annual meeting of the American Political Science Association, New York, 1994).

[24] Suzuki, *Zen and Japanese Culture,* 28.

Many and the Many in the One. The discovery is one of balance rather than hierarchy. This wisdom, Heidegger suggests, is already found in Heraclitus and Parmenides, who "were not yet 'philosophers.' . . . Heraclitus and Parmenides were 'greater' in the sense that they were still in harmony with the *Logos,* that is, with the 'One (is) all'" (*WP* 53). Harmony with this Logos, Heidegger relates, began to dissolve with the Sophists. It was broken by Plato through his insistence on a metaphysical knowledge that denies difference and celebrates uniformity. For Heidegger, however, "adequate knowledge" does not seek to overpower the many with the one. Rather, it marks "the total grasp of the harmony of multiplicity. . . . Identity is not the negative concept of the absence of all differentiation. It is, conversely, the idea of the unisonous unity of what is different" (*MFL* 68). The tensioned experience of the one as all is what allows our coming near to beings in a way that discloses rather than denies their Being.

Heidegger writes, "We believe we are at home in the immediate circle of beings. That which is, is familiar, reliable, ordinary. Nevertheless, the clearing is pervaded by a constant concealment in the double form of refusal and dissembling. At bottom, the ordinary is not ordinary; it is extra-ordinary, uncanny" (*PLT* 54). Once our coming near the simple no longer leaves us in awe, and the difference of the many is no longer grounded in the ever-sameness of Being, then the comfortable and familiar relationships we establish in the everyday become inauthentically experienced. The ordinary and familiar are the everyday grasped inauthentically, at face value. When experienced in appreciation of the everyday's "isness," in its uncanniness and nearness, however, the ordinary and familiar release their ontological potential. The everyday astonishes and liberates only once its notions of being and time become infused with interrogative refusal. To be liberated, in this sense, is disclosively to liberate. Our abode in Being is gained once our abode in the familiar circle of things is disrupted, and deepened, by ontological questioning.

Dwelling in Time and the Leap to Being

Our capacity fully to dwell in the world ironically rests on our capacity for alienation from the conventional and habitual. Experiencing uncanniness of the ordinary, for Heidegger, exposes the limitations of everyday concepts of time and being (*HCT* 156). Within Zen literature, a similar orientation is promoted. The sutra or Buddhist scripture describes the foundation of all things as "No-abode," signifying a disposition of ontological homelessness. "'No-abode' or having no abiding

place anywhere," means that "the ultimate source of all things is beyond human understanding, beyond the categories of time and space."[25]
Dōgen, a thirteenth-century monk who is credited with taking Zen to
Japan from China, offers support for this understanding in a way that
further illuminates Heidegger's thought. His chief work is, strikingly,
entitled *Being-time*. According to Dōgen, Being-time means that "time
is already being; all being is time."[26] Dōgen, like Heidegger, opposes the
absolute validity, though not the occasional utility, of metaphysical and
commonsense conceptions of time, such as the inauthentic notion of
time wherein "time flies"; that of clock time by which we measure; and
that of eternalism wherein another realm of time subsumes worldly time
(as inferior). In their stead, Dōgen proposes Being-time, which bears a
resemblance to Heidegger's notion of "ecstatic temporality." Both effectively identify time as the unconcealment of Being in the world.[27] Enlightened or authentic human being, in projecting its being as doing and
its doing as being, experiences the identity of Being and time. Usually,
time is conceived as the duration that marks the changing appearance of
beings. Herein human being thinks, speaks, and acts in the medium of
time's passage. Authentic or enlightened human being, on the other
hand, thinks, speaks, and acts the disclosure of Being as time.

With the disclosure of Being as time, everyday things and events are
experienced in their nearness and manifold simplicity. Heidegger interprets Nietzsche's description of the eternal recurrence in terms of this
achievement: "It is not merely that another series of happenstances unfolds; what is different is the *kind* of happening, acting, and creating.
Color, the very look of things, their *eidos*, presencing, Being—this is
what changes" (*ERS* 131–32). In like manner, Seigen Ishin (Ch'ing-
yuan Wei-hsin) states that "before a man studies Zen, to him mountains
are mountains and waters are waters; after he gets an insight into the
truth of Zen through the instruction of a good master, mountains to
him are not mountains and waters are not waters; but after this when
he really attains to the abode of rest, mountains are once more mountains and waters are waters."[28] It is not that mountains, water, and
color themselves change as we experience in turn their ordinariness or

---

[25] Ibid., 201.

[26] Dōgen, *Shobogenzo: Zen Essays by Dōgen*, trans. Thomas Cleary (Honolulu: University of Hawaii Press, 1986), 104.

[27] The chief difference is that Heidegger emphasizes human finitude while Dōgen focuses on impermanence. In turn, Heidegger tends to separate Dasein from other beings
(nature), and the personal, ethical realm from the ontological. Dōgen, on the other hand,
proposes a more naturalistic, holistic, and existential relation. See Heine, *Existential and
Ontological Dimensions of Time*, 60, 144–46.

[28] Suzuki, *Zen Buddhism*, 14.

their strangeness, their distance or their nearness. Mountains, water, and color continue to exist as before. The experience of their relation to Being, however, changes the way of our Being-in-the-world just as the way we are in the world changes our experience of beings.

This newfound way of worldly dwelling has characteristic features. The simple, Heidegger indicates, befalls one suddenly but then requires a long time to mature.[29] A relation to Being is achieved only by "our moving away from the attitude of representational thinking. This move is a leap in the sense of a spring. The spring leaps away, away from the habitual idea of man as the rational animal who in modern times has become a subject for his objects. . . . The spring is the abrupt entry into the realm from which man and Being have already reached each other in their active nature, since both are mutually appropriated, extended as a gift, one to the other" (*ID* 32–33). Nearness is achieved in an initial leap, which, having been made, might be approached with increasing frequency and assuredness. But the nothingness of Being continues to haunt us. The dreadful sense of "No-abode" lingers. The anxiety of the abyss of Being is not lost. The goal, one might say, is somehow to become at home in the middle of a leap.

The leap to the nearness of Being is also a leap into the abyss (*Abgrund*). It is analogous to the leap into the void, or *sunyata,* advocated in Buddhist thought. One leaps beyond the representational world, beyond conceptualization and logic, into the realm of what might be called intuition. Doubts linger about whether one should abandon the conceptual realm, with its reassuring foundations of logic and reason. In the East, the answer has been consistently more affirmative than it has in the West. The Zen tradition firmly maintains that the intuitive experience of reality must not be stymied by conceptual categories, logical restrictions, or rational systematizations.[30] In the Rinzai sect of Zen, for example, the gaining of intuition is aided by meditation on koans. Koans are terse paradoxes. A well-known koan, for instance, asks one to determine the sound of one hand clapping. Perhaps the most famous koan asks simply 'What is the nature of Mu?'" A commentator explains: "Mu is the expression of the living, functioning, dynamic Buddha-nature. What you must do is discover the spirit or essence of this Mu, not through intellectual analysis but by search [*sic*] into your innermost being."[31] In experiencing the nature of reality the Zen disciple

[29] Heidegger, "Pathway," 70.

[30] Daisetz Suzuki informs us that "strictly speaking, Zen has no philosophy of its own. Its teaching is concentrated on an intuitive experience, and the intellectual content of this experience can be supplied by a system of thought not necessarily Buddhistic." Suzuki, *Zen and Japanese Culture,* 44.

[31] Kapleau, *Three Pillars of Zen,* 142.

finds that linguistic, conceptual, and logical distinctions are unhelpful. A koan has no intellectually satisfying answer. Representational language fails to grasp its significance. As Takashina remarks, "though we try to understand this [koan] with the discriminating intellect, it will never be understood. . . . Zen meditation means to cut off at the root the mind which thinks 'I understand it', and to enter the state where there is no impure discrimination, and that one who rests satisfied at the stage of intellectual understanding is far from the goal of Zen."[32] Forced to confront the limits of rational inquiry and of representational and conceptual language, those contemplating a koan are prompted to leap toward an intuitive level of experience, gaining direct exposure to the Buddha-nature that pervades life. The "correct" answer to a koan effectively unasks the koan; the "correct" answer demonstrates not only that the question is unanswerable but that it remains, most fundamentally, unaskable.

Heidegger sets himself off from the Western tradition by answering in a fashion much like that of his Eastern counterparts the question of whether we dare quit the realm of logic, representation, and rational conceptualization. Philosophy, for Heidegger, takes on the task of making "the obvious incomprehensible and the unquestioned something questionable . . . of shocking common sense out of its presumptive self-glorification . . . of arousing us so that we become awake to see that, with a lot of hullabaloo and expenditure of activity, we wander around for the most part exclusively in the superficial regions of our existence, in intellectual matters as well!" (*MFL* 5–6). Rather than relying on pithy anti-intellectual puzzles to be contemplated in silence, Heidegger leads his readers beyond the merely conceptual, rational, and representational grasp of reality by way of poetic speech. An important difference exists between the approach to language taken by Heidegger and that taken by those in the Zen or Taoist tradition.

Within much Eastern thought, language is shunned along with intellectual analysis as a hindrance to intuition. "The name is but the guest of reality," Chuang Tzu admonishes, reflecting the typically Eastern worry that too often our linguistic visitations are mistaken for truth itself.[33] Silence, not speech, is the characteristic Taoist or Buddhist activity. The Tao Te Ching plainly states: "Abstaining from speech marks him who is obeying the spontaneity of his nature."[34] Conceptual thought and logic employ language as a tool to excavate knowledge. The leap demanded of Zen and Taoist practitioners, however, precludes

---

[32] Quoted in Edward Conze, ed. and trans., *Buddhist Scriptures* (New York: Penguin, 1959), 143.

[33] Chuang Tzu, "Writings of Chuang Tzu," 1:170.

[34] Lao Tzu, "Tao Te Ching," in Legge, *Texts of Taoism* 1:65.

such a utilitarian (linguistic) approach to enlightenment. Zen monks are routinely upbraided when their answers to koans evidence a belief that the answer sought is to be discovered *in* words, that the answer is somehow *about* words. The best answer is frequently mute, perhaps accompanied by movements or gestures that indicate the presence or experience of the Buddha-nature. Kensho, in turn, is often achieved when the monitor or Roshi (master) supervising meditation strikes a monk with a baton to focus his attention. The blow, more than any lecture, brings the monk a direct experience of the nearness of things. When language is engaged, Zen Buddhists take it not as a representation of reality but as the coming to bear of reality itself. In Zen, "experience and expression are one."[35] Like Heidegger, Zen Buddhists and Taoists hold that authentic words do not so much symbolize or represent beings as disclose Being. The language pertinent to Zen and Taoist practices, like Heidegger's, invokes rather than defines or describes.

Heidegger is disdainful of crassly utilitarian understandings of language. But freedom, Heidegger has no trouble affirming, may be exercised in speech, whose praises he frequently sings. However, before we drive a linguistic wedge completely between Heidegger and the Eastern tradition on this score, we might listen attentively to Heidegger's own words. He states, "Only because in everyday speaking language does *not* bring itself to language but holds back, are we able simply to go ahead and speak a language, and so to deal with something and negotiate something by speaking. But when does language speak itself as language? Curiously enough, when we cannot find the right word for something that concerns us, carries us away, oppresses or encourages us. Then we leave unspoken what we have in mind and, without rightly giving it thought, undergo moments in which language itself has distantly and fleetingly touched us with its essential being" (*WL* 59). Most fundamentally, language touches us, and displays our freedom in speech, not when we utter particular words but when we are confronted with a reality that words cannot limn. Language's mute message, its *"peal of stillness,"* shelters that which "by its essential nature remains unspoken" (*PLT* 208; *WL* 188). Language does not exhaust Being through verbalization. Rather, it allows us to discern Being's inexhaustibility through the gestures of a poetic disclosure that intimates its own limitations. To reach, and leap beyond, the limits of language whether in silent meditation, in struggle with koans, or in poetic-philosophic questioning—is precisely to experience an ineffable, inexhaustible reality. Heidegger was fond of Parmenides' dictum, "One should both say and think that Being is." This, in effect, is Heidegger's chant of Being.

[35] Suzuki, *Zen and Japanese Culture*, 6.

Like the Zen chant of Mu, it fosters the profound realization that *Being is*—not because (the word) "Being" is, nor because we can say that Being is. To say and think that Being is is to say and think what lies beyond the horizon of everyday time and space, and thus beyond the horizon of (representational) language and thought. Being is disclosed most fundamentally by a questioning conducted in the silence of answers.

Along with Eastern sages, Heidegger identifies our "being there" as truth itself, a truth that must first be experienced and only subsequently be given over to the realm of evaluation (*WBG* 213). Restricted from the utilitarian employment of language or conceptual cogitation as a means of achieving the leap of intuition, Heidegger advocates a patient and will-less waiting. "Genuine patience is one of the basic virtues of philosophizing," he writes, "a virtue which understands that we always have to build up the pile of kindling with properly selected wood so that it may at one point catch fire" (*HPS* 73). Likewise, within the Zen tradition, "Self-realization is not a matter of step-by-step progress but the result of a leap. Until your mind is pure you cannot make this leap."[36] In Zen practice, the preparation of the kindling is achieved through disciplined daily regimens and long hours of meditation. Meditational practice is aimed at purifying the mind, freeing it of conceptual prejudices and logical constrictions. Kensho marks the explosion into flame. Intellectual stimulation is never a direct means to enlightenment in the East. At most it constitutes a form of mental gymnastics. It builds strength so that one may eventually unburden oneself of the crutches of belief and logic and directly approach the Buddha-nature.

Heidegger identifies releasement as that which allows our intuitive leap to Being. The closest Eastern equivalent of Heidegger's notion of releasement is the Taoist understanding of *wu wei*.[37] "Wu wei" is often translated as "noninterference." It refers to a disposition of unattachment wherein willful behavior is suspended. One stills and empties oneself, abjuring willfulness in patient preparation for the vision of what is. Lao Tzu affirms that "if any one should wish to get the kingdom for himself, and to effect this by what he does, I see that he will not succeed. The kingdom is a spiritlike thing, and cannot be got by active doing. He who would so win it destroys it; he who would hold it in his grasp loses it. . . . the kingdom is made one's own (only) by freedom from action and purpose."[38] Similarly, Heidegger writes that "in-dwelling in releasement . . . mean[s] exulting in waiting, through which we

---

[36] Kapleau, *Three Pillars of Zen*, 227.

[37] Graham Parkes also observes this parallel. See Parkes, *Heidegger and Asian Thought*, 85.

[38] Lao Tzu, "Tao Te Ching," 1:71–72, 100.

become more waitful and more void. . . . [It is] pure resting in itself of that willing, which, renouncing willing, has released itself to what is not will" (*DT* 82, 85). Taoist freedom is much like Heidegger's disclosive freedom. Released from willfulness, one achieves as a witness what one is denied as a master and possessor.

Releasement does not signal passivity, a lack of power to act, or a denial of the will to live (*DT* 80). Releasement fosters an active Being-in-the-world, one whose dynamism arises out of the absence of attachment to specific models of the future. Taoists have a similar perspective. Chuang Tzu asserts that "he who practises the Tāo, daily diminishes his doing. He diminishes it and again diminishes it, till he arrives at doing nothing. Having arrived at this non-inaction, there is nothing that he does not do."[39] Similarly, Buddhist practitioners seek releasement from will or craving so as to be free from karma. Karma is the repository of the dispositions that have actuated thoughts, words, and deeds throughout one's life.[40] Bad karma accumulates from volitional actions engaged in for negative purposes. The accumulation of karma ensures one's rebirth, signifying that one has failed to gain release from the cravings and willfulness that turn the wheel of samsara. The Buddhist tradition is grounded on the original realization of its founder, Gautama, that escape from the cycle of birth and death perpetuated by karmic actions requires the knowledge that craving is the cause of all suffering. One must resolve to gain release from all craving. However, this resolve to gain release must not amount to just another craving.

This paradox has given rise to much discussion and commentary within Zen (and Taoist) circles. There is, for example, the story of a Zen monk who reputedly asked Daishu Ekai: "What is great *nirvāṇa*?" The T'ang master answered, "Not to commit oneself to the karma of birth-and-death is great *nirvāṇa*." When the monk followed with the question: "What, then, is the karma of birth-and-death?" Ekai could only respond: "To desire great *nirvāṇa* is the karma of birth-and-death."[41] Willfully to crave nirvana, the T'ang master indicates, is to perpetuate the conditions that hinder releasement. Nirvana, the cessation of all craving and suffering and the escape from the wheel of samsara, cannot be an achievement of will. For those within the Zen and Taoist traditions, as for Heidegger, freedom is achieved in releasing oneself from willful thought, speech, and action. However, in speaking of freedom only in a worldly context, Heidegger avoids the doctrinal aspects of certain Eastern traditions. By abstaining from beliefs in rein-

[39] Chuang Tzu, "Writings of Chuang Tzu," 2:59.
[40] See Conze, *Buddhist Scriptures*, 139.
[41] Suzuki, *Zen and Japanese Culture*, 139.

carnation and the nirvanic afterlife, Heidegger maintains the skepticism he rightly identifies as the medium of philosophic thought.

Releasement is to be sought with resolute determination. But it is only truly achieved once one no longer wills it. Resolute determination in the absence of willful striving constitutes waiting. The groundwork for this position is laid in Heidegger's critique of subjectivism. Metaphysical subjectivism culminates in the (Nietzschean) will to will, and the rule of enframing. Releasement marks the successful struggle against subjectivism wherein the subject/object dichotomy no longer structures perception and action, and the will to will is placed in abeyance. At this point one may act in and on the world without at the same time becoming invested (as a subject) in the bending of reality (as an object) to the dictates of will. The Taoist and Buddhist traditions both reinforce this position. One of the most prominent themes of the *Tao Te Ching*, the works of Chuang Tzu, and the Buddhist sutras is the self's struggle against itself as a willful subject. Taoist and Zen adages and commentaries constantly circle around this paradox, while meditational and other disciplines attempt to cut through it. We read in Seng-Ts'an's poem "On Believing in Mind":

> Abide not with dualism
> Carefully avoid pursuing it.
>
> . . . .
>
> The subject is quieted when the object ceases,
> The object ceases when the subject is quieted.
> The object is an object for the subject,
> The subject is a subject for the object;
> Know that the relativity of the two
> Rests ultimately on one emptiness.[42]

As Thomas Merton characterizes Zen practice in general: "Zen is the ontological *awareness of pure being beyond subject and object,* an immediate grasp of being in its 'suchness' and 'thusness.' "[43] Within the Buddhist tradition, this capacity for nonwillful action is incarnated in the Arahant, a saintly figure who no longer accumulates karma. The

---

[42] Quoted in Conze, *Buddhist Scriptures,* 172.

[43] Thomas Merton, *Mystics and Zen Masters* (New York: Noonday Press, 1967), 14. Within the Indian tradition, the understanding of *atman* signals a similar release from subjectivism. For an attempt to integrate this understanding with Western ecological concerns, see Arne Naess, "Identification as a Source of Deep Ecological Attitudes," in *Radical Environmentalism: Philosophy and Tactics,* ed. Peter List (Belmont, Calif.: Wadsworth, 1993), 24–38. In promoting an expansion of the self or *atman* that dissolves subjectivity, however, Naess and other deep ecologists typically fail to recognize otherness. I argue this point in "Nature and Freedom: A Heideggerian Critique of Biocentric and Sociocentric Environmentalism," *Environmental Ethics* 17 (1995): 171–90.

Arahant's past doings, carried out without willfulness, no longer determine his present actions or dispositions, nor do his present dispositions
and actions, similarly experienced and engaged in without craving, constrict his future. Herein freedom is most purely manifest, in that the
Arahant's wordly actions remain unrestricted by habit and convention
and unstructured by the aggregate residue of dispositions. His freedom
is a spontaneity uncluttered by subjectivity. Yet this freedom is never
the freedom simply to do what one pleases. Rather, it is the freedom of
a witness who everyday and anew affirms the abiding Buddha-nature of
all that is, including the Buddha-nature manifest in the mundane limitations of human being. The Arahant's freedom is exercised not in sovereignty, but through a disclosive worldly dwelling. The *Genjokoan*, by
Dōgen, a commentary whose title has been translated as *The Way of
Everyday Life*, illustrates the nature of this openness to the world:

> That the self acts upon and confirms the
> myriad things is delusion
> That the myriad things act upon and confirm
> the self is enlightenment.[44]

Entering the Marketplace

In an effort to integrate the exploration of everyday freedom, timely
dwelling, and Heidegger's hesitant gesture toward the East with the
question of politics, we might examine Leo Strauss's severe criticism of
the Heideggerian vision. Strauss writes:

> There is no room for political philosophy in Heidegger's work, and this may
> well be due to the fact that the room in question is occupied by gods or the
> gods. . . . Heidegger's philosophy of history has the same structure as Marx'
> [*sic*] and Nietzsche's: the moment in which the final insight is arriving opens
> the eschatological prospect. . . . Heidegger's philosophy belongs to the
> infinitely dangerous moment when man is in a greater danger than ever
> before of losing his humanity and therefore—danger and salvation belonging
> together—philosophy can have the task of contributing toward the recovery
> or return of *Bodenständigkeit* [rootedness in the soil] or rather of preparing
> an entirely novel kind of *Bodenständigkeit*: a *Bodenständigkeit* beyond the
> most extreme *Bodenlosigkeit* [loss of rootedness in the soil], a being at home

[44] Other translations of *Genjokoan* include *The Issue at Hand* and *The Actualization of
Enlightenment*. See Dōgen Zenji, *Shobogenzo*, trans. Kosen Nishiyam and John Stevens
(Sendai, Japan: Daihokkaikaku, 1975); Dōgen, *Shobogenzo*; and Dōgen, *The Way of
Everyday Life: Zen Master Dōgen's Genjokoan with Commentary*, trans. Hakuyu Taizan
Maezumi (Los Angeles: Center Publications, 1978).

beyond the most extreme homelessness. . . . A dialogue between the most profound thinkers of the Occident and the most profound thinkers of the Orient and in particular East Asia may lead to the consummation prepared, accompanied or followed by a return of the gods. That dialogue and everything that it entails, but surely not political action of any kind, is perhaps the way. Heidegger severs the connection of the vision with politics more radically than either Marx or Nietzsche. One is inclined to say that Heidegger has learned the lesson of 1933 more thoroughly than any other man. Surely he leaves no place whatever for political philosophy.[45]

Strauss touches on many of the most salient features of both Heidegger's thought and that of his critics. However, I take issue with Strauss on two related points, and in so doing mark the "room" in Heidegger's work for political philosophy.

First, Strauss assumes that the dialogue with the East prepares the way for an eschatology with dangerous political consequences. Yet Heidegger's dialogue is firmly grounded in an appreciation of the inexhaustible riches of the mundane and the everyday. Inauthenticity, for Heidegger, is not to be banished from our lives, as Marx hoped to banish capitalists.[46] What Strauss fails to discern is that Heidegger celebrates "waiting" (for the gods) as a way of being in the world, not as an "awaiting" of a millenarian epiphany. Waiting constitutes a responsible dwelling in, not an escape from, our worldly domicile and its obligations. The ontological discovery of home that ensues from such waiting is grounded in a historically and socially embedded life. Moreover, we may think through this ontology, beyond Heidegger's own words, to posit this life in terms of a globally oriented, democratic politics. Today, the terms *globalization* and *democratization* frequently signify economic and cultural homogenization. They increasingly refer to little more than the universalizing of Western patterns of production and consumption, reflecting the hegemonic reach of stock markets and cinemas. In this light, the contemporary philosophic and political task is twofold. We must struggle against the tribalism that prevents our fully acknowledging the humanness of others. At the same time, we must resist the technological homogenization that prevents our fully acknowledging the otherness of humans. The dialogue with the Eastern other that Heidegger initiates and this chapter underlines may be seen as a gesture in this direction.

Second, there is no denying that Heidegger's philosophy is occupied

---

[45] Leo Strauss, *Studies in Platonic Political Philosophy* (Chicago: University of Chicago Press, 1983), 30, 33, 34.

[46] Nietzsche was not a millenarian, though in his last frenzied years he came close. He assumed that the decadent would be with us always.

more with fostering the "responsibility to otherness" than with fostering the "responsibility to act."[47] For some, like Strauss, this signals the
abandonment of politics as we know it. But the witnessing of difference
that the responsibility to otherness entails is not irresponsible, inactive,
or politically insignificant. Human being, engaging its disclosive freedom in the witnessing of difference, is a doing. The challenge of political philosophy is to sacrifice neither human being to doing nor human
doing to being. As William Barrett, an avid reader of Heidegger and a
collaborator with Daisetz Suzuki, wrote: "The truth of human life must
perpetually lie in the tension between Being and doing. We can never
resolve the question exclusively in favor of one or the other side. All our
doing must take place within the context of Being, with its mystery
present and alive to us. Otherwise we are simply scurrying around
aimlessly in the mazes of our own contrivance. On the other hand, to
seek absorption in Being, as an escape from the tasks of ordinary life,
can only lead to quiescence and boring repetition. Man is the creature
who must live in perpetual tension between these opposites. He *is* their
tension and copresence."[48] Political philosophy pertains to the study and
appreciation of the perpetual tension between our essence and our actions, our identity and our engagements. In investigating Heidegger's
understanding of a disclosive freedom that is grounded in this tensioned
copresence, political philosophy comes to life.

The point is perhaps best conveyed by returning again to Eastern
thought and offering a commentary on the "Oxherding Pictures," a sequence of ten drawings originally attributed to the twelfth-century Zen
master Kuo-an Shih-yuan (Kakuan Shien). The sequence depicts the developing stages of the pursuit of enlightenment in the metaphor of herd-
ing oxen. The ox is symbolic of the elusive Buddha-nature that exists
within all, the herder of the aspirant in its pursuit.[49] The first drawing is
called *Seeking the Ox*. At this stage the aspirant remains lost. Without
spiritual guidance only a haphazard search for the way is possible. The
next drawing depicts finding the tracks. The Buddhist scriptures (sutras)
and teachings have been discovered and they strike a certain chord in
the seeker. A superficial knowledge of the nature of the search has been
gained, but many judgments are still impossible at this conceptual level
of understanding. With the first glimpse of the ox, one achieves kensho,
the momentary experience of the realization of Buddha-nature through

[47] Stephen K. White suggests this useful distinction in "Heidegger," 80–103. See also
White's *Political Theory and Postmodernism* (Cambridge: Cambridge University Press,
1991).

[48] William Barrett, *The Illusion of Technique* (Garden City, N.Y.: Anchor Books,
1976), 322.

[49] See Kapleau, *Three Pillars of Zen*, 241, 313–25.

meditation. But without continuing work all may still be lost. The subsequent drawing portrays catching the ox. Discipline has yielded a more stable and enduring experience of enlightenment, but the ox does not take easily to the bridle. There is a struggle with its wild movements and yearnings. Constant vigilance is required. Then the ox is tamed. One realizes that the delusions and wildness of the self that accompany catching the ox are themselves of the mind and, like everything else, are subsumed under the Buddha-nature. Discipline becomes less a war with inner demons than a serene participation in a nondualistic reality. With the struggle all but over, the seeker rides the ox home. Herein ego, subjectivity, and willfulness begin to dissolve, evaporating completely once one learns to forget both the ox and the self. Returning to the source now comes quite naturally. Without the need to strive, beyond discriminations of subject and object, one fearlessly immerses oneself in the world. No longer does ego-bound craving induce willful action, yet there is nothing one does not do. The last drawing is called *Entering the Marketplace with Helping Hands*. In the marketplace, one ceases to identify with esteemed forerunners or particular doctrines and traditions. One even ceases to differentiate between enlightenment and non-enlightenment. All attachment, including attachment to one's Buddha-nature, ceases. Instead, one enters into the everyday world, struck by its awesome simplicity, exchanging with those one meets whatever one has to offer.

This final stage is emblematic of the goal of the Mahayana school of Buddhism, from which Zen derives. Herein one aspires not so much to escape worldliness and temporality as to become an integral and active participant in it—but with a self-awareness that precludes the cravings and attachments that dominate conventional life. Enlightenment, or satori, leaves one fully in-the-world-with-others and yet at home in the nothing of Being that all beings share. As Daisetz Suzuki describes it, "*Satori* finds a meaning hitherto hidden in our daily concrete particular experiences, such as eating, drinking, or business of all kinds. The meaning thus revealed is not something added from the outside. It is in being itself, in becoming itself, in living itself. . . . [in] the 'isness' of a thing, Reality in its isness."[50] Having wagered the self in the valiant pursuit of enlightenment, the aspirant reclaims a home in the profound depths of the everyday world. Entering the marketplace, the seeker rediscovers the extraordinary task of escorting mortals.

Contrast the final stage of the Zen aspirant with another well-known, but unhappy, reentry into a marketplace. Nietzsche's madman, running into the market square, first announces to a bewildered crowd, "God is

---

[50] Suzuki, *Zen and Japanese Culture*, 16.

dead. God remains dead. And we have killed him."[51] Greeted with silence and derisive laughter, the madman retreats, believing that his
"time is not yet." Many ears were deaf to Nietzsche's call. In response,
Nietzsche construed his freedom as a sovereign solitude. Nietzsche's attempt to overcome his time and spurn his worldly cohabitants constitutes an ontological refusal no less resentful for its heroic dimensions.[52]
Heidegger offers an alternative vision. The groundlessness of human
being and the death of God prompt an interrogative openness, a
thoughtful and thankful relationship to the inexhaustible reality of the
everyday world. Resoluteness is not the transformation of the self into a
self-sufficient ego that might stand above and beyond time and space,
but the situating of the self within a shared abode. To be authentic is
resolutely to reenter the marketplace with helping hands. These hands
of flesh and blood may then be made available for the ongoing tasks of
building and preserving—the tasks of dwelling.

Freedom is found in the thoughts and words and deeds that deliver us
most profoundly into the world. Here we have the opportunity to become not masters and possessors of freedom, but, as Heidegger writes,
its "steward" (*Verwalter*) (*G* 31:134). It is indeed a paradox that human freedom is not gained through sovereign power but arises out of
our guardianship of worldly boundaries. But then, Lao Tzu had already
observed some twenty-five hundred years ago that "the movement of
the Tao / By contraries proceeds."[53] With this kept well in mind, the
enigmatic nature of a freedom discovered in finitude need not derail our
resolve to exercise its potential.

[51] Nietzsche, *Gay Science*, 181.

[52] Once again, I am underplaying Nietzsche's fecund heterogeneity. One may interpret
the eternal recurrence not only as an effort at self-appropriation, but as a gesture of
self-dispersal. For the recurring self to be what it is, the bounded world must also be (and
have been) what it is (and was). Accordingly, one may desire the eternal recurrence not as
a means of celebrating the creation of the sovereign self as a timeless work of art, but as a
means of celebrating the historical world, of which the self constitutes a timely fragment.
See Richard White, "Zarathustra and the Progress of Sovereignty from the Overman to
the Eternal Recurrence," *International Studies in Philosophy* 26/3 (1994): 107–15.

[53] Lao Tzu, "Tao Te Ching," 1:83.

Conclusion _____

Freedom Manipulated . . . this could be the
title of our half-century.
   (Jean-Luc Nancy, *The Experience of
   Freedom*)

THE BEGINNING of the tradition of Western philosophy was heralded by
Socrates' effort to shock Athenians out of particular social and political
habits. The tradition of Western philosophy ended with Nietzsche's effort to shock his readers into admitting that humanity amounts to nothing but the invidious decay of such habits. This final shock gives birth
to the postmodern world of the Last Man and the Overman—he who
abandons himself to whatever social and political habits are most comfortable and consoling and he who forgoes all such conventional anesthesia to engage in the heroic feat of self-creation. An apt description of
this postmodern world is that it is quickly becoming shockproof. That
is, the Socratic and Nietzschean legacies are themselves in jeopardy.
Neither active nor passive nihilists are much fazed by philosophic
trauma. "The shock effect of Catastrophic nihilism," Cornel West observes, "is now boring and uninteresting." Even the death of God, Maurice Blanchot suggests, "can no longer move us, so familiar has it become."[1]

Our jaded, postmodern times constitute an analogue to Nietzsche's
own decade of silence. The technological frenzy of the former and the
mental and physical paralysis of the latter have essentially the same
effect. Both mark the end of philosophic work that profoundly questions Being. Both mark the death of "the invisible" lamented by Rainer
Maria Rilke. A verse from Rilke's *Elegies* begins: "For Beauty's nothing
but the beginning of Terror we're still just able to bear, and why we
adore it so is because it serenely disdains to destroy us." Writing to his
Polish translator, Rilke offered this explanation:

> Transitoriness is everywhere plunging into a profound Being. And therefore
> all the forms of the here and now are not merely to be used in a time-limited
> way, but, so far as we can, instated within those superior significances in

[1] Cornel West, afterword to *Post-analytic Philosophy*, ed. John Rajchman and Cornel
West (New York: Columbia University Press, 1985), 259; Maurice Blanchot, "The Limits
of Experience: Nihilism," in *The New Nietzsche: Contemporary Styles of Interpretation*,
ed. David Allison (Cambridge, Mass.: MIT Press, 1977), 121.

which we share. . . . [I]n a purely mundane, deeply mundane, blissfully mundane consciousness, to instate what is HERE seen and touched within the wider, within the widest orbit—that is what is required. Not within a Beyond, whose shadow darkens the earth, but within a whole, within THE WHOLE. . . . Yes, for our task is to stamp this provisional, perishing earth into ourselves so deeply, so painfully and passionately, that its being may rise again, "invisibly," in us. . . . Even for our grandparents a "House," a "Well," a familiar tower, their very dress, their cloak, was infinitely more, infinitely more intimate: almost everything a vessel in which they found and stored humanity. . . . On us rests the responsibility of preserving, not merely [the] memory [of these mundane things] (that would be little and unreliable), but their human and laral worth. ("Laral" in the sense of household-gods.) The earth has no other refuge except to become invisible: IN US who, through one part of our nature, have a share in the Invisible, or at least, share-certificates, and can increase our holding in invisibility during our being here.[2]

In a world fast becoming shockproof, the invisible becomes mute as well. The imperative to instate the here and now in the whole, in Being, resounds a weakened call. "All essential philosophical questioning is necessarily untimely," Heidegger says (*IM* 8). But what is untimely in Heidegger's philosophy is precisely its call to timeliness: its call to safeguard invisibility in the visible, to shepherd Being in the permanent everywhere, to dwell in an age of increasing homelessness, to care for the earth and restrain technology in an age of possessive mastery.

I have argued that this call musters our potential for disclosive freedom. Such a mustering is imperative in a world where human possession and mastery is endlessly creative of those "empty, indifferent things, pseudo-things" that Rilke in the same letter identifies as "dummy-life." The real danger of this world is that dummy-life has become all too seductive. It is replete with comfort and the enchantments of hyperproductivity. It is also replete with "liberation." Freedom is everywhere sought . . . and everywhere supplied. Yet this marketing of freedom has real costs and dangers—philosophical, political, and ecological. In his essay "Home of the Free," Wendell Berry notes the modern desire to be "free of the 'hassles' of mortality" and to be liberated from the "life cycle." This desire garishly evidences itself in advertisements urging us to free ourselves from the "inconveniences" and "inefficiency" associated with the daily maintenance of life. We are to gain this liberation by purchasing machines or hiring hands, such that we might distance ourselves as much as possible from mundane caretaking. "Of course," Berry observes, "the only real way to get this sort of

---

[2] Rilke's letter of November 13, 1925 to Witold von Hulewicz, in Rainer Maria Rilke, *Duino Elegies*, trans. J. B. Leishman and S. Spender (New York: W. W. Norton, 1939), 128–29.

freedom and safety—to escape the hassles of earthly life—is to die. And what I think we see in these advertisements is an an appeal to a desire to be dead that is evidently felt by many people. These ads are addressed to the perfect consumers—the self consumers, who have found nothing of interest here on earth, nothing to do, and are impatient to be shed of earthly concerns." Berry suggests that real freedom cannot be won by escaping from or shunning the demands and limits of earthly life. It arises only by "living in the world as you find it, and by taking responsibility for the consequences of your life in it."[3] As Berry and others have documented, the ecological and political costs of freedom understood as a liberation from the responsibilities of caretaking are quickly becoming insupportable.

The best testimony to our living in a postindustrial world is, perhaps, the increasingly widespread concern about ecological devastation. The best testimony to our living in a postmodern world, perhaps, is the persistent denial or dismissal of our philosophic devastation. In the latter case the devastation is frequently celebrated as a liberation. Frederic Jameson observes that the concepts of "alienation, anomie, solitude, social fragmentation, and isolation" that characterized the modern self in the "age of anxiety" are "no longer appropriate in the world of the postmodern." But, Jameson concludes, the "liberation from anxiety" that triumphs in postmodernity also signifies a "liberation from every other kind of feeling as well, since there is no longer a self present to do the feeling. This is not to say that the cultural products of the postmodern era are utterly devoid of feeling, but rather that such feelings . . . are now free-floating and impersonal and tend to be dominated by a peculiar kind of euphoria."[4] Much postmodern theory fails to address this threat of euphoric disengagement and the dummy-life it propagates. Thus postmodern theory amounts, as some critics have charged, to a "spectacular PR maneuver" that makes conformism with socioeconomic and cultural conventions palatable. In this sense, postmodern theory has "succeeded in repackaging and marketing . . . what had been previously bemoaned as ontological *Angst* into *playfulness* and *joy:* transcendental homelessness for the me-generation."[5] Intent on being playful, postmodern theorists often remain oblivious to or glibly dismissive of the philosophic passion with which their forerunner, Fried-

---

[3]Wendell Berry, *The Gift of Good Land* (San Francisco: North Point Press, 1981), 184–87.

[4] Frederic Jameson, *Postmodernism; or, The Cultural Logic of Late Capitalism* (Durham, N.C.: Duke University Press, 1991), 11, 14–16.

[5] Russell Berman and Paul Piccone, "Hidden Agendas: The Young Heidegger and the Post-Modern Debate," *Telos* 77 (Fall 1988): 118.

rich Nietzsche, rejected complacency. Like the Last Men, they content-
edly announce their freedom as an anxiety-free homelessness . . . and
blink. Despite its endless celebration of the erosion of all philosophic
foundations, postmodernism has thus become a stable answer for many.
This anwer—signaling the end of profound questioning—is no less regrettable because it is grounded not in faith or reason but in their facile
rejection.

Heidegger illustrates the philosophic danger before us. We should listen to his warning with care: "For us, questioning means: exposing
oneself to the sublimity of things and their laws; it means: not closing
oneself off to the terror of the untamed and to the confusion of darkness. To be sure, it is for the sake of this questioning that we question,
and *not* to serve those who have grown tired and their complacent
yearning for comfortable answers. We know: the courage to question,
to experience the abysses of existence and to endure the abysses of existence, is in itself already a *higher* answer than any of the all-too-cheap
answers afforded by artificial systems of thought."[6] Such words might
well inspire us to embrace worldly life without resentment for its contingency and finitude, and to transform this message into a political
sensibility. Indeed, that has been my project.

But these words, like the philosopher who wrote them, also strikingly
illustrate the political dangers of the postmodern age. Philosophy, even
a philosophy of limits grounded in questioning, cannot immunize us
from self-deception and the most dangerous political fictioning. Indeed,
Heidegger's admonitions to spurn "cheap answers" and "artificial systems of thought" were given in a 1934 speech that propagandized the
myth of a people's organic unity and immanent destiny. Its immediate
goal was to encourage his fellow Germans to ratify Hitler's fait accom-
pli of quitting the League of Nations. We must listen to this ominous
message with care as well, for Heidegger's call to profound philosophic
interrogation was directly followed by another call that betrays the former terribly. He concludes his speech: "Our will to national (*völkisch*)
self-responsibility desires that each people find and preserve the greatness and truth of its destiny. . . . The Führer has awakened this will in
the entire people and has welded it into *one* single resolve. . . . Heil
Hitler!"[7] In one way at least, Heidegger is the consummate postmodern:
his study reveals that thought, like speech and action, is inherently am-

[6] Heidegger, "Political Texts," 106–107.

[7] Heidegger's disastrous wedding of philosophy to politics recalls Nietzsche's flirtations.
"Hitherto there have been a thousand goals, for there have been a thousand peoples,"
Zarathustra observes. "Only fetters are still lacking for these thousand necks, the one goal
is still lacking." Nietzsche, *Thus Spoke Zarathustra*, 86.

biguous, fraught with dangers, and chronically susceptible to coopta-
tion. But that is only to say that philosophically no less than politically,
freedom and vigilance must go hand in hand.

With this in mind, one should exercise caution and judgment in any
attempt to shock people out of social and political habits. Despite their
tendency to foster philosophic complacency, for instance, there is a
much-needed political security fostered by liberal conventions. Unim-
pressed with this security, Heidegger asks if we have "the courage for
the single question as to whether the West still dares to create a goal
above itself and its history, or whether it prefers to sink to the level of
the preservation and enhancement of trade interests and entertainments,
to be satisfied with appealing to the status quo as if this were absolute"
(WPK 91). The menace of Heidegger's question is that its prescription
of a society with an overarching goal and a singular, regimented purpose—with "*one* single resolve"—courts fascism. It bespeaks not the
overcoming of subjectivism, but its dangerous conversion from an individualistic to a collective force. Historically and theoretically, when individualistic subjectivism has been rejected it has been rejected mostly in
the name of collective subjectivism. This is the story of modern fascism
and communism. This is the dangerous conversion that liberalism
rightly combats. At the same time, in the age of an impending ecological
catastrophe largely attributable to the unrestrained growth of "trade
interests" grounded in negative liberty, the courage to challenge the status quo is imperative.[8] A successor to liberal ideology that remains
equally effective at opposing fascism and other antidemocratic forms of
rule has yet to gain a full voice. But I believe it has begun to show its
colors, and they are mostly shades of green.

We are, or should be, beyond the dangerous hope that a single political system or ideology might right the world. The world was not made
for such righting. As William James wrote, "Things are 'with' one another in many ways, but nothing includes everything, or dominates over
everything. The word 'and' trails along after every sentence. Something
always escapes. 'Ever not quite' has to be said of the best attempts made
anywhere in the universe at attaining all-inclusiveness. The pluralistic
world is thus more like a federal republic than like an empire or a
kingdom. However much may report itself as present at any effective
center of consciousness or action, something else is self-governed and
absent and unreduced to unity."[9] Human beings are part of this plural-

---

[8] Hegel already warned us that "when liberty is mentioned, we must always be careful
to observe whether it is not really the assertion of private interests which is thereby designated." Hegel, *Philosophy of History*, 430.

[9] William James, *A Pluralistic Universe* (Cambridge, Mass.: Harvard University Press,
1977), 145.

istic world. This, I have argued, is the meaning of Being-in-the-world-with-others. Perhaps Heidegger's ontology really is the stultifying monism that William James discouraged. Perhaps it has too dangerous an affinity with empire, and an alternative philosophic federation allows a more fruitful relationship with politics. I believe, however, that Heidegger's Being, unlike Plato's Idea, Hegel's Spirit, or even Nietzsche's Will to Power, is not the despotic unifier that James rightly feared. The freedom fostered by disclosive thought, speech, and action bespeaks the capacity of human being to abide by and affirm otherness. Indeed, its embrace constitutes perhaps the only viable challenge to the technological reduction of the world to standing-reserve, to a uniform dummy-life. The unity of Being is not to be feared as a form of homogeneity. Its identity is born of and sustained in difference. But in celebrating difference we must not make the mistake of denying Being. Even the indelibly pluralist James admitted that the "'multiverse' still makes a 'universe.'"[10] Likewise, Heidegger proposes that all diversity rests on a more encompassing unity, a unity, however, that is defined by its preservation of difference. What better foundation might there be for a political theory?

Heidegger's counsel regarding *Being and Time* might be extended to his entire corpus. He considered it "a *way* and not a shelter. Whoever cannot walk should not take refuge in it. A way, not 'the' way, which never exists in philosophy" (*ST* 64). In these pages I have used Heidegger as a bannister for philosophic reflection and political theorizing. The intent was that he not become a crutch. An uncritical dependence on Heidegger would constitute the greatest betrayal of his most fundamental thought, namely, that profound questioning—the human capacity resolutely to say yes *and* no—is the essence of human freedom. I have sought to explore the politics that accords with this freedom. It is a politics confronted with the task of preserving the earth from the destructive effects of a legacy of liberty understood as possessive mastery. And it is a politics that entails escorting our fellow men and women through life in a manner that safeguards and celebrates the capacity of each, every day, to partake of a disclosive freedom whose depths cannot fully be plumbed. It is, in short, a politics of worldly dwelling, rife with ambiguities and burdened with anxieties, but not for that reason without hope.

[10] Ibid., 146.

Index